**Individual
Development
and
Social Experience**

BY JENNIFER HILTON

The Gentle Arm of the Law

published by Educational Explorers (1967)
and in paperback by Transworld Publishers Ltd (1973)

Individual Development and Social Experience

SONJA HUNT, M.A., Ph.D.
Lecturer in Applied Social Psychology
at Liverpool University

JENNIFER HILTON, M.A., Dip. Crim.
Directing Staff at the National Police College

London   George Allen & Unwin Ltd
Ruskin House   Museum Street

First published in 1975

ISBN 0 04 150055 6 paperback
     0 04 150056 3 hardback

Printed in Great Britain
in 11 *point Baskerville type*
by Clarke, Doble & Brendon, Ltd,
Plymouth

Acknowledgements

We wish to thank Professor John Cohen of Manchester University, without whom the idea of the book would not have become actuality, and the numerous colleagues and friends who have by their comments given us varying degrees of inspiration and encouragement. We are grateful to those who have read earlier versions of parts of the book and made detailed criticisms. Our greatest debt is to those people from a variety of professions who have been subjected to the basic material of the book in lecture form during the past two years. By their questioning and arguing they have helped us to clarify our thinking and test our assumptions. Thank you also to Joe for his patience, moral support and practical help and to our most efficient typist, Mrs Margaret Young.

Contents

Illustrations

Introduction

This book is concerned with the psychological development of an individual throughout the life span. In looking at the principal influences on that development we have tried to reconcile some of the major theories in psychology. Different views of Man are often presented as if they are incompatible with each other. Sometimes Man is made to resemble a passive automaton waiting for the environment to provide a stick or a carrot; sometimes Man is described as an autonomous and curious explorer fighting desperately to maintain his integrity in the face of environmental pressures. Any 'either-or' formulations of a complex creature such as Man can only over-simplify the issue. He may easily be both at times active and exploratory and at others prodded into action.

There is a wealth of sources and material concerning human experience and behaviour, some more reliable than others. The basis of reliability in science is the reproducibility, or otherwise, of some result from a particular investigation. In a science like physics this is easier to achieve since one can count on certain aspects of inanimate matter remaining constant from one occasion to the next. This is by no means true of human beings in psychological experiments, since the way they behave is highly susceptible to influences from the social, emotional and physical conditions in which they are acting. Moreover they bring with them all sorts of preconceptions and misconceptions about the situation. Thus the data of psychology are hedged around with ifs and buts whose elucidation waits upon further research.

Psychologists have produced an enormous volume of research material and a diversity of theories in the short history of their subject. In a book such as this it would be an impossible task to include all the topics, notions and themes that are in existence. Some selection is inevitable.

The assumptions which run throughout this book and which have influenced our choice of theories and material are that each individual has a unique core of personality which is acted upon, but not obliterated by, social events; that development continues up to and past middle age, not coming to an end at adolescence; and that every person does have an element of choice in whether or not to accede to or to defy the demands of others. We also assume that there are some areas of human experience which are, at present, not accessible to the investigations of psychologists and not explainable in terms of any current theories of human behaviour. Such things as love, anguish, joy and despair are as mysterious to us now as they were to the ancient Greeks.

The easier it is to control the variables operating in a situation the more reliable are the generalisations made from observation and experiment. Thus, the early part of the book which concerns itself with the developing child contains more 'hard' data than the later parts which are concerned with adulthood and thus much more with the social psychological aspects of experience. The ratio of speculation to information may be said roughly to increase in psychology as individuals exist longer in the world.

There is often some confusion between the field of psychology and those of psychiatry, psychoanalysis and sociology. Psychology may be defined as the study of the experience and behaviour of individuals. It includes such topics as learning, memory, perception, social influences, beliefs, childhood experience and the effects of growing older. Psychiatry is a medical discipline which involves the diagnosis and treatment of mental disorders. Psychoanalysis refers to the method of treatment and the theory of mental functioning first formulated by Sigmund Freud and which interprets current behaviour in terms of the dreams and memories of childhood. Although some psychiatrists may practise psychoanalysis, it is mainly practised by lay analysts who do not have to be members of the medical profession. Whilst Freud's theories form a part of psychology, psychoanalysis constitutes a form of therapy. Sociology is the study of groups of people from whole societies to smaller communities and attempts to explain certain social phenomena in terms of the structure and interaction of these groupings. In terms of the understanding of human beings it is not very useful to compartmentalise areas of human experience into separate disciplines in this way and there is a movement now towards the initiation of more interdisciplinary research and co-operation.

Psychology, as has often been pointed out, is still at an early stage of its development. During the last few decades, however, a solid core of knowledge about human development has been gathered. It has been suggested[1] that psychology is a subject which is still at the stage where it can be understood by most people (unlike, say, bio-chemistry) and since its discoveries are within common experience they are rapidly assimilated through the mass media into common knowledge. They may then no longer be thought of as psychological discoveries, but as 'common sense'.

The results of painstaking research do not always at first seem credible, as shown by medieval man's reluctance to believe that the earth was whirling around the sun and by the reluctance of eighteenth-century physicians to accept that washing their hands after examining patients could help to cut down infection. Nowadays the effects of depriving babies of stimulation, security or attention are almost universally recognised, but it took years of repeated research before it was accepted by institutions that babies should not be left alone to look at blank ceilings for long periods of time.

A common charge against psychology is that it wraps up its commonplace findings in an elaborate jargon like five pennyworth of chips in *The Times Literary Supplement*. Some jargon is indeed quite unnecessary and may serve merely to disguise poverty of insight. However, it is important for all members of a discipline to agree on certain definitions of words, so that they are always used in the same way, unlike everyday usage. Some apparent jargon acts as useful shorthand expressions, but mystification is likely to occur, because it is assumed by many non-psychologists that terms like 'ego', 'intelligence', 'personality' and 'attitude' refer to concrete entities as do 'liver', 'heart' and 'brain', whereas they are merely useful labels for hypothetical constructs.

Two of the main aims of this book are to avoid compartmentalisation of topics and to avoid jargon wherever possible.

Some shorthand terms are so useful that they have been retained after a short explanation.

Generally graduate students in psychology have learned to be questioning and sceptical and to be aware of the complexities involved in human behaviour. They are less ready to provide and seek for neat solutions or unambiguous answers to social problems. Practitioners such as doctors and social workers, on the other hand, are required by the nature of their work to try and do just that. They may, therefore, be somewhat disappointed by the caution of psychologists in putting forward suggestions for the alleviation of human suffering or techniques for the control of anti-social behaviour. We cannot claim to be supplying socially valuable techniques in this book, but we do believe that we are offering insights into human behaviour which may assist those who have to try and solve the problems of society.

Although psychology has not yet developed a clear underlying philosophy or an adequate methodology it is at that exciting stage where arguments are stimulating and research illuminating, where theories become popular and then drop out of favour. This can sometimes be irritating and confusing, but it is indicative of progress and lively debate.

In the early part of the book we include several studies of animal behaviour. A mini-zoo is now a stable part of the luggage of psychology. Pavlov's dogs, Köhler's apes and the thousands of white rats belonging to the behaviourists have been joined by pigeons, geese and ten-spined sticklebacks belonging to ethologists like Konrad Lorenz. Latterly, studies of apes and monkeys in their natural environment have given leads to the possible origin of some human attributes.

Many psychologists believe that research into animal behaviour has no relevance whatsoever for human beings, because the fact that we possess language and culture overrides any common factors. We believe, however, that the investigation of animal behaviour can provide useful insights for theory-building and hypothesis-testing about Man. The fact that young monkeys brought up in isolation show severe disturbances of behaviour at adulthood throws new light on the deprivation experiences of human children. Animals can be used where ethics would rule out the use of human subjects and, because of faster breeding rates, the heredity of experimental animals can be controlled and thus used to assess the contributions of learning to a piece of behaviour uncontaminated by genetic effects.

Recent years have seen a rise in the popularity of psychology, reflected in its appearance in the curricula of professionals such as nurses, social workers, doctors, managers and policemen. High expectations have been generated. It is assumed that the study of psychology can aid in the understanding of people and provide explanations for such problems as drunkenness, violence and inter-racial conflict. Whilst it is true that psychologists can contribute to the understanding and explanation of human behaviour, their discipline covers only some of the multiplicity of interacting factors – economic, political, historical and sociological – which influence the life of man.

Psychology does not know how to make people 'good' or happy and offers no prescriptions for a contented and fruitful life. It can, however, point to those experiences which may be guaranteed to make people unhappy, to grossly disturb or stunt human potential. It may also, by pointing to the enormous complexity of human beings, their frailties as well as their strengths, help to create a tolerance and sympathy for people, so that those charged with their care or supervision may think twice or three times before carrying out programmes which intervene in human adaptation.

It is possible to make generalisations, albeit tentatively, about new-born infants whose behaviour is initially governed more by physiology than by thought. As individuals pass through childhood to adulthood they become more and more individual, although given superficial similarities by the demands of culture and social convention. They thus become ever more likely to be exceptions to general rules. We suggest, therefore, that the evidence of the later chapters be viewed more critically than that of the earlier ones and that it be weighed in the balance against the reader's experience and practical

B

knowledge. Knowledge grows most strongly in a soil of objections, questions and arguments. We hope this book will be provocative of all three.

REFERENCE

1 G. Miller, *Psychology: the science of mental life* (Harmondsworth, Penguin Books, 1966).

1
The Variety of Man

What a piece of work is a Man!
Shakespeare, *Hamlet*

One of the several peculiarities of the brain of Man is its ability to speculate upon its own nature and origin. How did we get to be the way we are? Are our destinies and characters fixed at birth by inheritance whether we are Eskimoes, Papuans or Scottish landowners? Or do the experiences that we undergo from birth determine our individuality?

During the nineteenth century these conflicting points of view were encapsulated in the 'Nature versus Nurture' debate. On the side of Nature were those who believed that inheritance was all – a point of view which was echoed in the hymn – *'The rich man in his castle. The poor man at his gate. God made them high or lowly. And ordered their estate.'* On the other side of the argument were the Environmentalists who, like the Jesuits, considered heredity to play only a tiny part in the development of character, being rapidly overlaid by learning. Echoes of this debate are still with us, for example, in the use of such terms as 'maternal instinct', in the current controversy concerning the intelligence of different ethnic groups, and in the perpetual popularity of horoscopes. The two extreme points of view can be envisaged, on the one hand, as seeing human beings as apples with a hard central core of inherited and unchangeable characteristics, and on the other, as conceiving of them as more like onions built up of layer upon layer of experience, but with no fixed centre.

Modern psychology no longer indulges in this kind of 'either-or' argument, and most psychologists agree that the identity of any human being is a consequence of the interaction between the genetic material with which an individual is provided at conception and the myriad events in that individual's life. It is the interplay between 'Nature' and 'Nurture' which is responsible for the uniqueness of each of us.

Man is, moreover, the product of millions of years of evolution during which numerous species came into being and disappeared again, leaving only their fossil remains. The reason for their disappearance seems to be related to changes in the environment which were inimical to their survival. One of Man's greatest assets is his ability to adapt to a wide variety of situations and climates, often by changing the situation to suit himself.

EVOLUTION

The concept of evolutionary advance, that is, the development of greater complexity and adaptability in species, is based upon several fundamental conditions.

Within any animal species no two individuals are identical. The effect of this variability is to give some of them a greater chance of survival if the environment changes. For example public health authorities are becoming worried about the increase in the rat population in spite of large-scale efforts to keep this down by using certain poisons. What seems to be happening is that some rats are, because of particular and tiny differences in their body chemistry, more resistant to these poisons than other rats. The rats without resistance are killed off, but the others are able to survive and pass on their protective chemistry to their offspring, thus producing a new generation of rats relatively immune to old methods of extermination. So a change in the environment, i.e. the introduction of poison, was fatal for some rats, but allowed others, because of variability, to survive in even greater numbers. A further example of the advantage of variability for survival is industrial melanism. In industrial towns many different species of moth are dark in colour, whilst the same species in the country are light-coloured. The dark moths (melanics) are at a greater advantage in the town where, against the grimy walls, they are difficult for predators to spot. The country moths, however, in the cleaner atmosphere, are protected by the fact that they are light in colour. Each colour, in its own environment, is at a selective advantage. What if that environment changes? This is what has happened in some towns, where, because of new laws about industrial pollution and the cleaning of buildings, the dark moths became conspicuous against the light walls and thus easily detected and eaten. The few light moths who had somehow managed to survive in the town now found themselves at an advantage and the result has been a tremendous increase in the number of light-coloured moths found in industrial areas.[1]

As environments change, so different varieties of animal, insect or plant, will be more successful. The more flexible and adaptable an animal is, the more likely it is that it will be able to settle down in a variety of different environments. The vital factor is the ability to live long enough to produce offspring – this is the 'survival of the fittest' upon which the concept of 'natural selection' rests. When Darwin coined these terms in his book *Origin of Species*,[2] some of his contemporaries extended his concept of 'survival of the fittest' to apply to social conditions and used it to justify social inequalities on the grounds that the poor were poor because of their 'natural' inferiority. This came to be known as 'Social Darwinism'. By 'fittest', however, Darwin did not mean the richest, or even the strongest or healthiest of the species, he meant the best fitted to the environment and, therefore, the best fitted to reproduce its own kind.

Like changes in the environment, changes in behaviour from, say, tree-dwelling to plains-dwelling, from eating nuts and berries to eating seeds, will discriminate in favour of differently adapted bodily forms. This selection of the best adapted physiques can be seen, for example, in the fact that small animal species tend to be larger the farther away they are from the equator (larger bodies have a relatively smaller surface area and so lose heat less rapidly). Puffins increase in size by over 1 per cent for every degree of latitude they live further north.[3] Different feeding habits have evolved both within and between species so that they do not compete for the same food. Thus the beaks of birds who eat insects are adapted for catching them, whilst those birds that prefer nuts or seeds have beaks which can crack and peck.

The variability of individuals which is so essential to their survival is brought about by two principal factors. Firstly, sexual reproduction, which ensures that genetic material is mixed together. In species like the single-celled amoeba, reproduction consists of the splitting of the one cell into two, each of which is exactly the same genetically; one generation of amoebae are almost exact replicas of any other generation. During sexual reproduction, however, each parent contributes something different and no organism produced in this way is ever precisely like its parents.

Secondly, there are processes which produce wholly original changes in genetic material. These changes are known as random mutations and may be triggered off 'spontaneously' (that is to say by unknown events) or by radiation from the environment such as X-rays. Many mutations are harmful and are responsible for a variety of human disorders, including some types of subnormality like mongolism and phenylketonuria (a condition in which a mutant gene prevents the body from breaking down certain chemicals). Unless phenylketonuria is quickly diagnosed in infancy (by a urine test) and a special diet observed, these chemicals build up and the child becomes mentally defective.

Some mutations confer an advantage if they lead to the organism becoming better adapted to its environment (as was the case with the melanic moths) by being better able to compete with rivals or to escape enemies more easily. Harmful mutations often die out as their effects can be severe enough to prevent the organism affected from reaching maturity and reproducing. Successful mutations on the other hand will, by definition, tend to be preserved. It is also quite possible that some mutations will survive to be passed on because they are not harmful, even if they are not particularly useful. Natural selection favours successful or non-harmful mutations in such a way that what was once an extremely rare characteristic becomes, in time, an extremely common one. The fact of sexual reproduction speeds up this process for it increases the possibility of the combination of favourable genes from different individuals.

LEARNING ABILITY

Adaptability is not only achieved by changes in bodily form, but also refers to the ability to learn new behaviour, to voluntarily adjust to changes in the environment. This type of adaptability tends to increase with increases in the complexity of the brain of the animal, and would seem to be at its most extreme in Man, who, as far as we can tell, has the greatest ability of all species to learn from experience. The wide distribution of *Homo sapiens*, from the sub-zero temperatures of the Arctic circle to the equatorial heat of Africa, is partly a consequence of our variability in physique and appearance, but it is also due to our ability to adapt our behaviour to the demands and material resources of the situation. Thus, in Alaska, igloos have been found to be ideal for keeping out the Arctic cold, whilst in jungle clearings grass huts are most efficient for combining protection from the sun with the capacity to let through the slightest breeze.

The evolution of adaptability has gone hand in hand with the evolution of the brain. In animals lower down the evolutionary scale the functions of the brain are concerned mainly with controlling and satisfying bodily needs, making sure the animal gets food, oxygen, drink and, to ensure the survival of the species, sex. These needs can, in an unchanging environment, be satisfied for generation after generation by means of inherited patterns of behaviour that are triggered off by some internal stimulus, e.g. feeling hungry or thirsty and coming into contact with an appropriate external stimulus, food or water. It is essential that the animal should be able to maintain its body in the requisite state of equilibrium in order for it to survive. Going without food, water or oxygen for longer than a certain time is bound to result in death. The process by which a constant internal state is maintained in an organism is known as homeostasis. The brain contains homeostatic mechanisms which are sensitive to deficiencies in the body. For example, if oxygen is getting short the animal begins to breathe faster thus eliminating carbon dioxide more rapidly and taking in as much oxygen as possible. Similarly there is a homeostatic regulator for temperature. When body temperature rises above a certain level the animal begins to sweat, perhaps to pant, thus getting rid of excess heat. To some extent the needs for food and water are controlled by homeostatic mechanisms. When sugar in the blood falls below a certain concentration this automatically triggers off a process whereby the liver begins to release some of its store of sugar into the blood stream. Similarly, when the body is running short of water the constituents of the urine become more concentrated.

There is, naturally, a point at which homeostatic control becomes inadequate for survival and the animal will be impelled into activity, looking for a place with more fresh air, a meal, a source of liquid. In lower animals the larger part of the brain is taken up with this constant need to maintain the equilibrium of the body.

In Man the satisfaction of physiological needs is coped with by only a very small part of the brain, the so-called 'lower centres' which form the bulk of the brain in animals such as rats, fishes, birds, etc. In Man large areas of the brain remain free to learn, the neo-cortex overlays the lower centres and dominates them to some extent. Thus, in Man, the lessons of experience are brought to bear on the necessities for survival.

The lower, more primitive, parts of the brain remain recognisable from one species to another, although they differ in size. For example, the olfactory area of a dog's brain is about a hundred times larger than the same area in a man's brain. As we proceed up the evolutionary scale the size of the neo-cortex increases and it becomes more convoluted (this increases the surface area) and possesses a larger number of brain cells connected to each other in ever more complex ways.

The ability of human beings to learn and remember enables them to control and channel biological drives. In the brain this is effected by the many connections linking the upper, learning areas of the brain with the lower, instinctive centres. Many basic bodily functions are, therefore, in Man surrounded

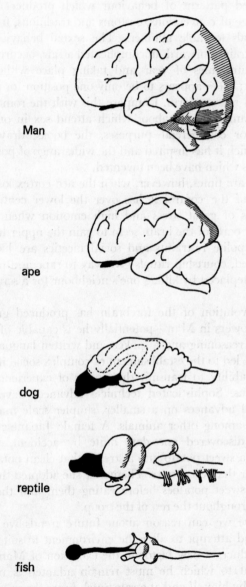

Figure 1   Comparative sizes of the brain

by learned patterns of behaviour which produce a tremendous range of conventions, customs and traditions, from courtship rituals to table manners. The sexual behaviour of the rat is a straightforward, uncomplicated affair, occurring at the appropriate times of year and taking place without much preamble; there appears to be only one position for mating to which all rats conform. Compare this with the romantic daydreams, anxiety and taboos which attend sex in our society, its use for commercial purposes, the books, drawings and music which it has inspired and the wide range of postures and variations which have been invented.

There are times, however, when the neo-cortex loses a large amount of the control it has over the lower centres. These are times of great stress and high emotion when the more primitive parts of the brain seem to gain the upper hand. This is when polite restraints and social niceties are likely to be abandoned, courtship rituals give way to rape and table manners are replaced by killing one's neighbour for a scrap of stale bread.

The evolution of the forebrain has produced great intellectual powers in Man – potentially he is capable of memory, learning, reasoning and a spoken and written language. These gifts have led to the establishment of complex social institutions and the ability to transmit the lessons of experience to later generations. Sophisticated technical advances have resulted. Technical advances on a smaller, simpler scale may also be observed among other animals. A female Japanese macaque monkey discovered one day, quite by accident, when she dropped a sweet potato into a stream that clean potatoes were pleasanter than dirty ones. Thereafter she adopted the habit of washing sweet potatoes before eating them and the practice spread throughout the rest of the troop.[4]

Because we can reason about future trends we can plan ahead and attempt to alter the environment to suit ourselves. This produces a new factor in the evolution of Man. The environment to which he must remain adapted is now being changed by himself and at a rate much faster than would occur naturally. An environment altered by technology, although it can become physically safer and more comfortable, can also bring undesired and unpredictable changes in terms of pollution, noise and depleted resources that may be harder to adapt to than we at present realise.

We pride ourselves on our ability to learn, to adjust, to create. The dinosaurs have become objects of derision, because they were unable to keep pace with their environment and so became extinct. Dinosaurs, however, survived for 140 million years whilst *Homo sapiens* has lasted, so far, about 2 million. During this time the speed of change has accelerated with every century due to the transmission of acquired knowledge. It has taken a mere 10,000 years to advance from Stone Age to Space Age and we are now communicating 10 million times faster, travelling 100 times more rapidly and using up the world's resources 1,000 times more quickly than we were a century ago.[5]

Our species probably started life in scattered, wandering bands, which competed with each other for scarce food resources, living on their wits and learning to eat anything even remotely nourishing. The competition for food probably made rival bands antagonistic and our present high-density living may be conflicting with a need for space which is a hangover from our hunting ancestors.

Social and political institutions may also run counter to the evolutionary forces which lead to successful adaptation. Rigid barriers between groups of people on the grounds of social class, nationality or religion artificially restrict mating patterns and so reduce the chances of new combinations of genes and favourable mutations coming together.

Improved medical techniques, which are a consequence of Man's capacity for communication, co-operation and creativity, enable children who possess harmful genes to survive, to marry and pass on the harmful material to their offspring. There is a form of eye cancer in children (retinoblastoma) which is almost always fatal if not treated. Natural selection would have removed a disadvantageous gene from the population. Now with proper treatment some 70 per cent of sufferers survive and carry on the gene responsible to the next generation.[6]

LIVING IN GROUPS

Most animals, even the most primitive, have social groups which help with adaptation and survival. The larvae of barnacles, given the choice, are attracted towards a rock covered with other barnacles rather than towards an empty rock.[7] This gregariousness arises not out of affection for their fellows but probably because where one barnacle can survive so can another.

Division of labour, found in many animal species and in insects, can give a more efficient and skilled work force than non-specialisation. Hunting is more effective if several animals co-operate. Wolves, for example, when hunting in packs, divide themselves into those who harry and surround the prey and those who capture and kill.

Ants have a rigid system of dividing up group tasks. Not only do the workers, drones and queen have their work-roles which are determined by genetic differences,[8] but there are also 'slave' ants stolen as larvae from other colonies, who work as excavators, feeders and nurses to the young of the colony.

To keep a group together strong feelings of loyalty are vital. This often involves hostility towards other groups. Group solidarity in insects is maintained by touch, smell and sound, a sort of genetic programme for team spirit. If, as has been done, a termite is removed from its home-colony and coated with a 'foreign' smell and then replaced, it will be attacked by its former workmates. Conversely, a 'foreign' termite coated with the correct smell will be accepted into a strange colony.[9]

There is some evidence that social groupings may also play a role in keeping a population stable relative to the food supply. It has been suggested that the flocking of starlings at twilight is an example of this. If the flock is too large it divides the following day to seek fresh feeding grounds.[10]

Many species that live in communities have ranking orders in which some animals are dominant over others. There are examples of this in chickens, goats, bears, lions, gorillas – and Man. Where animals live in the wild, if food is short the subordinate ones may be excluded from eating and so only dominant animals survive. Equal shares might result in the whole group perishing. The phenomenon of territoriality may work in a similar way. Those animals which fight for territories – birds, dogs, fish, deer, apes, etc. – tend to defend larger areas when food is short. Often the obtaining of a mate is dependent upon the male possessing a territory. Thus, when territories are larger more animals do not mate, and the next generation is smaller. Both dominance and territory can act so as to have a regulative function for the species.

In Man both dominance hierarchies, e.g. the army and territorial fighting do occur, but it would be a mistake to ascribe these to the same origins as for animals. Man's social and political institutions are an obvious complicating factor.

In higher animals co-operation becomes less dependent on built-in urges toward concerted effort and more a voluntary affair reaching, sometimes, what, in a human context, would be called friendship. Dolphins will support a sick fellow dolphin on the surface of the water so that his blow-hole is left clear and he can breathe. Dolphins will also co-operate on a task even when they cannot see each other, but must communicate by sound only. In one experiment two dolphins were placed in separate but adjacent tanks each of which contained a lever. When a light came on which was visible to only one of the dolphins, a fish was delivered if the dolphins pushed their levers simultaneously. This they very quickly learned to do, even though only one of the dolphins got the fish.[11] Chimpanzees have also been observed to display examples of teamwork. If a heavy box containing food is placed outside a cage containing two chimpanzees, and if the box is attached to a rope within the reach of the animals, they will co-operate in pulling the box towards them, even when only one is hungry.[12]

THE SOCIAL LIFE OF MAN

Social groupings such as families and tribes do convey evolutionary benefits. They can help to ensure the survival of the species by co-operation and by passing on to subsequent generations the accumulated wisdom of the past. To re-introduce the apple and onion analogy: the central core of personality may be the result of eons of evolutionary change and the particular hereditary make-up of any individual, but the layers that are added through learning and experience result from the interaction of the person with other people.

One big difference between the social life of Man and that of animals is that Man can choose which groups he wants to belong to, except, of course, for the family group. Humans appear to be sociable creatures. The 'Nature' argument would be that this is due entirely to in-built mechanisms deriving from the evolutionary advantages of belonging to a group. The 'Nurture' argument would be that sociability is learned from others at a very early age. It seems more likely that, whilst the underlying motivation may be innate, the forms that sociability takes are learned. As we shall see in a later chapter, infants do seem to be born with a tendency to form attachments to significant people in their vicinity, but the social conditions must be such as to allow this to occur.

Social grouping is a fact all over the world, but there is wide variation in local customs concerning the organisation of the groups. Some of these may be explained as valuable adaptations to local conditions. Polyandry among the Nayar of India ensures that, despite low fertility due to inadequate diet, the women are likely to conceive and produce heirs. On the other hand monogamy seems to be related to the inheritance of property and the need for a wise father to know his own child.

Family life takes a variety of forms from the intense nuclear group of western society to the amorphous extended relationships of some African tribes. Families may recognise either a man or a woman as their head and property may be inherited either through male or female lines. In some orthodox Hindu families three or four generations will live together and the lifetime of experience of the oldest man is recognised, in that his is the deciding voice in all matters affecting the family or any member of it. Playfellows and spouses are chosen by the family and no one has an individual social existence.

In matrilineal societies succession to status positions and inheritance is passed from a woman's brother to her son. Among the Nayar people the tie between brother and sister is regarded as more important than that between husband and wife. After marriage women remain in the household of the brother where they are visited by their husbands. There is no expectation of an emotional involvement between spouses and the children of a union belong not to the father but to the brother. Thus physiological and social fatherhood are separated and a high divorce rate is normal.

As with genetic material so in social life variability conveys advantages. Rigid patterns of thought and behaviour can become maladaptive in changing circumstances. For example, the idea that a large number of children is a blessing, a sign of virility and an economic advantage, is taking a long time to die and is, in the meantime, endangering whole populations (including our own) whose resources are limited. The notion that man is born to work, indeed must work to support himself and society, is another deeply engrained principle in our lives. The whole organisation of society revolves around this belief – the economic system, the educational system and the provision of leisure activities. Yet it is possible that not too far in the future people will have to be paid not to work and children will have to be educated to another kind of existence than a nine-to-five working life. A society which presents its members with only one prevailing and rigid view of life will find change much more hazardous and full of conflict than one where alternative life styles are already in existence.

One common experience of all men is death, but attitudes to it and its consequences vary widely and show how flexible Man can be. In western society, for example, as in others, it is assumed that the heirs will inherit any property. Muslims, however, believe that we should not build up lasting property in this life and so the beautiful Turkish palaces on the shores of the Bosphorus are made of wood, not stone. The Navajo Indians burn all the belongings of the deceased so that no polluted object will pass, even accidentally, to a living person. Some Australian Aborigines break up the skeleton of the dead person, pounding the skull to fragments so that he cannot harm them and breaking the leg bones so that he cannot run after them.

Differences in behaviour between human groups are due to

the vagaries of the environment and the accidents of history. Beneath the mosaic of surface forms are universal human concerns – care of children, possession of property, sex, death, survival.

Social phenomena do suggest that adults are just as emotional as small children, although they have learned more strategies for disguising their feelings. Most societies erect elaborate systems of thought to explain away that which is threatening to the society. The presence of 'deviants' such as the mentally ill, the violent, the delinquent, remind people of human frailty, therefore such deviants must be put 'beyond the pale', so that their behaviour can be regarded as having no relevance for the rest of mankind.

A complex technological culture helps human beings to protect themselves against irrational fears. Darkness and loneliness are vanquished by electric light and television. The handling of dead bodies is undertaken by professionals. Social taboos against overt aggression, unsanctioned sexual behaviour and painful frankness help to damp down emotions which might disrupt smooth social interaction.[13][14]

The need for social controls suggests that human beings are born with dangerous drives which have to be thwarted in the interests of the whole group. This was Freud's belief and in one form or another it has had a profound effect on social policies. An alternative view is propounded by other theorists such as Maslow,[15] Rogers[16] and Marcuse.[17] They incline to the philosophy that Man is basically good, but becomes warped by the pressures and corruption of society, so that true human potential is stunted.

Attempts to adapt to the demands of society can, quite obviously, be disastrous for some individuals, for example, the businessman who develops ulcers or coronary heart disease in his efforts to conform to the idea that people should be successful and rich. On a national level, German conformity to demands for *'lebensraum'* led to the devastation of much of western Europe. Non-conformity and criticism are of as much benefit to society as conformity and acceptance.

HUMAN NATURE

The extent of Man's inborn drives has not yet been fully established. One school of psychology, the Behaviourists, sees Man as driven principally by the need to avoid physiological distress – hunger, thirst, pain, sexual deprivation. They consider that more complex motives such as ambition are learned through the association of particular actions with the satisfaction of these basic needs. Ambition can thus secure the satisfaction of physiological needs by acquiring the money to buy food, drink, warmth and women (or men!). This viewpoint suggests that motivation is primarily homeostatic and directed at keeping the body in a state of comfortable balance. It is the basis of some utopian (some would say nightmare) visions of the future, for example, Aldous Huxley's *Brave New World*,[18] B. F. Skinner's *Walden Two*.[19]

Man does, however, appear more complex than the limited automaton outlined by the behaviourist imagination. Searching, seeking, trying to make sense and to find meaning are also aspects of human behaviour. Curiosity and the need to explore manifest themselves even in the humble rat. Chimpanzees will solve problems without reward just, it would seem, for the pleasure of doing so. In Man, the popularity of activities which in no way make for greater comfort, suggests that he too needs the stimulus of risk-taking, the thrill of exploration, and the satisfaction that comes from achievement, whether it is completing *The Times* crossword puzzle, winning at darts or penetrating the Amazon jungle. The explanation that a mountain is climbed 'because it's there' is an expression of Man's need for challenge and excitement. The mental stimulus of such pursuits as collecting stamps or scientific research is sought for its own sake and not to satisfy physiological needs, either directly or indirectly.

It does not seem, therefore, that we are purely passive creatures waiting to be prodded into action by some biological deficiency, but rather that we actively seek new information and fresh experiences. The physiological needs of the body are, nevertheless, basic to our survival. A starving man has no interest in climbing mountains or in complex intellectual

c

dilemmas. Needs vary in importance and in the order in which they need to be satisfied.

Apart from in-built needs which serve to preserve life and prompt exploration, most of Man's needs are socially learned and may vary from one culture to another. Because human beings develop in social groups they have a superficial similarity to other members of their tribe, family and culture. Nevertheless, few people conform wholly to the customs and conventions of their cultural setting. Each individual has a different life history, so that the onion layers of social learning are never identical. The uniqueness of the individual core affects all subsequent learning and ensures that people react differently even to identical situations.

It is very difficult, indeed impossible, at this stage of psychological knowledge to find psychological theories which are completely predictive of human behaviour, for one would have to specify each individual characteristic of the person and each facet of the particular time and situation. The most a psychologist can do is to try and formulate general laws of wide applicability within which individual differences of constitution, past experience and present personality must be taken into account.

REFERENCES

1 J. A. Bishop and P. S. Harper, 'Melanism in the moth Gondontis bidentata: a clime within the Merseyside conurbation', *Heredity, 25* (3), (1970), 447–56.
2 C. Darwin, *The Origin of Species* (London, John Murray, 1859).
3 J. Prevost and J. Boulier, 'Vie sociale et thermoregulation chez le manchot empereur', *Aptenodytes Forsteri Alanda, 25* (1957), 167–73.
4 M. Kawai, 'Newly-acquired pre-cultural behaviour of the natural troop of Japanese monkeys of Koshima Island', *Primates, 6* (1965), 1–30.
5 T. Dobzhansky, *Mankind Evolving: the evolution of the human species* (New Haven, Yale University Press, 1962).
6 T. Dobzhansky, 'The present evolution of Man', *Scientific American, 609* (1960).
7 R. Brown, *Social Psychology* (New York, The Free Press, 1965).

8 S. F. Light, 'The determination of the castes of social insects', *Quart. Rev. Biol.*, *17* (1942), 312–26.

9 V. H. Dropkin, 'Host specificity relations of termite protozoa', *Ecology*, *22* (1941), 200–22.

10 V. C. Wynne-Edwards, *Animal Dispersion in Relation to Social Behaviour* (Edinburgh and London, Oliver & Boyd, 1962).

11 R. Stenuit, *The Dolphin: cousin to Man* (Harmondsworth, Penguin Books, 1971).

12 M. P. Crawford, 'The co-operative solving of problems by young chimpanzees', *Comp. Psychol. Monog.*, *14*, No. 68 (1937), 1–88.

13 D. O. Hebb, 'Emotion in man and animal: an analysis of the intuitive processes of recognition', *Psychol. Rev.*, *53* (1946), 88–106.

14 D. O. Hebb, 'Temperament in chimps. I: Method of analysis', *J. Comp. Physiol. Psychol.*, *42* (1949), 192–206.

15 A. Maslow, *Motivation and Personality* (New York, Harper & Row, 1954).

16 C. Rogers, *Client-centred Therapy: its current practice, implications and theory* (Boston, Houghton Mifflin, 1951).

17 H. Marcuse, *One-dimensional Man* (London, Routledge & Kegan Paul, 1964).

18 A. Huxley, *Brave New World* (Harmondsworth, Penguin Books, 1955).

19 B. F. Skinner, *Walden Two* (New York, Macmillan, 1962).

2

Embryonic Man

All nature is but art unknown to thee,
All chance, direction which thou canst not see.
Alexander Pope, *An Essay on Man*

Each of us is born into the world with a unique genetic inheritance, although parts of it will be shared with our fellow human beings. There are similarities and dissimilarities between babies at the moment of birth. All need food, water and care, and share features of appearance, but each has had a somewhat different experience in the womb and each is provided with a central nervous system which differs in the amount of nervous activity going on in it; each also has an autonomic nervous system of slightly different responsiveness, so that babies differ in alertness and sensitivity to stimulation. These differences, together with hormonal variations, physical condition and built-in drives and reflexes, form the core of the baby's personality. This core is acted upon by many experiences and events from conception until death. The nutritional, social and psychological environment will all affect the layers of personality that are laid down around the central core.

Even identical twins with the same genetic constitution as each other are affected by their different experiences in the womb (the supply of oxygen, nutrition and available space vary). What is subsequently learned from experience constructs a framework of perception into which we slot all events; people select and learn different things even from an identical environment and the effect is cumulative.

The actual chemistry of the brain is altered by learning[1][2] and since, at birth, our brain chemistry is unique, the results of learning interact with this uniqueness to produce ever greater individual differences. This individual variability has survival value as we have already noted in Chapter 1.

THE MECHANISM OF INHERITANCE

The individuality in the genetic make-up of the newly conceived embryo is due to the random shuffling of parental genes. Genes are coded combinations of chemicals, the exact constitution of which is still under investigation. It is these chemicals which determine the hereditary characteristics of us all. The genes are carried on chromosomes which have a long, thread-like appearance and are present in the nuclei of our body cells. Each cell has a nucleus containing twenty-three pairs of chromosomes, except for the sex cells, specialised for reproductive purposes, which contain twenty-three single unpaired chromosomes.

The cells that make up the body and brain carry out all the processes essential to the sustaining of life : the exchange of oxygen for carbon dioxide, the creation of energy from food. Cells have specialised roles as bones and skin, nerves, muscles and internal organs, the constituents of the blood, hair, and so on. The nucleus of each cell is surrounded by a lumpy jelly-like substance containing microscopic structures which carry out the chemical operations of living. Each nucleus has embedded in it the chromosomes which map out the individual's characteristics, such as eye colour and height, shape of the nose, length of fingers, complexion, and thousands of other details of appearance. Although these kinds of characteristics have an hereditary basis they can be affected by environmental factors such as nutrition. Some psychological attributes like intelligence, temperament and activity/passivity also probably have an hereditary component.

The sex cells, sperm in men, ova in women, contain only twenty-three single chromosomes. It is when a sperm and an ovum unite that they create cells containing twenty-three pairs. Sperm and ova are produced in the male testes and the female ovaries respectively, by a special and complicated process known as meiosis.

Meiosis

A layer of cells in the ovary or testis produces cells known as oocytes and spermatocytes respectively. These cells have the usual twenty-three pairs of chromosomes. Each of these will eventually divide into four, producing four ova in the case of the female, one of which is viable and three abortive, and four spermatozoa in the case of the male, all of which are viable.

In these oocytes and spermatocytes the pairs of chromosomes at a certain stage come together so that their matching parts are exactly opposite. Each pair of chromosomes behaves in the same way. They then twist around each other. Each pair of coiled chromosomes then divides lengthwise into four strands known as chromatids. Still coiled tightly together, the chromatids stretch outwards and, because of the tension created at certain points, they split at one or more areas of tension. The loose ends of the chromatids then rejoin with the parts of the chromatids belonging to the chromosome partner. The position and number of splits is variable so that the re-joining mixes varying blocks of genes from each chromosome. This process creates new combinations of genes.

The four newly constituted chromatids begin to uncoil and at the same time combine back into two chromosomes. These start to move toward the edges of the nucleus and during this movement they once again split lengthwise into chromatids. Each of the four chromatids now moves to one of the four quarters of the nucleus and the nucleus and cell divide into four. The result of the meiosis is the production of four cells from one, each of the new cells containing a nucleus with twenty-three single chromosomes, one chromosome from each of the original pairs.

The cells so produced are the sex cells, none of which contains the same gene combinations as any other. At fertilisation the fusion of sperm and ovum brings each single chromosome a partner and the fertilised egg develops into cells containing twenty-three pairs of chromosomes, one of the pair donated by the male and the other by the female. It is a matter of chance which sperm, out of the millions that are released, fertilises the ovum – the laws of inheritance appear to be based on chance occurrences. The likelihood that a second child would

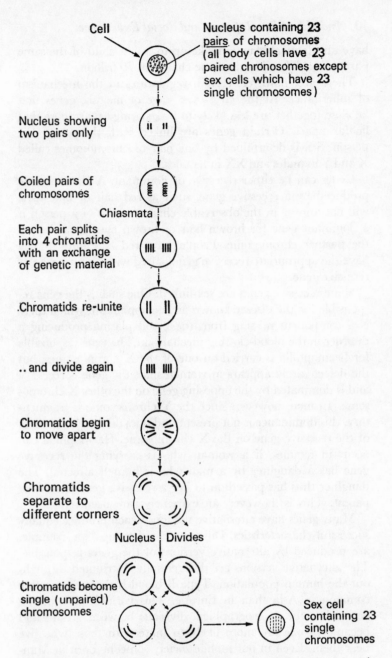

Cell

Nucleus containing **23**
pairs of chromosomes
(all body cells have **23**
paired chromosomes except
sex cells which have **23**
single chromosomes)

Nucleus showing
two pairs only

Coiled pairs of
chromosomes

Chiasmata

Each pair splits
into 4 chromatids
with an exchange
of genetic material

.Chromatids re-unite

.. and divide again

Chromatids begin
to move apart

Chromatids
separate to
different corners

Nucleus : Divides

Chromatids become
single (unpaired) chromosomes

Sex cell
containing 23
single
chromosomes

Figure 2 Meiosis: Process which produces sex cells (sperms and ova)
and which shuffles hereditary characteristics

have an identical genetic make-up to a first child of the same parents is $(\frac{1}{2}^{23})^2$ or less than one chance in 70 trillion.

There are, however, certain regularities in the mechanism of inheritance. At the cross-over stage of meiosis, genes that lie close together are less likely to be separated than those that lie far apart. Certain genes are linked with the sex of the person. Sex is determined by one pair of chromosomes called X and Y in males and XX in females.

Genes can be either recessive or dominant. A characteristic produced by a recessive gene, such as red hair or blue eyes, will not appear in the observable characteristics of a person if a dominant gene for brown hair or brown eyes is carried on the partner chromosome. People have red hair only if they have the appropriate recessive gene paired with another similar recessive gene.

Some recessive genes are sex-linked. One such is the gene responsible for the disease known as haemophilia in which there is a component missing from the blood plasma producing a disorder in the blood-clotting mechanism. The gene responsible for haemophilia is carried on one of the X chromosomes, but the defect rarely appears in women since the gene is recessive and is dominated by the opposing gene on the other X chromosome. In men, however, since the Y chromosome is fragmentary, this dominance is not present and does not mask the effect of the recessive gene on the X chromosome. Haemophilia can occur in females, if a woman who is carrying the recessive gene has a daughter by a man who is himself affected. The daughter thus has passed on to her a recessive gene from each parent. This is, however, an extremely rare occurrence.

Many genes have alternative versions which produce equally successful characteristics. Different blood groups, for example, are produced by alternative versions of the genes responsible. The alternative versions are differentially distributed throughout the human population. Type B blood is three times more common in Asia than in Europe. This variable distribution occurs because of geographical divisions between groups and because people are more likely to mate with those who live near them. Even in our mobile society someone born in Manchester will more probably marry a Mancunian than a Liverpudlian. In consequence, groups are inclined to share physical characteristics such as skin colour as well as having common cultural patterns. However, a comparison of the frequency with which alternative versions of genes are found in different ethnic groups shows that there is greater variation in the individuals within a population than there is between the means of different populations.

Certain genetic abnormalities may profoundly affect the development of the individual: some produce physical, some mental, abnormality, and usually a combination of both. One such condition is mongolism which can be 'regular', i.e. produced by an extra chromosome, so that there are forty-seven instead of forty-six. This occurs because the twenty-first chromosome splits, during meiosis, into three instead of two. There is also a condition known as 'translocatory' mongolism which is produced by an uneven exchange of genetic material so that one chromosome is unusually long. Mongolism occurs in two out of every thousand children born in Europe and the risk of having a mongoloid child increases with the age of the mother.

Phenylketonuria, mentioned in the last chapter, is the consequence of a recessive gene and occurs in only one in 40,000 children in Europe. Some disorders are transmitted by dominant genes, for example, Huntington's Chorea. Those suffering from it invariably pass on the disease to half their children. The manifestations are progressive degeneration of the brain tissue resulting in involuntary movement and violent uncontrolled behaviour. These symptoms do not show themselves until adulthood by which time the tragic inheritors have probably produced another afflicted generation. There is no known cure and the course of the disease is inevitable.

EMBRYONIC DEVELOPMENT AND ENVIRONMENT

After an ovum has been fertilised it divides and multiplies many times to form the embryo. All the cells contain identically structured chromosomes, but they start to develop different functions depending on their location. Groups of cells differentiate into brain, liver, heart, skin, hair and so on.

What a cell becomes depends, at least in the early stages, upon its position relative to the other cells. If a group of cells is transplanted in the laboratory from a region that will later become skin and is placed in a region that will subsequently become brain, then they, too, will become brain cells.[3] Similarly if potential brain cells are transplanted at an early stage to a group of cells destined to become skin, then they will develop into skin cells. At early stages of development cells produce structures that are programmed in conjunction with surrounding structures. However, if the cells are transplanted after they have begun to develop their special characteristics then they retain that form even if moved to another part of the body.

The pre-natal conditions of the womb provide a constant and protective environment for the embryo. Temperature, pressure, oxygen and salt balance are all maintained at a constant level which is very important for the foetus, since any variation in these can endanger its development. Although the foetus and the mother have separate bloodstreams, the blood capillaries of both come into close proximity in the placenta and substances are able to diffuse across from one bloodstream to the other.

Both physiological changes and psychological changes in the mother can affect the foetus since both may alter the chemical composition of her blood and so affect the foetal bloodstream via the placenta. Drugs, hormones, antibodies, antigens, food, oxygen, all these diffuse across from the mother's blood to that of the foetus. The close association between the maternal bloodstream and that of the embryo enables the mother to nourish the foetus and remove waste materials and carbon dioxide via her own body, but it can also lead to the introduction of harmful substances.

Expectant mothers given increasingly heavy doses of sedative drugs seem to have babies who, at birth, are less attentive to their surroundings than other babies.[4] Large doses of quinine, morphine and barbiturates may adversely affect the foetus[5] and mothers who take heroin can produce babies who are addicted to the drug at birth.[6]

Infectious diseases such as syphilis, tuberculosis and rubella

(German measles) may be transmitted through the placenta. During the first three months of pregnancy rubella may cause abnormalities such as cataract, deafness and mental deficiency.[7] Other non-infectious conditions of the mother, like diabetes and hypertension, are associated with an above average incidence of spontaneous abortion and still births.[7]

The mother's diet also affects the development of the embryo. Despite great variations in maternal diet the foetus manages to maintain the content of its blood in a fairly constant state and even when the mother is under-nourished the embryo gets more than its fair share of nourishment. Because, however, the foetus is growing rapidly it can at certain periods of its growth be more seriously damaged than the mother by her poor diet.[5] [8]

The effects of malnutrition

During embryonic development the number of nerve cells in the brain increases at an average rate of 20,000 a minute, but there are certain critical periods in the development of the brain when it undergoes spurts in its rate of growth. At these times it is particularly vulnerable to under-nutrition. These periods of rapid brain growth occur both whilst the child is in the womb and in the first months of life. The best estimate of the time of brain growth spurts in Man is given by Dobbing as being probably during the last three months of gestation and the first eighteen months of infancy.[9] There is growing evidence that severe malnourishment at these times can stunt the development of the brain. To what extent this is related to later retardation in the child remains so far unknown.

There can be little doubt, however, that there is a critical period during the first months of life when the damage produced by malnourishment has serious and perhaps a permanent consequence for the child even if its circumstances improve. There is an association between protein-calorie malnutrition in infancy and backwardness in psychological development.[10]

One study compared twenty calorie-deficient children aged 11·8 to 43·5 months with nineteen normal children on a sorting task indicative of cognitive development. The malnourished children performed worse than the controls and the effect was greatest for the younger children. After twelve weeks of remedial treatment the differential between the two groups remained.[11] A similar study by Cravioto[12] looked at young children in hospital who had suffered severe malnutrition. The older the children were on entering hospital the more closely during treatment did they approach the motor and intellectual norms for their age despite having been well below par on their entry. Those infants, on the other hand, who were under six months of age when they entered hospital never made up their deficiencies. It is believed that malnutrition of a child under one year for a period lasting more than four months results in severe retardation which cannot be corrected.[13] However, a word of caution must be injected here. It is extremely difficult to establish a clear causal connection between malnutrition and retarded mental development since malnutrition is nearly always accompanied by poor socio-economic conditions, bad housing, high infection rates and general disadvantages which may have been present for generations. Cobos[14] reports that the prevalence of malnutrition in his studies has always been related to other indices of deprivation such as large families, overcrowding, low income and poor level of education in both mother and father. It is difficult to conduct research which controls for factors such as these, although attempts have been made to conduct studies comparing an ill-nourished child with a sibling which has been well nourished.[14] [15] Apparently, where malnutrition is common, it is not unusual to find one child getting an adequate diet whilst its brothers and sisters are near starvation. In these studies the malnourished children are invariably found to do worse on developmental tests than their better-fed sibling. Again, however, some of this effect could be due to parents showing a preference for one child and, therefore, encouraging it in other ways, or to the fact that the better-nourished child might have more energy and motivation to carry out the tests. Thus it would appear impossible, at present, to separate out the effects of malnutrition alone on psychological functioning, but it is likely that if a foetus or an infant is under-nourished at certain critical periods of its growth there will be associated effects on its later intellectual development.

Certainly, in rats, Dobbing found that even mild under-nourishment of the foetus resulted in measurable deficiencies in brain size, cell number and lipid composition that were irreversible.[16]

We tend to associate malnutrition with the materially less fortunate parts of the world, but it can occur in rich countries such as Britain. For example, under-nourishment sometimes occurs in the later-born children of ill-nourished mothers, where there are disturbances in the mother-child relationship, for instance failure to provide adequate food and, in cases of emotional upset, either refusal to eat, or altered intestinal motility and consequent decreased absorption of foodstuffs into the bloodstream.

The effects of the mother's emotional state

A second class of factors which may affect the development of the foetus is less directly attributable to the physical condition of the mother, but may arise from her emotional state during pregnancy. It is probable that the effects of emotion in the mother are transmitted to the embryo through the changes it brings about in her physiological condition.

The old wives' tale of pregnant women eating strawberries and producing babies with strawberry-shaped birth marks, or being frightened by a mouse and having a child with a mouse-shaped mole are no longer believed by the majority of people, but it is well known that stress and anxiety affect the level of various chemicals in the bloodstream and that, in this way, the mother's emotional state can have repercussions upon the child she is carrying. Much of the evidence for this comes from animal studies, for in these cases it is easier to control effects which arise out of the animal's heredity or environment and which might become confused with effects due to its experiences in the womb.

The living conditions and heredity of laboratory animals can be standardised so that there are no confounding factors, and reliable control groups can be obtained for comparison purposes.

In a study by Thomson and his associates, pregnant rats were subjected to stressful electric shocks. Pregnant rats from the same litter acted as controls, so that heredity was held constant. When the offspring were born they were cross-fostered, that is, the offspring of the rats which had been stressed were brought up by the mothers in the control group and the offspring of the mothers in the control group were reared by the mothers who had been stressed. This cross-fostering ruled out the possibility of a mother who had been made anxious influencing the behaviour of her offspring after they were born. The experimenters found that the offspring of the rats who had received the stressful stimulus during pregnancy were more emotional, less active and slower to learn than were the offspring of the control group.[17] Even the use of rats does not rule out the existence of complicating factors, e.g. different supplies of milk in stressed and unstressed mothers. Some investigators have found opposite effects to those reported in Thomson's study – that the offspring of mothers who had received shocks were less emotional, more active and quicker to learn.[18] These contradictory results could be due to different experimenters using different strains of rats, so that heredity must be taken into account when generalising from the results of particular experiments. Nevertheless, whatever the effect may be, such experiments do demonstrate that emotional experiences during pregnancy have consequences for the offspring.

In human beings there is some evidence that prolonged emotional stress during pregnancy can lead to increased activity and a lower birth weight. More active foetuses tend to become babies prone to stomach upsets, restlessness and irritability.[19] Increased foetal activity is also produced by prolonged activity, fatigue or anxiety in the mother which can alter the carbon dioxide and lactic acid levels in the blood of the embryo. Fear and anger in the mother have been found to increase foetal pulse rate, presumably because of the effects of adrenalin in the blood and it has been suggested that constant and intense maternal anxiety causes imbalance in the autonomic nervous system and disfunction in the stomach of the foetus, heart spasms, and later, emotional maladjustment in the infant.[20] As with the studies on malnutrition one should beware of generalising from these studies of maternal emotional stress in humans because of the confounding effects of heredity and the later handling of the young infant by the mother. Nevertheless, studies which monitor the immediate effects of a particular maternal state and compare the condition of the foetus before and after the particular stress, show that there is an increase of several hundred per cent in foetal body movements and this can persist for several weeks.[7]

One might expect that in our society an illegitimate pregnancy would be fraught with stress for the mother. A careful study by James[21] suggests that the disproportionate number of stillbirths to unmarried mothers may, partly at least, be a consequence of psychological and social stress. (The excess of stillbirths to unmarried women over married women is 32 per cent for those under 20 years of age, 37 per cent for those aged 20–24 and 40 per cent for those aged 25–29.) James' study controlled such factors as socio-economic status, time of conception (which apparently, but not surprisingly, varies with the warmth of weather in the unmarried) and the use made of ante-natal services. He suggests that some of the very large discrepancy may be accounted for by the prolonged worry which is the usual concomitant of an illegitimate pregnancy.

It is debatable whether other stimuli experienced by the mother can affect the foetus. Loud noises, pressure and vibration are probably buffered by the protective layer of the amniotic fluid which surrounds the embryo, together with the uterus and the maternal abdominal wall. Research has been done on the effect of reducing the abdominal pressure on the foetus. Initially it was claimed that this led to superior intellectual and motor development by giving the foetus an extra supply of oxygen.[22] Liddicoat, however, in a study which was better controlled than earlier ones, found no differences in intelligence between the children of mothers who had had abdominal decompression during pregnancy and those who had had ordinary physiotherapy. Both these groups produced children, who, at three years of age, were of slightly higher I.Q. than a control group whose mothers had had no antenatal treatment.[23] The results can probably be explained by the higher intelligence and greater solicitude of those mothers who seek ante-antal care.

Sorting out the differential effects of genetic factors and pre-natal experience is very complex. Many studies with humans have to rely on the memories that women have of their pregnancies. Memory is notoriously susceptible to blurring, reconstruction, wishful thinking, etc., and is rapidly overlaid by, and confused with, subsequent events.

Mothers whose children attend child guidance clinics tend to report a higher than average number of complications in pregnancy, but this could merely mean that the woman has the type of personality which could both give her a difficult pregnancy, or cause her to remember it as being so, and adversely affect the behaviour of her child. There need be no direct relationship between a child's behaviour and any adverse experiences in his mother's womb.

Experiments with animals suggest, as one would expect, that there is an interaction between genetic and other pre-natal factors. This can be shown by making use of a technique for transplanting embryos from one womb to another. First, rats are bred to produce two distinct strains, one highly emotional and one very placid. The female rats are then made pregnant by male rats from their own strain. The pregnant rats from each strain are then divided into two groups. In one group the pregnancy is left to continue normally. In the other group the embryos are transplanted into rats of the opposite strain, i.e. the mothers 'swap' embryos so that the embryos from half of the highly emotional mothers will develop in the placid mothers, and the embryos from half the placid mothers will develop inside the highly emotional mothers. If genetics was all important one would expect the offspring to compare with their parents in emotionality. In fact what happens is that those offspring from the highly emotional mothers which are transplanted into the placid mothers are not so emotional as their brethren who grew inside their own mothers. The offspring of the placid rats brought to term in highly emotional mothers are more emotional than their brethren who were left alone.

Thus, the emotionality which is a consequence of genetic inheritance is modified by the experience of the offspring within the womb.

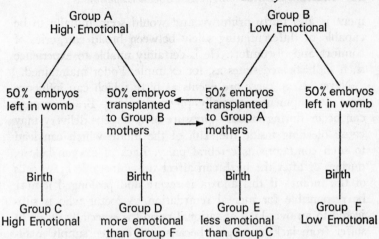

Figure 3   Transplantation of embryos from one strain of rats to another to show the interaction of heredity and pre-natal environment

BIRTH

It has been suggested by some writers, especially those of the psychoanalytic school, that the actual process of being born may have traumatic emotional consequences for a child. They believe that the child experiences the birth as separation and rejection and that the anxiety which is an accompaniment of these sentiments is re-experienced throughout life on occasions of helplessness and loss, so that the person so afflicted may feel a desire to return to the safety of the womb. The sensation provided by the womb, they suggest, is a warm and cosy condition of 'oneness' with the mother. It is from this idyllic state that the infant is precipitated into the cold, harsh world where he must fend for himself.[24] There is absolutely no reliable evidence on this point. Those patients who have produced 'memories of the event'[25] have probably been prompted by the analyst and then had their recollections extensively interpreted. The underdeveloped state of the brain of the neonate makes it highly unlikely that memories of this kind could be laid down, nor can small infants form such concepts as 'oneness' and 'separateness'. The newborn child's emotional equip-

D

ment is also fairly primitive and would seem initially to be capable of differentiating solely between broad categories of comfort and discomfort. He is certainly unable to experience such sophisticated states as, for example, Fodor maintained.

Nevertheless, there are events at birth which can influence later development, especially physical injury. Brain damage can occur during labour – pressure or a forceps delivery may cause bleeding inside the skull of the infant which can lead to such conditions as cerebral palsy. Lack of oxygen before, during, or after the birth can affect the vulnerable brain cells of the infant – if this anoxia is severe and prolonged it may be responsible for mental retardation. A foetus who is subjected to an over-long gestational period is especially prone to suffer from lack of oxygen, because the oxygen supply available from the mother tends to decrease in the last weeks of pregnancy.

A study of five-day-old neonates compared those who had suffered from oxygen lack with those who had not. Those who had been deprived of oxygen were less sensitive to pain, less mature in motor development and the pupils of their eyes showed a weaker reflex response to variations in light intensity. They were also more irritable and tense. A follow-up study three years later found them still to be comparatively backward both in physical and mental skills.[26]

Unmarried mothers, older mothers and first pregnancies are prone to produce premature babies.[7] [27] [28] Babies can be adversely affected by being born prematurely, although the proportion who are is very small. A tiny minority of those of low birth weight (which, of course, includes the premature) are in danger of mental retardation. There is also some evidence that the premature are susceptible to behaviour disorders as they grow up, e.g. speech and reading difficulties, to be clumsy and either over- or under-active and to have visual defects.[29] Some of these effects suggest mild but diffuse brain damage of some kind, but some of the differences from full-term babies could be due to anxious and overprotective reactions on the part of the family when faced with a premature baby. Disease,[28] undernourishment and low social status in the mother are also associated with short-term pregnancies, so that when considering the effects of prematurity itself, it is difficult, in follow-up studies to disentangle them from the consequences of an adverse environment. Babies who go the full term of pregnancy, but who are lighter than the requisite weight for their date of arrival, also seem to be at risk. A birth weight which is below average has been found to be associated with hyperkinetic behaviour, low achievement and I.Q. scores and poor school performance. In a study of nineteen monozygotic and fifty-eight dizygotic twins, wherever there was a difference in I.Q. score it was the lighter twin at birth who had the lower score, even when the weight difference was as small as 10 per cent.[30][31][32][33]

In all these effects it is obvious that it is the interaction of genetic, pre-natal and post-natal environment that is important in influencing the development and behaviour of the child. This interaction of constitutional and situational factors will continue to be stressed in later chapters.

REFERENCES

1 H. Hyden and E. Egyhazi, 'Nuclear RNA changes of nerve cells during a learning experience in rats'. *Proc. Nat. Acad. Sci. U.S.*, *48* (1962), 1366–73.

2 H. Hyden and E. Egyhazi, 'Glial RNA changes during a learning experience in rats'. *Proc. Nat. Acad. Sci. U.S.*, *49* (1963), 618–24.

3 H. Waddington, *The Strategy of the Genes* (London, Macmillan, 1957).

4 G. Stechler, 'New-born attention as affected by medication during labour', *Science, 144, whole No. 3616* (1964), 315–17.

5 L. W. Sontag, 'The possible relationship of pre-natal environment to schizophrenia', *The Etiology of Schizophrenia* (New York, Basic Books, 1960).

6 R. W. Cobrinik, T. Hood Jr and E. Chusid, 'The effect of maternal narcotic addiction on the new-born infant. Review of the literature and report of 22 cases', *Pediatrics*, *24* (1959), 288–304.

7 M. F. Ashley Montagu, *Pre-natal Influences* (Springfield, Ill., C. C. Thomas, 1962).

8 B. S. Burke, V. A. Beal, S. B. Kirkwood and H. C. Stuart, 'Nutrition studies during pregnancy', *Amer. J. Obstet. Gyn.*, *46* (1943), 38–52.

9 J. Dobbing, 'Undernutrition and the developing brain: the relevance of animal models to the human problem', *Amer. J. Dis. Child, 120* (1970), 411–15.

10 B. F. Monckeberg, *FAO/WHO/UNICEF Protein Advisory Group Bulletin, 11* (1971), 9–17.

11 L. M. Brockman and H. N. Ricciuti, 'Severe protein-calorie malnutrition and cognitive development in infancy and early childhood', *Devel. Psychol., 4* (1971), 312–19.

12 J. Cravioto, 'Mental performance in school-age children', *Amer. J. Dis. Child., 120* (1970), 404–10.

13 H. P. Chase and H. P. Martin, 'Undernutrition and child development'. Paper read before a conference on neuropsychological methods for the Association of impaired brain functioning, in the malnourished child. Palo Alto, Calif. (1969).

14 F. Cobos, 'Malnutrition and mental retardation: conceptual issues' in *Lipids, Malnutrition and the Developing Brain* (Ciba Foundation Symposium, Elsevier, Excerpta Medica, 1972).

15 J. Cravioto, C. Pinero, M. Arroyo and E. Alcalde, 'Nutrition in preschool and school age', *Swedish Nutrition Foundation Symp. VII*, 85–9, K. Blix (Ed.), (Uppsala, Almquist & Wiksell, 1969).

16 J. Dobbing, 'Undernutrition and the developing brain', *Handbook of Neurochemistry, 6*, A. Lajtha (Ed.), (New York, Plenum Press, 1971).

17 W. R. Thomson, J. Watson and W. R. Charlesworth, 'The effects of pre-natal maternal stress on offspring behaviour in rats', *Psychol. Monog., 76, whole No. 38* (1962).

18 L. J. Grota, 'The effects of pre-natal stimulation upon subsequent behaviour and physiology of the rat', *Diss. Abstr. 24* (9), (1964), 3847–8.

19 E. K. Turner, 'The syndrome in the infant resulting from maternal emotional tension during pregnancy', *Med. J. Austr., 1* (1956), 221–22.

20 A. Davids, R. H. Holden and G. B. Gray, 'Maternal anxiety during pregnancy and adequacy of mother-child adjustment eight months following child birth', *Ch. Devel., 34* (1963), 993–1003.

21 W. H. James, 'The effect of maternal psychological stress on the foetus', *Brit. J. Psychiat., 115* (1969), 556–9.

22 O. S. Heyns, *Abdominal Decompression,* a monograph (Johannesburg, Witwatersrand University Press, 1963).

23 R. Liddicoat, 'The effects of maternal ante-natal decompression treatment on infant mental development', *S. Afr. Med. J., 42* (1967), 203–11.

24 J. A. C. Brown, *Freud and the Post-Freudians* (Harmondsworth, Penguin Books, 1961).

25 N. Fodor, *The Search for the Beloved* (New York, Hermitage Press, 1949).

26 F. K. Graham, R. G. Matarazzo and D. M. Caldwell, 'Behaviour differences between normal and traumatized newborns, II: Standardisation, reliability and validity', *Psychol. Monog., 70* (1956), 21.

27 C. M. Drillien and R. W. Ellis, *The Growth and Development of the Prematurely Born Infant* (Baltimore, Williams & Williams, 1964).

28 M. M. Shirley, 'Development of immature babies during their first two years', *Ch. Devel., 9* (1938), 333–46.

29 M. D. Braine, C. B. Heimer, H. Wortis and A. M. Fredman, 'Factors associated with impairment of the early development of prematures', *Monog. Soc. Res. Child Devel., 31* (4), (1966), Serial No. 16.

30 J. B. Arey and J. Dent, 'Pathological findings in premature infants', *Amer. J. Clin. Pathol.*, *20* (1950), 1016–25.
31 G. Weiner, 'Psychological correlates of premature birth: a review', *J. Nerv. Ment. Dis.*, *134* (1962), 129–44.
32 C. M. Drillien, 'Possible causes of handicap in babies of low birth weight', *J. Obstet. Gynaec. Brit. Comm.*, *72* (1965), 993–7.
33 J. A. Churchill, 'The relationship between intelligence and birth weight in twins', *Neurology, 15* (1965), 341–7.

3

Infant Man

*Language was not powerful enough to describe
the infant phenomenon.*
Charles Dickens, *Nicholas Nickleby*

There are several basic theories in psychology which concern themselves with the development of the child, for example those of the Freudian school, Piaget, and the Behaviourists. Although each tends to use its own kind of language, so that at first reading they appear to have little in common, their ideas are by no means antagonistic, but can be seen to be complementary, throwing light from different directions and illuminating several aspects of the child's development. Thus Piaget is interested primarily in thought processes, Freud in emotion and the Behaviourists in behaviour.

The newly born child is already unique due to his hereditary characteristics and to his experiences before and during birth. All babies, however, unless grossly abnormal, do behave in certain similar ways. This behaviour is initially in the form of reflexes, but learning rapidly establishes other patterns of response.

Both 'instinct' and 'reflex' have precise technical meanings in psychology, unlike their diluted form in everyday speech. A *reflex* is a purely nervous and muscular response such as the knee-jerk response to a tap on the knee, or coughing in response to irritation of the throat. The basis of a reflex is an inherited nervous pathway which 'short-circuits' stimulus and response via the spinal cord, so that higher brain processes need not be involved.

The popular use of the word *instinct* occurs in two ways, either as in 'I applied the brakes instinctively' or as in 'He has an instinct for business'. In the first example the sentence

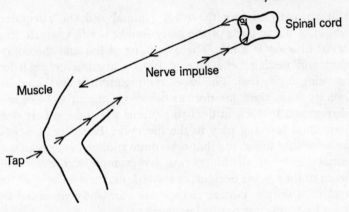

Figure 4   A reflex response (knee jerk)

refers to a complex learned skill and in the second it can be taken to refer to a particular aptitude. As we shall see these meanings fall well outside the limits allowed by psychological definitions. There are two principal ways in which psychologists use the term 'instinct'. One of these is derived from the study of animals in their ethology and refers to behaviour, and the other is psychoanalytical and regards instincts as the driving forces underlying behaviour. Both definitions, however, have elements in common.

INNATE TENDENCIES — THE ETHOLOGICAL
APPROACH

Ethologists regard instincts as complex patterns of behaviour. To conform to their definition the behaviour must fulfil certain conditions. It must be universal in a species; it should be relatively stereotyped in appearance so that every time it occurs it should follow a similar pattern, as with the mating behaviour of the rat; and it should manifest itself at the first opportunity without having been learned from another member of the species, that is, it must be built in to the animal genetically.

On this definition instincts can be regarded as chains of co-ordinated responses that are laid down in the genetic code of a species and that have been adopted by natural selection because of their survival value in the course of evolution. They will normally involve the whole animal and the integrated action of many parts of the body (unlike a reflex which may occur in a single limb). The swimming of fish and the courtship and nesting behaviour of birds may thus be regarded as being instinctual. The lower the organism is on the evolutionary scale, the more does its behaviour appear to be rigidly determined by such instinctive patterns and the less part does individual learning play in the life cycle. However, it would be a mistake to assume that even quite rudimentary organisms cannot learn at all. Flatworms, for example, can eventually learn to turn to left or right, or towards darkness or light, at the end of a simple T-maze if they are constantly rewarded by food for taking one particular course.[1]

The fixed action pattern of an instinct is triggered by an appropriate signal, called by ethologists a 'sign stimulus' from the environment. Studies of the natural environments of animals, birds and fish have identified some of these sign stimuli. For example, the courtship ritual of the male tenspined stickleback is elicited by a certain aspect of the appearance of the female, her swollen belly. If a series of life-like wooden models of female sticklebacks is presented to the male, no response is elicited, whereas he will court a crude, but appropriately swollen, shape.[2]

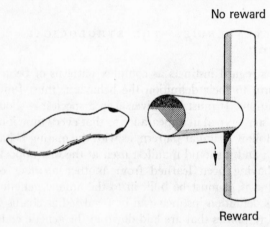

No reward

Reward

Figure 5   This flat-worm after a sufficient number of trials will learn always to turn to the right at the end of the 'T' maze

In baby birds various signals act as sign stimuli. Young thrushes gape for food only at models of their parents which are of a certain size and above their own eye level. Young herring gulls, who peck at their parents' beaks to obtain food, will peck at models of adult herring gulls' heads only if there is a red patch on them.[3] A robin in defence of its territory will attack intruders; if such a robin is presented with a stuffed adult robin, a stuffed juvenile robin and a bundle of red feathers, he will direct as many aggressive responses towards the red feathers as he will towards the dead adult, but the juvenile model elicits hardly any such behaviour – it has no red breast.[4] Thus there are critical elements in the stimulus situation which call forth particular kinds of responses.

To establish whether behaviour is learned or instinctive it is necessary to isolate an animal from birth and bring it up without contact with other members of its species, so that opportunities for learning are absent. Reed buntings reared in this way from hatching will, when mature, sing the correct reed bunting song. Male rats brought up in isolation will at puberty (three months of age) display the usual mating pattern of the species at their first contact with receptive females.[5] This instinct for mating, however, is not the case with animals higher up the evolutionary scale. Chimpanzees reared in isolation have great difficulty in establishing sexual and social relationships when they grow up.[6] In higher species mating depends less on instinct and more upon opportunities for learning.

Some behaviour which appears to be instinctual – unlearned, stereotyped and universal in a species – may in fact be learned at a very early stage in the animal's life. Kuo[7] reared chicks in isolation and found that they showed a pecking response from the moment of hatching, apparently an in-built pattern of behaviour. Further investigation revealed, however, that whilst the chick is still in the egg, its head is stimulated by the yolk sac which moves rhythmically in time to contractions of the fluid in the egg, synchronous with the heart beat of the chick. Head-lunging is, therefore, well-established even before the chick hatches, but it is not independent of experience.

Other apparently unlearned patterns of behaviour only appear at the requisite time if the animal is living in its proper environment and has the normal life experiences of its species. The dichotomy between learned and unlearned behaviour may not, therefore, be very useful. The maternal behaviour of a female rat, for example, normally takes the form of nest-building, cleaning and retrieving the young. If a pregnant female rat has been brought up in a special environment, where she has been fed on powdered food from an immovable container, lived on a wire mesh floor so that faeces have fallen through, and been deprived of material to manipulate, move about or explore, then she becomes a very inadequate mother and her 'maternal instincts' are severely disrupted.[8] Thus the appearance of even maternal behaviour is not unrelated to opportunities to explore and manipulate. Some apparently instinctive actions may not automatically result from a genetic programme, but rather may be dispositions to act in particular ways in response to particular environments.

A contributory factor in instinctive behaviour is the internal condition of the animal. Is there a state of tissue starvation or hormonal imbalance or an excess of some particular hormone, any of which could affect food- water- or sex-seeking behaviour? Rats, for example, do not mate unless the female is at the appropriate stage – oestrus – in her hormonal cycle and castrated rats will mate if given an injection of the male sex hormone, testosterone.[9]

There is an interaction between all these factors. The genetic plan, past experience, internal condition and external stimuli must be present together for the instinctual behaviour to occur. The pattern of behaviour which is produced may, moreover, vary with the sign stimulus, for example, at the appropriate time of year the male stickleback's sex hormones make him either attack red-bellied males or court swollen-bellied females.[10]

The limitation of instinctive behaviour is that it can be maladaptive. If there is some gross change in the environment the animal is still stuck with the old behaviour which may no longer be of any value. It is possible for an instinctive pattern to be triggered by an inappropriate stimulus, so that the animal is endangered. For instance, small fish who think they are about to eat a juicy worm may find themselves instead being swallowed by an angler fish who lies buried in the mud waving a worm-like process above its head.[11]

There seems to be an impulsion within the animal to perform certain acts. In the absence of the appropriate stimulus it may try to carry out the behaviour in a way which is undesirable. For example, a bird deprived of nest-building materials may pull out its own chest feathers in order to make a nest. Thus the drawback of instinctive behaviour is that it is not very flexible or adjustable to environmental circumstances.

Some programmes of behaviour are completely inflexible. The reed bunting, for example, can sing only its own song even if brought up with other species of bird. Other programmes may be more 'open', with some patterns being responsive to learning. A chaffinch reared in isolation produces only a shortened chaffinch song. If he is then put with linnets he will add part of the linnet repertoire, but if next placed with his own species he will sing the full chaffinch song and abandon the linnet notes.[12]

A completely closed programme of behaviour means that the animal cannot adapt to a changed environment. The more 'open' the programme the greater the flexibility of the animal and the more chances it has of survival. The higher the animal the fewer fixed reactions it has and the more does the upper brain overcome the automatism of the lower centres.

Man may have innate dispositions of the kind we have been looking at but these are rapidly overlaid and altered by learning. A limited range of behaviour – crawling, walking and babbling, for example – does develop without learning, but is dependent upon maturation and exercise. Eating, drinking and sex are universal human activities, but they have different manifestations in different people. Man's great ability to learn means that behaviour can become flexible enough to enable survival in a variety of environments and in the face of changing circumstances, but it also means that during our long period of learning we are helpless and dependent.

INNATE TENDENCIES – THE FREUDIAN VIEW

A rather different view of instinct was formulated by Freud,[13] although it shares the ethological philosophy that an organism is born with a disposition to perform certain acts and with certain needs and that the aim of behaviour is to return the organism to a state of quiescence.

Freud believed that the human being is an energy system. Energy from food is expended in activity, both physical and mental. Mental energy was called by Freud 'psychic energy' and is said to carry out psychological work – imagining, thinking, remembering, perceiving. Psychic energy, he believed, was channelled by the instincts. The function of the instincts was to satisfy basic needs, such as hunger and sex. Freud constructed a model of mental processes composed of three elements : the Id, Ego and Superego. The Id is present from birth but the other two develop later.

The function of the Id is to gratify the instincts by any means available. It is said to be governed by the pleasure principle. It is the hedonist and 'spoiled child' within us all, for it is concerned only with subjective reality and is responsible for impulsive behaviour. The Id does not think, it wishes or it acts.

As a human baby is not in a position to satisfy its own needs, it must, therefore, inevitably suffer some frustration, because of delay in the gratification of its needs. In Freud's view this frustration gives rise to what he called 'the primary process', that is the imaging of the desired object. Since the Id is only in touch with subjective reality, for the Id an image is the same as a real object in the outside world as, in Freud's words, 'the mirage of oasis is real to the thirsty traveller'. The Id has no means of distinguishing reality from fantasy, or satisfactory from non-satisfactory objects. Thus an infant under the impetus of a strong feeling of hunger may attempt to eat a piece of coal.

It is obvious that the wishes of a child are not sufficient to ensure its satisfaction. In order to survive it must learn to distinguish between fantasy, imagination and reality and it must learn to interact with other persons in the vicinity. Initially all control over the infant's behaviour is imposed from outside. One of the major achievements of a society is the way in which this external control gradually moves inward, so that by adulthood most people have developed some degree of self-control which enables them to adapt to those around them and to the exigencies of the environment.

The subjective reality of the infant, then, gradually gives way to, but is not replaced by, a recognition of physical reality, for example, that coal does not satisfy hunger, that fire will burn; and of social reality, that there are certain accepted ways of doing things, certain behaviours which are more desirable in the eyes of one's parents than others. Of course, this social reality will vary slightly from family to family and even more with social class and culture.

It seems that inherent in the development of the child is conflict between its own demands and those of others and between itself and things, for instance its ability to manipulate a toy – witness the intensity of the concentration and ultimate rage of a baby who is just not capable of grasping a particular toy. Out of this conflict comes knowledge and growth, as the child learns to come to terms with reality. In Freudian terms, the child develops an Ego – a self – which is governed by the 'reality principle', reality being that which exists in the world outside the infant. The aim of the Ego is to postpone activity until the actual object which will satisfy a need is available, in the case of hunger an edible object. This process involves a delay in gratification whilst exploration of the environment takes place and is known as the 'secondary process', the discovery of reality by means of a plan of action based upon thought and reason. The secondary process is thinking and problem-solving.

The Freudian view of instinct and the ethological view have much in common. Both assume that the organism is impelled into activity by some internal lack and that the aim of behaviour is to restore some kind of internal equilibrium. Both believe that a certain amount of energy is available for the satisfaction of needs. Just as the 'Id' may act in defiance of reality when a need is strong, so a strong disposition to perform an instinctual act may lead a bird to pluck out its own feathers to make a nest. Freud's 'primary process' refers to the built-in abilities of the infant, e.g. all infants must have the ability to form mental images soon after birth, otherwise, in the absence of language, they would not be able to retain what they had learned. We may compare this in-built ability with the term 'instinct' in the ethological sense although it is much more flexible, since the content of the images will vary with the experience of the child. The 'secondary process' of learning is what, at its highest level, frees Man from the fixed action patterns of lower animals; we may regard it as an example of the control of the neo-cortex over the lower brain. The Ego, the sense of self-identity and mastery over the environment grow out of our capacity to learn, to speculate, to remember and to integrate our knowledge.

Freud's formulation provides a useful model for looking at the transition from mindless gratification-seeking to realistic thought which is achieved by learning.

EARLY LEARNING

Apart from their genetic equipment, human babies are born with a number of reflexes and several biological needs, plus an ability to retain images of some kind. These attributes constitute the basis for future learning.

The biological needs are for oxygen, food, water and elimination of waste products, etc. Many of the reflexes are designed to serve these basic needs and include yawning (present five minutes after birth), turning the head if the cheek is touched (essential for breast-feeding), sucking, swallowing, pushing salty objects from the mouth, head shuddering to a bitter taste, crying and coughing.

Some 'social' expressions such as grimacing spontaneously or to an unpleasant stimulus, and smiling when well-fed or tickled under the chin, appear in the first weeks of life. Newborn babies can also squirm, arch their backs, grasp with their hands, show the knee-jerk response and a pupillary response to light, and boys are capable of penis erection. If held up with the feet touching a flat surface new babies can make stepping movements, the rudimentary precursors of walking.

Piaget,[14] a Swiss writer on child development, considers the reflexes to be the basic material upon which elaborate edifices of behaviour are built through learning. During the first period of a child's life, which he calls the 'sensori-motor', the child moves from the reflex level of existence to achieve co-ordination and organisation of his senses and his actions. It involves relatively simple perceptual and motor adjustments to the world, rather than, as will happen later, symbolic representations of the world in thought. This stage is thought to occupy about the first two years of life during which the child is building up conceptual structures which Piaget calls 'schemata'.

Probably the best way to think of a schema is as an internal representation of some body of knowledge, a model of reality inside the mind which is a product of actions and their consequences. Piaget suggests that there may be many separate schemata, for different areas of existence, which may link up with each other, or at some point coalesce into a larger schema. For example, when people begin to study a new topic, such as psychology, they may begin by compartmentalising the material in their minds, constructing a separate schema unconnected to the rest of their knowledge; later, however, this material will begin to overlap with, and link up to, other areas of experience.

A schema, then, starts in a very small way, in the newly born from a reflex action. Gradually, the infant accumulates experience which can either be 'assimilated' into the schema or the schema can 'accommodate' itself to the event. By assimilation Piaget means that events, perceptions, actions can be fitted into the framework of reality that already exists. By accommodation he means that, since some experiences are not capable of being assimilated, perhaps because they are very discrepant to existing concepts, then models of reality must be altered to take the new event, perception or action into account. In adult life accommodation may become more difficult and some people may find themselves disturbed by novel ideas or strange behaviour because their basic constructs are threatened with demolition or reconstruction.

Piaget uses the 'sucking schema' to illustrate how a simple reflex can develop into a complex web of inter-related ideas. In the course of his sucking activities the baby finds out that some things are suckable, some are not, some suckable objects relieve his hunger, some do not, some suckable things are part of himself (a thumb), some are not (a corner of a sheet). Thus merely through this simple form of activity the infant is learning the qualities of objects, the difference between edible and inedible, and he is also learning to differentiate himself from the rest of the world. This distinction between himself and the other things, other people, is quite a sophisticated one and the child takes some time to learn it.

As the schema grows, chance occurrences (thumb-sucking, perhaps) become intentionally sought and the baby will suck his thumb intentionally or seek his mother's breast or the teat of a bottle. The initial reflex thus becomes a complex pattern of purposive behaviour.

Combined with reflex behaviour it would seem that the infant also has an innate disposition to explore the environment. Initially this will be mainly by using his eyes, then fingers, and as he grows it will involve the whole body and mind. Piaget called this urge to explore 'the need to know'. It drives the baby into conflict between what it cannot do and would like to do, between what it knows and what it would like to know. As was noted in the discussion of Freud's ideas it is this discrepancy between physical, social and subjective reality which instigates exploration and the growth of knowledge. Thus the baby's experience of the world develops and the number and complexity of his schemata increase.

The natural curiosity of children means that the infant is interested in any new occurrence. If he accidentally produces a novel event he will tend to repeat the action that brought it about until the novelty finally wears off. A baby with a toy suspended over his pram may first of all knock it accidentally as he waves his arms about. This sets the toy in motion and excites his interest; he attempts to repeat the action and succeeds in hitting the toy on purpose. Thus the infant is developing ideas of causation and of his own power to effect changes in his environment, and he is increasing his repertoire of behaviour. Similarly, a child may exasperate his mother by throwing some article of shopping out of his pram. She retrieves it only to see it disappear over the side once more, a cycle which may go on for some time during which the child may change his focus from, say, a tin of beans to the pillow to a toy. Irritating as this may be for the mother it is an essential part of the learning experience of the child. He is finding out what happens as a consequence of his actions. Anything which is 'moderately novel' is likely to attract the child's attention. Something which has no relation to something already in his experience is likely to be ignored since it has no link with an existing schema. Something highly familiar has little interest value.

The infant gradually learns about physical and social reality through his interaction with people, things and events. Most of what he learns is not taught to him by others but arises out of the associations he makes between one event and another and the consequences of his actions. The early learning of the child would seem to take place principally by means of two processes which have been extensively described by the Behaviourist school of psychologists. It is this early learning which builds up the schemata of the child and, in Freud's term, is the basis of the secondary process.

Classical conditioning

The phenomenon of classical conditioning was first described in detail by Pavlov[15] in the 1920s when he was conducting experiments on the digestive processes of the dog. It is now known to occur in many animal species and is easily demonstrable in the human baby. For example, if a nipple is placed in a baby's mouth it will start to suck. If this placing of the nipple is preceded on several occasions in succession by the sound of a buzzer then after about a dozen such pairings of nipple and buzzer the baby will begin to show the sucking response to the buzzer alone.[16] Thus a reflex which once appeared automatically in response to one particular stimulus can now be elicited by an entirely different stimulus. In this case the nipple is referred to as the unconditioned stimulus which produces the unconditioned response of sucking, the buzzer then becomes the conditioned stimulus to the conditioned response of sucking and learning is said to have taken place.

Classical conditioning has certain characteristics. For example, in the experiment just described, if, after the establishment of the conditioned response to the buzzer, a bell had been rung, or a gong banged, then the conditioned re-

E

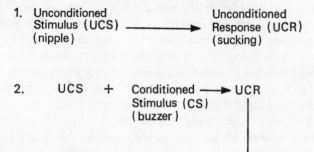

Figure 6   Establishment of a conditioned response of sucking to the sound of a buzzer

sponse of sucking would also have occurred (albeit less vigorously) to these noises – in other words a conditioned response to other stimuli of a similar nature. A conditioned response will suffer extinction if one continually presents the conditioned stimulus without the unconditioned stimulus so that if one sounded the buzzer over and over again without ever presenting the nipple, the sucking response to the buzzer would eventually die away. In other words the response must be reinforced from time to time by the presentation of the original stimulus. One can manipulate the phenomena of generalisation and extinction to teach a baby to discriminate between, say, two sounds of different pitch. First, by establishing a conditioned response to a tone o one pitch, because of generalisation the response would also occur in modified form to the tone of the second pitch. Now by consistently reinforcing the first tone and not the second, one can teach the baby to make discriminations of pitch. This method has obvious practical applications, for example one could test quite small babies for colour blindness by establishing a conditioned response to a light of a particular colour, and by selective reinforcement of different coloured lights, test its ability to discriminate between them.

In an experiment by Marinesco and Kreindler[17] a metronome was sounded for fifty seconds and followed immediately by twenty seconds of a weak electric shock to the baby's leg.

After twelve pairings of this nature a conditioned response of leg withdrawal was established to the sound of the metronome alone. The initial response of the infant was at first rather diffuse, i.e. although the shock was received by one leg only, the baby's reaction was movement of the whole body. As conditioning proceeded, the infant began to discriminate and the response narrowed down to involve only the appropriate leg. This illustrates a common aspect of the child's learning, the gradual limitation of certain responses to certain situations, so a small baby trying to grasp a toy which is just out of reach begins by making generalised movements of the whole body, waving both arms and legs about in its efforts to reach its goal. Eventually, however, the child begins to learn that all this is not necessary and it begins to reach with one hand only.

Whilst it seems likely that much of the early learning of the infant takes place by this pairing of new stimuli with reflex responses, some learning may occur merely by exposure to stimulation without the need for reinforcement. Later in life, especially with the development of language, more complex and intentional ways of learning become possible.

It has been pointed out that the fact that babies normally adapt to a feeding schedule during their first week of life suggests that they become conditioned to a particular timetable.[18] That the babies are not just responding to the stimulus of bottle or breast is shown by the fact that they exhibit spontaneous anticipatory behaviour, such as increased activity, before feeding. This early adaptation of a primitive biological drive is perhaps the first example of the development of self-regulation in a human being.

Classical conditioning may also assume an aversive form, by producing an unpleasant reaction in the child. Watson, one of the most influential of the Behaviourists, demonstrated the effects of aversive conditioning on an eleven-month-old child called Albert.[19] Albert was introduced to a tame white rat with whom he enjoyed playing. One day as Albert played with the rat a gong was struck by a steel bar right behind Albert's head. This had the effect of making Albert jump quite violently. (The response of 'jumping' is known as the startle response and it appears to be an innate reflex.) Subsequently, every time Albert reached for the white rat, the same thing happened. The startle response is accompanied by a variety of autonomic nervous responses, such as increased heart rate, holding of the breath and a 'butterflies in the stomach' feeling. These reactions are similar to those which accompany fear. Eventually, after this constant pairing of the rat with the noise, a conditioned fear response was established in Albert and he would no longer go anywhere near the rat. His aversion generalised to a dislike of furry objects in general, including beards.

This generalisation of a conditioned fear response may account for many simple phobias, such as agoraphobia or

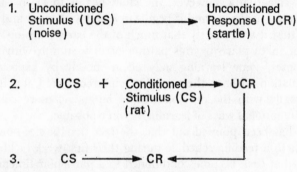

Figure 7   Establishment of a conditioned fear response

claustrophobia, where frightening experiences become associated with particular, but possibly irrelevant, aspects of a situation, such as being on a train or being alone. This kind of conditioning involves some signal in the environment (in Albert's case the white rat) that warns that something unpleasant is going to happen (a loud noise). This anticipation then triggers off an increased flow of adrenalin which leads to the physiological changes which are experienced as unpleasant. Later in the child's development this kind of reaction may be how the conscience is formed – the thought of carrying out a forbidden act makes the child feel anxious as he anticipates his mother's anger and he stops short.

This response of internal organs to external stimuli has been demonstrated in several Russian experiments following in the steps of Pavlov. In one of these[20] surgical patients had a pressure gauge inserted into the bladder, the gauge being linked to a manometer so that the subjects could see the pressure which was recorded. They were given drinks and came to associate the desire to urinate (UCR) with a certain recorded bladder pressure (UCS). Unknown to the participants, at a certain stage in the experiment, the manometer was uncoupled from the pressure gauges in their bladder and falsified mano-meter readings were presented. Although the reading on the manometer had no connection with the actual bladder pres-sure, subjects reported the desire to urinate (CR) when the readings were at or above the level they had previously learned to associate with this need. Moreover, low readings failed to produce a urination urge even when the actual bladder pres-sure was very high.

Other physiological changes can also occur as conditioned responses. The dilation and constriction of the blood vessels of the stomach have been conditioned to words such as 'warm' and 'cold' even though the subjects were unaware of the state of their stomachs.[21] Such interoceptive conditioning would account for the infant's ready adaptation to a feeding schedule and for the adult's hunger at regular mealtimes regardless of the need for food.

Where a stimulus is ambiguous, or if it is not clear which of alternative available responses is appropriate, confusion and distress can be caused. Pavlov taught his dogs to salivate, using meat as the unconditioned stimulus, to a circle drawn on a card, but he taught them, by conditioned discrimination, not to salivate in response to a drawing of an ellipse. The dogs were then presented with shapes which approached increas-ingly to a position halfway between a circle and an ellipse. In this situation the dogs developed 'experimental neurosis' and became restless, withdrawn and began to whine. In a similar way to present a child with a situation of inconsistent reward and punishment can make him uncertain as to whether his behaviour is right or wrong and can be equally disturb-ing.

The important points about classical conditioning are that it works on reflex responses which are already present in the child's repertoire and which are elicited by some stimulus. Through conditioning, the response becomes associated with a new stimulus by means of the two stimuli occurring several times very close together in time and space. Generalisation of a response may account for some phobias where the original experience is severe enough to establish an avoidance reaction, which is in itself rewarding because it stops the anxiety. Unfortunately this prevents discrimination learning from taking place, since if the person is reacting to all members of a particular conceptual class, avoiding all members of it will prevent the development of the ability to differentiate between them. For example, a child who is bitten by an Alsatian dog may develop a conditioned fear response not only to Alsatians but to dogs in general and to other species of animal. If the child then shuns further acquaintance he does not have the opportunity to learn that not all Alsatian dogs and animals are going to bite him.

The conditioning of internal responses to external stimuli has implications for the development of psychosomatic disorders such as ulcers, since particular situations may constantly elicit, say, gastric changes which eventually become pathological.

Instrumental conditioning
The phenomenon of instrumental (sometimes referred to as operant) conditioning is particularly associated now with the name of B. F. Skinner,[22] who has developed a number of practical uses of Behaviourist theory.

Instrumental learning is dependent, initially, on the trial and error behaviour of the animal or person who is engaged in exploration of the environment. Some actions are found to be rewarding, either because of the reactions of other people, or because of the power of the action to satisfy some need. The child learns to behave in certain ways because these are reinforced or rewarded by food, comfort or social approval in the form of a smile. Infants appear to find the sight of a human face particularly rewarding[23] and they respond with interest and reflex smiles. The baby's smile is rewarding for the mother and may in turn 'condition' her to spend more time leaning over the cot and talking to him. On the other hand some of the baby's responses will be discouraged, either deliberately by parents or by the fact that they have an unpleasant outcome or because they are not reinforced by reward. Rewards may be positive or may be the ending of some unpleasant state, feeling cold, hungry or uncomfortable.

Instrumental conditioning does not involve a specific response to a specific stimulus in the environment. It is rather that some of the behaviour emitted by the child is encouraged and so is likely to be repeated in similar circumstances, and the rest is discouraged by punishment or indifference and vanishes from his repertoire. Thus purposive patterns of behaviour develop.

As with classical conditioning there must be some consistency of reinforcement to establish a response, and the response is also subject to generalisation, extinction and discrimination.

An example of spontaneously emitted behaviour which is reinforced selectively is speech. All babies begin to babble at a certain age. Initially the babbling is very similar in all babies regardless of nationality. It thus contains the sounds of languages other than the baby's own. Gradually as other people respond to and reinforce the sounds of one particular language the other sounds begin to disappear. An English mother will smile and encourage, by her repetition, sounds made by the baby which approximate Ma-ma and Da-da. The baby learns that she is pleased when he says something that sounds like Da-da to his father, but less pleased if he calls his father Ma-ma. Thus he learns to discriminate between the names of the adults in his life. (This early trial and error in respect of language and the operation of reinforcement is clearly not the whole answer to language acquisition. This will be considered further in a later chapter.)

Many experimental demonstrations of operant conditioning are available. Greenspoon[24] provided a simple example of the use of social approval as a positive reinforcer of verbal behaviour. He instructed his subjects to talk about anything they liked. If during the course of conversation they uttered a plural noun, Greenspoon responded with 'Uh huh', at other times he said and did nothing. As the session proceeded there was an increase in the number of plural nouns emitted by the subject. Similarly, in another experiment the interviewer showed interest only when the subject gave an expression of personal opinion such as 'I think' or 'I believe that'. Such expressions became more frequent as the conversation went on.[25]

Children have also been taught to co-operate by the use of operant techniques. In an experiment by Azrin and Lindsley[26] children between the ages of 7 and 12 years were put together in pairs and seated at opposite sides of a table separated from each other by a wire screen. In front of each child were three holes and a stylus. The children were shown that the stylus would fit into the holes, but were given no other instructions. They were, however, told that they would receive a sweet occasionally. Unknown to the children, if each of them placed the stylus in the hole which was directly opposite that of the other child, and if they did this within 0·04 seconds of each other, then a red light would go on and a sweet would be delivered to one of them via a chute. At first the children engaged in a lot of random trial and error behaviour, but all learned the secret in the first ten minutes and co-operated to get sweets which they divided between them.

In order to develop conditioned responses and form new associations between two events or objects it is evident that they must occur in close succession and that there should be some kind of motivation in the learner, that is, a particular want or need should be present, whether material or social, inborn or acquired. Acquired needs have a large cultural element as with needs for prestige, power, achievement and social recognition. Thus as well as being based upon the pleasant or unpleasant outcome of a response, learning may also result from the satisfaction of desires that are acquired through training in the particular cultural values of the society within which the child grows up.

Positive reinforcement is more effective when it does not occur on every occasion of the emission of the response, as though it is worth working harder for a rare reward. Negative reinforcement, that is, some kind of punishment, may be effective in extinguishing a response in a child, but it may be merely suppressed and return with undiminished vigour once the fear of punishment is removed.[27] Punishment also has emotional side-effects like increased arousal, crying, discouragement and loss of sensitivity to environmental cues – as these side-effects diminish so does the effect of the punishment. It is, moreover, sometimes difficult for a child to know which of a set of associated events, objects or actions is directly related to the punishment. This is especially the case where no explanation is given by the parent. In extreme cases the child will come to associate a parent with punishment rather than his own misdeeds and thus learn to avoid the parent. Or he may learn to conceal his behaviour rather than learn some system of moral principles.

Instrumental conditioning, then, works by the selective reinforcement, by reward or punishment, of the trial and error behaviour of the child, so that some responses become stamped in and others tend to fall away. Whether or not the reinforcement is effective will depend upon the state of the child, whether he or she is motivated in some way, and on whether there is a clear connection between the response and the reinforcement.

Some practical applications
Both classical and instrumental conditioning have been used, mainly in clinical situations, to bring about some desired change in the behaviour of an individual.

Aversive conditioning has been used with alcoholics. In this case the person learns to associate taking a drink with feelings of extreme nausea. For example, the patient is given an injection or a tablet which, combined with alcohol, will produce severe vomiting. Thus as soon as the person has a drink he or she is violently sick. Some success in curing drinking problems has been achieved in this way, although there is always the possibility that once away from the clinic the conditioning will wear off.[28] Similar techniques have been tried with smokers with less success.

The cure of simple phobias such as that which was deliberately induced in Albert can be achieved by means of a 'desensitisation' process, which attempts to reverse the original conditioning by replacing the fear response to certain objects or situations with feelings of relaxation. In the case of Albert, for example, one would construct a list of situations and objects which elicited the fear reaction and place them in order according to the amount of reaction that was present. Perhaps one would see that Albert was not very keen on men with beards, and that he was terrified of white rats. Between these two extremes there would be a hierarchy of situations from those which frightened him least to those which frightened him most. Starting with the thing that made Albert least afraid – let's say a photograph of a bearded man – Albert would be encouraged to look at this whilst being maintained in a calm, relaxed condition, perhaps combined with a sweet. Once Albert could look at the photograph without the least sign of distress the therapist would go on to the next item on the hierarchy and so on until eventually, we hope, Albert would once more be able to play with the white rat. This method is sometimes referred to as 'reciprocal inhibition' since the therapeutic technique elicits responses that are antagonistic to the original fear responses. This method has been very successful with a variety of simple phobias such as fear of heights, spiders, cats, open spaces and so on, but it is not so efficient where the phobia is part of an underlying and more serious problem.

Operant techniques have been used to shape the behaviour of disturbed children and adults. For example, Hingten and his associates[29] worked with autistic children who showed no social interaction, were verbally deficient and repetitious in behaviour. They were trained to operate a lever to obtain coins which could be used to buy biscuits and sweets from an automatic dispenser. The children were then put in pairs and each child eventually learned that he could only get a coin when a light of a particular colour came on. Subsequently the apparatus was arranged so that either child could only get a coin by co-operating with the other child. Over time, the social interaction of the children increased in the laboratory situation, but didn't continue when the children were back on their hospital ward, probably because no intermittent reinforcement was provided outside the experimental situation. Such experiments thus require the help of the hospital staff who could be taught to carry on reinforcement techniques in normal living conditions on the ward.

Another study by Wolf[30] used operant techniques with autistic children whose symptoms included hair-pulling, face-scratching and temper tantrums. (Quite often these forms of behaviour are inadvertently rewarded since they draw a lot of attention to the child who is thus being positively reinforced for the very kind of behaviour that one wishes to discourage.) On each occasion that some piece of undesired behaviour was displayed by a child, all social reinforcement was removed and the child was put in isolation for ten minutes. Any time that the child emitted a piece of behaviour considered desirable, mimicking a phrase for example, he was rewarded. Over a period of time this regime was found to strengthen the verbal repertoire of the children and to result in much less disturbed behaviour. The results, in this case, generalised to other types of situation.

There can be little doubt that some knowledge of the principles of conditioning would be a boon to parents who often reward or punish in a way which has the opposite effect to the one they wish to bring about. Consider a child who consistently pesters its mother to buy sweets when they are out shopping. Because the mother is preoccupied, this behaviour will be ignored sometimes, but when it reaches some unbearable peak of intensity she will probably capitulate and reward the behaviour by attention and sweets. Thus the child learns that its mother is inclined to ignore milder forms of pestering but that she is responsive to prolonged and intensive behaviour of this kind. Such a mother would tend to have a child who indulges in persistent, intense and prolonged attention-seeking behaviour. Where only responses of high frequency and strength are rewarded the child's behaviour is likely to attain this pitch, whether the responses are considered desirable or undesirable by the parent.

EARLY PERSONALITY DEVELOPMENT

The child begins to learn by the interaction of his reflexes and physiology with his social and physical environment. There is a gradual but cumulative growth of knowledge, because of the conflict between present abilities and the possibilities of experience.

Much of the early learning of the child will usually occur as a part of his relationship with his mother. Her treatment and attempts to control his behaviour have important formative effects on the development of his personality.

As the child learns to adapt to the demands of his environment, including the other people in his life, he begins to develop control himself, over his reactions and needs. The primary processes of the infant begin to give way through his sensory and motor experience, to processes that are concerned with problem-solving and the construction of a model of reality. He attempts to reach a balance in the conflict between his needs and his abilities, between his desires and the demands of others, and so his knowledge of the world develops. He learns that objects have a continuing existence though they may be out of sight, he learns that some objects roll when they are pushed and that some are immovable. He also learns that he has a separate identity of his own.

Freud[31] suggested that the areas of experience in which children are most likely to come into conflict with their parents can be divided into three. These areas represent stages of the child's development, passage through which is unavoidable and fraught with danger. He maintained that small children pass through oral, anal and phallic stages when parental reactions to, and control of, feeding, toilet training and genital play respectively can produce profound effects on the later personality of the child. Since the development of early feeding habits, control of elimination and sexual play are likely to involve intense parent-child interaction it is indeed probable that much of the early learning of the child will relate to these areas.

Freud believed that single traumatic events occurring during one of the stages of development could have long-term consequences for the individual's modes of adjustment to reality. Abrupt weaning, for example, was said to produce incomplete satisfaction of oral desires which could lead to a search for constant oral gratification in later life, such as thumb-sucking, pipe-smoking and compulsive eating. It is extremely difficult to gather evidence to support Freudian contentions of this nature and present-day investigation of child-rearing methods tends to focus on the whole context of mothering as being formative rather than on single incidents.

Ainsworth and Bell[32] have studied various kinds of feeding schedules – demand, fixed interval, flexible, inflexible – and, as a result of their findings, they suggested that the feeding schedule itself is largely irrelevant to the child's development. It seems to be the total response of the mother to the needs of the child that is critical. Those mothers who were sensitive to the cues and rhythms of their child had harmonious feeding sessions and this harmony was characteristic of other situations. Their babies cried less and learned more rapidly other ways of communicating than by crying. They were more tolerant of delays in being fed and had more regular physiological rhythms than did the children of less sensitive mothers. Babies whose mothers were less responsive to them took longer to learn to communicate, cried more and were more irregular in their habits. The fact that the babies had less control over the behaviour of their mother no doubt emphasised their dependence and heightened their frustrating experiences.

Feedback to an infant from his attempts at control seems to be important in the development of the self concept. Are his actions achieving the desired effect? In order to construct a stable world the infant must learn to anticipate the outcome of ing the behaviour of his mother – the higher will his expectancy lead to a cumulative expectation of success or failure. The more personal control the infant has over what happens – by regulating the behaviour of his mother – the higher will his expectancy of success become. The less control the infant learns he has, for example, by non-synchronicity between his demands and needs and their satisfaction by his mother, the less will he expect to have control over what happens to him.

In a study involving the development of visual attention and grasping in relation to the amount of environmental stimulation, carried out on babies from birth to age four months, it was found that exposure to a 'rich' environment, that is, one with plenty of changing stimulation, led to more rapid development of visual-motor skills than did a less rich environment.[33] [34] The author suggests that it is the opportunity to experience a wide variety of stimuli that facilitates the development of increasing levels of personal control. Relative deprivation of stimulation produces a retarded development of the skills necessary for this kind of personal power, and there is a gradual decrease in the number of self-initiated activities by the baby, because of the lack of feedback from his actions.

The first relationship of mother and child has been described by Erikson as one which generates relative degrees of trust and mistrust in the child.[35]

The consistency of the mother (or mother-substitute) in meeting the needs of the child leads to a sense of well-being and safety, feelings of being loved and cared for. It is only by learning that he can trust other people that the child can learn to trust and love himself and so develop a sense of his own continuing identity. If the mother is inconsistent, if the behaviour of the infant produces no satisfying feedback, the infant will have no one to rely on. (This can also occur when the mother figure is constantly changing.) He will be unable to adjust his rhythms to an irregular routine and he will feel uncomfortable and disturbed. Having no evidence for the efficiency of his own behaviour, having no faith in the inconsistent behaviour of other people, he will be unable to trust his ability to control his own behaviour. It may be that something of this sort is at the root of anxiety states in which the individual is frightened of losing control or of being unable to cope with a situation.

The 'mistrust' end of this dimension resembles a concept developed by a neo-Freudian writer, Karen Horney, that of 'basic anxiety' – a feeling of being lost and alone in a hostile world.[36] The child is dependent upon his parents for survival; unless he is sure of their unconditional love he is intimidated by them and made anxious. This anxiety, says Horney, can have unfortunate consequences: the child's use of energy is inhibited and his self-esteem is undermined. He feels hostile towards his parents but cannot give this free expression for fear of being deserted by them. He, therefore, grows up feeling that the world and the people in it, including himself, are dangerous and untrustworthy.

The growth of feelings of having some kind of minimum control over what happens to him encourages the child to further exploration and so to further psychological growth. Knowing that he is loved enables him to love others and gives a secure background against which exploration can take place. It also enables positive resolution of the inevitable conflict and frustration encountered by the child.

REFERENCES

1 H. B. Hovey, 'Associative hysteresis in marine flatworms', *Physiol. Zool.*, 2 (1929), 322–33.
2 N. Tinbergen, *The Study of Instinct* (London, Oxford University Press, 1951).
3 N. Tinbergen, *The Herring Gull's World* (London, Collins, 1963).
4 D. Lack, *The Life of the Robin* (Harmondsworth, Penguin Books, 1953), revised edition.
5 N. L. Munn, *Handbook of Psychological Research on the Rat* (Houghton-Mifflin, 1950).
6 H. F. Harlow and M. K. Harlow, 'Social deprivation in monkeys', *Sci. American*, 207 (5), (1962), 136.
7 Z. Y. Kuo, 'The influence of embryonic movements upon the behaviour after hatching', *J. Comp. Psychol.*, 14 (1932), 109–22.
8 B. F. Reiss, 'The effect of altered environment and of age on mother-young relationships among animals', *Ann. N.Y. Acad. Sci.*, 57 (1954), 606–10.
9 F. A. Beach, 'Instinctive behaviour: reproductive activities', in *Handbook of Experimental Psychology* (Ed. S. S. Stevens), (New York, Wiley, 1951), Ch. 12.
10 K. Lorenz, *On Aggression* (London, Metheun, 1966).
11 J. C. Field, 'Contributions to the functional morphology of fishes. II: The feeding mechanisms of the angler fish, *Lophius piscatorium Linneaeus*', *Zool. Africana*, 2 (i) (1966), 45–67.
12 W. H. Thorpe, 'The process of song learning in the chaffinch as studied by means of the sound spectrograph', *Nature*, 173 (1954), 465.
13 S. Freud, *The Ego and the Id* (London, Hogarth Press, 1923).
14 J. Piaget, *The Origins of Intelligence in Children* (New York, International University Press, 1952).
15 I. P. Pavlov, *Conditioned Reflexes*, trans. G. V. Anrep (New York, Dover Publications, 1927).
16 L. P. Lipsitt, 'Learning in the first year of life', in *Advances in Child Development* (Eds L. P. Lipsitt and C. C. Spiker), (New York, Academic Press, 1963).

17 G. Marinesco and A. Kreindler, 'Des reflexes conditionnels. I : L'organisation des reflexes conditionnels chez l'enfant', *J. de Psychol.*, *30* (1933), 855–86.

18 D. P. Marquis, 'Learning in the neonate: the modification of behaviour under the feeding schedules', *J. Exp. Psychol.*, *29* (1941), 263–82.

19 J. B. Watson, 'Conditioned emotional reactions', *J. Exp. Psychol.*, *3* (1920), 1–14.

20 E. Ayrapetyants, 'Higher nervous function and the receptors of internal organs' (Moscow, Akad. Nauk. SSSR, 1952).

21 A. T. Pshonik, 'Interaction of extero- and interoceptive conditioned vasomotor reflexes', *Dokl. Akad. Nauk. SSSR*, *67*, 1175–8.

22 B. F. Skinner, *The Behaviour of Organisms* (New York, Appleton-Century Crofts, 1938).

23 R. L. Fantz, 'Pattern discrimination and selective attention as determinants of perceptual development from birth', in *Perceptual Development in Children* (Eds A. J. Kidd and J. L. Rivoire), (London, International University Press, 1966).

24 J. Greenspoon, 'The reinforcing effect of two spoken sounds in the frequency of two responses', *Amer. J. Psychol.*, *68* (1955), 409–16.

25 W. W. Verplanck, 'The control of the content of conversation: reinforcements of statements of opinion', *J. Abn. Soc. Psychol.*, *57* (1955), 668–76.

26 N. Azrin and O. Lindsley, 'The reinforcement of co-operation between children', *J. Abn. Soc. Psychol.*, *52* (1956), 100–2.

27 W. K. Estes, 'An experimental study of punishment', *Psychol. Monog.*, *57* (1944), No. 263.

28 S. Rachman and J. Teasdale, *Aversion Therapy and Behaviour Disorders: an analysis* (London, Routledge & Kegan Paul, 1969).

29 J. N. Hingten, S. K. Coulter and D. W. Churchill, 'Intensive reinforcement of imitative behaviour in mute autistic children', *Arch. Gen. Psychiat.*, *17* (1967), 36–43.

30 M. M. Wolf, H. Mees and T. Risley, 'Application of operant conditioning procedures to the behaviour problems of an autistic child', *Behav. Res. and Therapy*, *1* (1964), 305-12.

31 S. Freud, 'Three Essays on the Theory of Sexuality', *The Complete Psychological Works of Sigmund Freud*, Vol. 7 (London, Hogarth Press, 1905).

32 M. D. S. Ainsworth and M. Bell, 'Some contemporary patterns of mother-infant interaction in the feeding situation', in *Stimulation in Early Infancy* (Ed. J. A. Ambrose), (London, Academic Press, 1969).

33 B. L. White, 'An experimental approach to the effect of experience on early human behaviour', in *Minnesota Symposium on Child Psychology*, Vol. I (Ed. J. P. Hill), (Minneapolis, University of Minnesota Press, 1967).

34 B. L. White, 'Child development research: an edifice without a foundation', *Merrill-Palmer Quart.*, *15* (1969), 49–79.

35 E. Erikson, *Childhood and Society* (Harmondsworth, Penguin Books, 1965), revised edition.

36 K. Horney, *The Neurotic Personality of our Time* (London, Routledge & Kegan Paul, 1937).

4

Development and the Family Environment

Children begin by loving their parents. After a time they judge them. Rarely, if ever, do they forgive them.
Oscar Wilde, *A Woman of No Importance*

The energy levels of babies are recognisably varied, even in the first few days of life. Some babies have more active central nervous systems than others. Some have more easily aroused autonomic nervous systems, that is they respond more readily with what in later life we call signs of emotion; pallor, flushing, increased heart rate and variations in digestion.

Several investigations have been carried out to try and determine if a baby is born with any psychological traits. In one longitudinal study of twenty-five infants the author maintained that certain aspects of personality had an innate basis because they persisted from birth into childhood and beyond.[1] The most persistent of these traits were motor ability, skill in manipulating objects and something called 'general development'. The most variable characteristics were the child's degree of sociability and responsiveness to stimuli. Another study by Washburn[2] found that it was the extent of a child's 'emotionality' (the amount of laughing and smiling he did) that endured well into the second year. It has also been found that a tendency to cry persists in this way.[3]

It is possible that inborn temperamental tendencies in infants are reinforced by the responses of parents and others. The amount of attention given to a very lively or irritable child is likely to be greater than that received by a more placid infant. In turn the child learns to respond to his parents in particular

F

and consistent ways because of the way they react to him. Such characteristics as 'passivity' appear to be very stable traits, persisting from infancy to adulthood[4] (passivity is defined as the avoidance of dangerous activities, timidity and conformity to parental wishes). Studies of twins who have been brought up apart do demonstrate the existence of personality similarities in the majority of cases,[5] which suggests that there may be some constitutional basis of personality, but twins of this type are so rare that the results from such studies can by no means be regarded as conclusive.

Many psychologists would probably agree that there is a nucleus of personality that is modified and overlaid by learning from the physical and social environment. Most studies, however, have found it impossible to control for the influence of parental attitudes and treatment and to isolate any clearly inborn psychological characteristics of the child. Since genetic factors affect hormone levels, physique, and levels of activity in the nervous system, which in turn affect the responses of the child, it does seem possible to say that there is an innate core to personality which is worked upon by experience. Those traits which most investigators agree have some consistency at all age levels of a child are motor and vocal activity, emotionality and passivity, all of which could well be related to genetic factors.

ATTACHMENT

Imprinting
The phenomenon of imprinting, which has been demonstrated to exist in animals, is an example of an in-built propensity that requires appropriate environmental stimuli for it to have the desired effect. At certain sensitive periods in the life of many young animals and birds (particularly those which are mobile from birth) it is important for their survival that they should identify and attach themselves to a member of their own species, usually the mother. This mechanism is most clearly apparent when it goes wrong. In many birds the attachment is made to any object that has the right sign stimuli of shape or sound, if it is present at the critical time. Young geese, for

example, will at a certain time attach themselves to any large and moving object. Thus they can become imprinted upon human beings or even upon a cardboard box on wheels.[6] For ducklings the critical sign stimulus is the sound of quacking. Hess[7] found that ducklings would follow a tape recorder moving on a trolley and emitting quacking noises, if they were exposed to it between the ages of ten and sixteen hours. The lower time limit is that age at which the bird can walk efficiently and the upper time limit seems to be related to the development of the fear response (80 per cent of ducklings show fear by the time they are one day old). Imprinting not only establishes a following response, but also establishes sexual responses. Lorenz raised a jackdaw which, at maturity, displayed courtship behaviour towards him, bringing him presents of grubs and worms.[6]

Whether inappropriate imprinting of this kind can be reversed is debatable and may be dependent upon whether or not the mechanism is 'open', for example, the grey-lag goose will follow any large moving object which is present at the right time, or 'closed', for example, curlews only become imprinted on curlews.[8]

Imprinting occurs in many species – dogs, sheep and goats, for example – and it appears to be a device for the establishment of social and sexual responses in the appropriate direction. The animal develops preferences in attachment that are normally restricted to its own species and that are laid down fairly quickly during a limited phase. The phenomenon is of obvious evolutionary advantage. Unions between different species are infertile and young who behave in a sociable way to an animal of a different species may find themselves in danger of being eaten by predators.

Human Attachment
The earliest socialisation of human beings has some of the characteristics of imprinting, since early learning experiences establish patterns of behaviour, habits and perceptions that persist and so determine adult responses.

Young babies respond with delight to the sight of a human face, initially to any human face, but this reaction gradually narrows down to the few adults whom they regularly encounter. Together with this developing recognition of parents (or substitutes) goes an increasing fear of strangers. The appearance of the fear response seems to depend upon maturation of an innate tendency. It is found universally and, as far as one can judge, appears spontaneously without the opportunity to have been learned. Its function may be to prepare individuals for life in a particular society whose laws can only be learned within the bounds of a deep emotional attachment.

Fear responses in babies to strange people and objects can be seen between the ages of six and nine months and their presence makes it difficult for the child to attach itself to a new person. Attachment shows itself in the child seeking to be near the preferred person. Once a bond has been formed between child and mother then separation becomes increasingly traumatic.

However, it is possible to argue that an infant's attachment to his mother is not innate but is a consequence of learning through association. She is the source of his comfort and stimulation. Much of the early social behaviour of infants is directed towards attracting her attention. Some of this behaviour will elicit more success than other forms. Laughing, smiling, crying, dropping toys, vocalising tend to be particularly successful and are reinforced and thus tend to persist. Responsive mothers may in this way unwittingly encourage patterns of behaviour that make their babies more demanding.

Moss[9] observed thirty mothers and their first-born children over a period of time, in eight-hour sessions. He found that at three weeks of age boys were held by their mothers twenty-seven minutes longer per session on average than were girls. At three months they were held fourteen minutes longer. At both ages girls slept approximately one hour longer during the period of observation. There was wide variability between infants, some slept for only two hours out of the eight whilst others were asleep for six hours. This would naturally have a considerable effect on their opportunities for stimulation, interaction and exercise. In general the boys slept less and cried more and so received more attention. Mothers were also more likely to stimulate boys, by tickling and picking up, but more likely to imitate the girls, by echoing their babbling noises, for example. This finding of a particular kind of differential treatment could account to some extent for the fact that boys tend to be more active and aggressive and girls tend to talk earlier. It is the feedback which the child gets from its own behaviour that is important. Mothers may also be more tolerant of demanding male children, classifying this kind of behaviour as an expression of masculinity, and thereby encouraging it more than in girls.

The intensity of the interaction which a child experiences during a particular period may account for the object of his attachment. As we shall see, this propensity to form an attachment may be confined to a particular period in the child's life which, although not necessarily critical, may represent the best time for it to occur.[10] There is some evidence that such a 'sensitive period' also applies in the case of the learning of the sex role, finding out which sex one belongs to and behaving in the appropriate way. A study of hermaphrodite children who had been reared from birth in one sex and later brought up as the opposite sex, showed that the amount of emotional disturbance they experienced was less if the change in sex role took place before the age of $2\frac{1}{2}$ years.[11] The authors suggested that this difference could be related to the presence of language in the older children. The tendency of human beings is to interpret present experience in terms of past events. It is easier to assimilate facts which fit into an already existing framework of concepts than it is to alter the framework to accommodate the complete re-orientation of the self-image which would be involved in a change of sex role. The development of a set of concepts relating to the self is greatly accelerated by the ability to speak, because the child now begins to think of itself in terms of, for example, 'boy', 'girl'.

A vital process in the infant's development is, as we have already noted in Chapter 3, the build up of schemata, models of the world within which the child can make sense of his experiences. Some of his early concepts relate to himself as distinct from others. This distinguishing of one person from another, one object from another, has to be learned. Piaget[12] believed that the concept of conservation – that is the nation that other objects and people continue to exist even when out of sight – is established at about three or four months of age. Up until then babies experience little distress if one mother figure has to be substituted for another. Once the child has grasped the idea that objects and people have a permanent existence, independent of their presence, then the idea that people and things can be lost is also there. The age when babies begin to search for lost playthings coincides with the age when loss of a parent by separation or death begins to have serious consequences.

Attachment is not solely conceptual awareness of permanence and impermanence, it also involves the establishment of a definite emotional bond between the child and the mother (or her substitute). Freud[13] believed that the basis of the child's attachment to his mother was the gratification of his oral needs and that this attachment underlies the secondary drive of liking for other people. The undelayed satisfaction of the child's hunger is said to make him feel warm and loved and this feelings becomes associated with the provider of the satisfaction.

Since Freud, studies with young monkeys have indicated that the basis of attachment is something other than the satiation of hunger. For monkeys, at least, contact with the mother's fur seems to provide greater comfort than being fed. Eight young monkeys were reared in separate cages with 'surrogate' mothers, that is, each monkey had available two substitutes for a mother. One of these consisted of a wire frame with nipples and the other of a fur-covered frame which did not provide milk. Although the young were fed by the wire mother they spent only half an hour per day clinging to it compared with an average of fifteen hours per day spent clinging to the cloth mother. If subjected to stress they invariably ran to the cloth mother for comfort.[14] Further experiments demonstrated the strength of the infants' attachment by the construction of 'rejecting' mothers which shook or tipped backwards dislodging the infants, or blew out high-pressure blasts of air. In spite of this treatment the infants could not be induced to leave their surrogate mothers and clung on even more tightly. Harlow[15] has suggested that the attachment is based upon 'contact comfort' which in real relationships is probably reciprocated by the mother. There is some kind of sensual satisfaction in the contact of the two bodies. This is commonly observed in humans where the fondling and picking up of babies provides a great deal of pleasure on both sides.

The clinging behaviour of human infants is reinforced, normally, by the pleasure that the person being clung to experiences. Attachment behaviour may also be strong even where the mother or her substitute is rejecting of, or even cruel to, the child.

DEPRIVATION – THE ROLE OF STIMULATION

Before birth a baby receives touch stimulation from the varying pressures in his mother's womb. After birth the range of stimulation increases enormously as the five senses come into play. It is known from studies of animals that normal development depends upon the quantity and kind of sensory information being fed into the maturing nervous system.

Chimpanzees reared in the dark, or with a translucent plastic dome over their heads, giving an unbroken visual field without form or pattern, are unable to discriminate between or recognise objects when they are released into a normal environment.[16] Similarly, animals deprived from birth of the normal experiences of sound and touch patterns are severely curtailed in their ability to recognise sounds or feel pain. This difficulty may, in part, arise from the need to interlock the different perceptual systems of looking, listening and touching so as to form an integrated concept of an object or event. If one system is disrupted then it may be difficult to fit incoming information from this system into the schemata already formed by the other senses. The comprehension of what we can see requires learning as well as adequate vision and neither can develop without the other. People born with cataracts who are successfully operated upon in late childhood, or when adult, learnt to recognise colours fairly quickly, but take months to recognise, say a triangle by sight alone and never acquire complete visual perceptual ability.[17] Lack of adequate levels of stimulation may also lead to atrophy of the parts of the nervous system that would normally deal with them. It does, moreover, appear to be disturbing. Blind children engage in a variety of 'stereotypic' activities such as head-rolling, rocking and head-banging. Brain-damaged, feeble-minded and autistic children show much more of such behaviour than do normal children. It may be that this is a re-sponse to lack of sufficient sensory input and is an attempt to establish a balance with the environment through self-stimu-lation.

There is some evidence that an 'enriched' environment providing high levels of stimulation may speed up the pace of development. In one study[18] two groups of rats of identical heredity received differing amounts of stimulation. One group was extensively handled during the first weeks of life and the other was not. The rats who had been handled between birth and weaning were more active and quicker to learn than the other group. Early handling has also been found to make rats less emotional and to promote an increase in the number of active brain cells.[19] Levine[20] suggests that mildly unpleasant experiences in infancy are not necessarily harmful or anxiety-producing. His rats were stimulated with electric shocks and gained more weight, were calmer and learned an avoidance task quicker than a control group. A rich early environment gives a rat comparatively high scores on maze tests of animal intelligence.

It has been suggested that the reason first-born children tend to be, on average, more gifted than later children is that they receive more attention and stimulation as an infant.[21] The further apart in time brother and sisters are born the higher are their I.Q. scores and twins tend to do worse than only children.

The upbringing of European and African children has been compared in Uganda.[22] Ugandans tend to give their infants a great deal of attention until the time they are weaned, they are rarely left alone, are carried about wherever the mother goes, and get plenty of amusement. After weaning, which is abrupt, they receive much less attention. The author found that prior to weaning Ugandan children were ahead of European children in respect of motor and intellectual development. After weaning this advantage was gradually lost. Ugandan children brought up the European way were compared with Ugandan children brought up in the traditional manner and similar differences were found.

The need for a varied and stimulating environment may well be related to the orienting reflex which directs our attention to new information and which is present from birth. This reflex shows itself in the familiar turn of the head towards some novel event and has a number of accompanying components – changes in blood pressure, increased heart rate, cessation of ongoing activity and attention to the new stimulus. The orienting response only occurs when a stimulus is somewhat unfamiliar and so is related to Piaget's concept of 'moderate novelty' as being essential for the arousal of interest. Orientation to novel stimuli may also be an important element of the curiosity and exploration displayed by both animals and human beings. Rats, for instance, will endure electric shocks to get from their nests to explore an unfamiliar area[23] and monkeys enclosed in a room will continually push at a heavy door in order to see what is going on outside.[24]

DEPRIVATION – THE ROLE OF PARENTS

The term 'maternal deprivation' has been used to cover a number of instances of disruption of an attachment bond which may adversely affect a child. It is important, however, to distinguish between separation and deprivation of care. The two conditions may occur simultaneously, but it is possible for an infant to be separated from his mother without otherwise being deprived, or to lack care, food or stimulation whilst still retaining a tie with his mother.

One of the foremost writers on the topic, John Bowlby, maintains that separation from, or lack of, a mother figure is more serious than privation, but, of course, a combination of the two is likely to be the most serious in its long- and short-term effects, and may happen when a motherless child is placed in an old-fashioned institution where individual attention is lacking. One must also distinguish between the loss of a mother (or father) and the total absence from birth of a mother or her substitute where there has been no opportunity for an attachment bond to form.

Generally it appears that privation leads to the retardation of intellectual growth, so that intelligence and language development are adversely affected, whilst separation leads to emotional and behavioural disturbance, although the latter may disrupt intellectual growth because of apathy, over-activity or interference with educational progress.

Pringle and Bossio[25] studied children in institutions and found that the most stable were those who had entered them after their first year of life, whilst the most severely maladjusted were those who had entered them earlier than this and had had no chance to form a stable and continuing bond with one individual. Children who enter institutions as early as six months and who remain there until at least 3 years of age are less able to form emotional bonds. According to Bowlby, they are in danger of facing the future as 'affectionless characters' – people who are unable to form close relationships and who appear to be deficient in sympathy and empathy for their fellows – although these individuals are not necessarily intellectually retarded. Their psychological condition is often exacerbated by the fact that these children who have not learned to love and to trust others are themselves often difficult to love. They are, therefore, unresponsive to, and as a consequence often unacceptable to, foster parents.

Bowlby[26] has said that mental health requires a warm and continuing relationship with a mother figure in which both find satisfaction, and that without this, the affectionless children become delinquent or suffer from depression, speech defects and a variety of emotional disorders. He maintains that loss of a mother by death before the age of 5 years is a significantly frequent event in the life history of those suffering from depressive illnesses. Latterly Bowlby has modified his position and now accepts that fathers and substitute mothers may prevent or repair the damage caused by separation from the mother.[27]

Studies of children reared in institutions yield conflicting results depending upon the type of care and attention given to the children, the tests that are used and frequent failure to distinguish between maternal, paternal, sensory and social deprivation. Deprivation may take several forms – no maternal care, several transitory maternal substitutes, or a broken home – any of which may be combined with lack of adequate stimulation. The latter can occur even with a 'good' mother who prefers quiet, passive children. Separation may also take on several aspects, through death of a parent, hospitalisation of parent or child, or divorce.

The effects which these events will have are highly dependent upon the child's previous and subsequent life experiences. An orphan brought up by warm, loving and stimulating foster parents will usually show few ill-effects. A child whose mother dies but who is in a supportive family atmosphere may show few scars.

It has been found that institutionalised children have a higher mortality rate, despite good medical care, than children brought up in their own homes,[28] and that they have motor and language retardation. In a study which matched children placed in a foundling home in infancy and subsequently transferred to foster parents when three years old, with a control group who had been fostered from babyhood, it was found that, compared to the control group, the children in the first group had lower I.Q. scores, lacked concentration and were backward in behaviour, language, emotional and social adjustment. These effects were said to be apparent even after ten years.[29] On the other hand, another study of children of nineteen to twenty-four months, who had spent the latter half of their lives in institutions, found that the children were healthy, well adjusted and of normal intellectual ability.[30]

The effect an institution has depends very much on its nature. If babies are left alone for long periods of time, lying on their backs with only a blank ceiling to stare at, they will be deprived of stimulation and opportunities for exploration. If they are only provided with the material necessities of food and cleanliness and are without the chance to form a close relationship then they will be deprived of affection.

The child's age when a separation occurs is also an important factor. The most severely disturbed children have usually entered the institution before one year of age, whilst the better adjusted have usually not been separated until after the age of three years.

An experimental investigation on monkeys has demonstrated the effects of deprivation at their most extreme.[31] Monkeys were reared either in isolation from birth or in age-mate pairs. In all instances they showed inadequate social behaviour, neither grooming each other nor indulging in spontaneous play. They were mute, indifferent to aggressive attacks and showed compulsive rocking and periodic outbursts of rage. The unmothered females either had to be taught to mate or were artificially inseminated. They became totally inadequate mothers, treating the resulting offspring with complete indifference or cruelty. A similar study in which two rhesus monkeys were reared in total isolation until the age of 2, found the animals to be impaired in all forms of social behaviour, never initiating social contacts, never displaying sexual or aggressive behaviour, and responding to aggression by withdrawal.[32]

Deprivation can thus have demonstrably severe effects, but whether it is inevitably disruptive depends upon how the child interprets his loss and his subsequent experience. Rheingold improved the social responsiveness of six-month-old institutionalised babies by giving them six weeks of intensive individual attention.[33] It seems that where institutions are able to provide this kind of individual care for every child the worst effects of deprivation can be avoided.[34]

Short-term separations, such as occur when a child must enter hospital, also have effects on the child, depending upon its age. Clear differences have been found in reaction to hospitalisation between children aged seven months and under and those aged over seven months.[35] The younger babies evinced little protest on initial separation, were normally responsive whilst in hospital even to strangers and settled down well. The older infants showed acute fretting, restlessness and over-activity which eventually led to withdrawal from contact. On return home the two groups again differed in behaviour. The younger ones seemed to be preoccupied with their environment, staring for long periods at previously familiar sights, whilst the older ones became, for varying periods of time, over-dependent and clinging to an uncharacteristic degree. The difference in reaction between the age groups would seem to be related to the age at which attachments are made. Infants whose social relationships have been clearly established and whose fear responses are fully developed are more likely to be disturbed by changes than those who have not reached this stage. One must also remember that for older children entry into hospital can mean a setback to their developing independence since they are in a situation where things happen (for them) in an apparently arbitrary way and where they have little power to influence events. Most hospitals have, now, recognised the disturbing effect that short-term separation from the mother can have and so provide for her presence where possible.

Most studies of deprivation have accepted the Western type of family as being a desirable norm. Erikson's basic trust concept implies that it is a relationship with one person that is vital to healthy development. In other cultures, however, children can apparently have several mother figures without suffering distress or damage. Children reared on kibbutzim in Israel grow up with a group of children of the same age under the care of a 'metapelet' who changes from time to time. The children usually see their parents at weekends when they go to stay with them. The greatest attachment seems to be towards the parents although the metapelets provide the major part of food and care; this is possibly because the parental relationship is more stable even though the interaction is less frequent. Basic trust seems to be achieved by these children because of a continuing relationship with the peer group and a desire to retain their companionship.[36] This supportive role of peers as parent substitutes is borne out by a study by Freud and Dann.[37] Six children of pre-school age lost their parents in concentration camps during the Second World War, and had remained together as a group in spite of several changes of camp and great hardship. They eventually ended up after the war in an English nursery. Although the children did have emotional problems as a consequence of their horrific experiences there was no evidence of the gross disturbance which one might have expected. The children seemed to have been protected by reason of the strong ties which they developed for each other. Experimentally the ameliorating effect of the presence of age mates has been demonstrated in another study by Harlow using monkeys as subjects. Monkeys were reared either in total isolation, or with their mother alone, or in groups of age mates, but without a mother, or in a normal group of adults and peers. As we have already noted, isolation has very deleterious effects on later behaviour, but Harlow found that the effects were nearly as bad for monkeys brought up with only their mother for company. Those monkeys brought up with a group of peers, but without a mother, showed few ill effects and were comparable in adjustment to the monkeys reared in a normal environment. Harlow did claim that the affectional bonds between mother and child were qualitatively different from those formed between peers.[38] This is not surprising, since the former relationship is based upon care-taking whilst the latter is based upon play activity to a much greater extent. The studies do, however, suggest that the long-term effect of bonds formed with peers is very similar to the effect of bonds formed normally with a mother.[39]

Nor is multiple mothering necessarily harmful. This occurs in home management training colleges in the USA where the children come from institutions and are cared for by students in houses and then are moved on to foster homes. Follow-up studies have revealed no impairment or disorder in these children.[40] Multiple-mothering, if adequate, could conceivably provide more stimulation and perhaps encourage a wider, more flexible range of social responses.

Until recently, investigators of deprivation have been mainly concerned with the role of the mother and her absence or inadequacy, but there is evidence to suggest that the presence of the father is also an important variable. In view of the fact that one study reported 30 per cent of a sample of infants to have formed a bond with their father rather than their mother[41] this is an area that needs much more investigation. This seems to bear on the fact that it has been suggested that it is not the absolute amount of time that a person spends with the child that leads to an attachment with that person, but rather the intensity of the interaction between them. Where there is a relatively unstimulating mother and a very attentive father, then the father is likely to become the attachment figure.[42]

Burton and Whiting[43] have produced anthropological evidence to suggest that boys raised in cultures where the father is habitually absent tend to have conflicts about their sex-role and to display exaggerated masculine behaviour. A study of 8- and 9-year-old Norwegian children whose fathers were sailors found that, compared to a control group, the boys were more immature and less well-adjusted to their peer group. The girls were said to be highly dependent.[44] A similar study in Italy, however, did not confirm these findings.[45] The Italian fathers were absent because of the financial need of the family and were idealised by their wives as an image for their sons to live up to. These studies suggest that father absence will be dependent in its effects upon the attitude of the mother to the absent father, and how far he is maintained as a meaningful part of the family. A study of father-absent families during the Second World War[46] found the boys to have 'feminine-type' fantasies, to show less masculine behaviour than boys with fathers at home, and to get on less well with peers.

The fathers of autistic children have been described, in one sample of 100, as being cold, undemonstrative, rigid in their attitudes to child-rearing and more interested in their work than their family.[47]

Some writers have reported more delinquency in families without fathers, but there are clearly more factors involved than mere absence of the father, including the reason for his absence, which could be prison, death, desertion, and the financial state of the family.

Crane studied pre-adolescent boys in Australia and found that delinquent groups were associated with poor paternal relationships, whereas gangs with more constructive aims had good relationships with their fathers.[48] Rejection of a boy by his father has been found to be associated with delinquency even where the relationship with the mother was satisfactory.[49]

Most of the evidence on the effects of absence of a parent or privation of some kind is retrospective, which means that it needs to be treated with caution – many other factors may cause retardation and/or emotional upset. Some general observations may, however, be made in summary : disruption of an attachment to a preferred individual usually causes acute distress which is most severe if the separation occurs when the child is aged between six months and 3 years. Before the age of six months a sense of the permanent existence of people is not developed and a bond rarely established. After the age of 3 the child is normally socially capable of interaction with other figures who can provide a substitute for the mother.

Distress consequent upon separation from the mother can be relieved by continued contact with a familiar figure such as a father, aunt or sibling. Infants who are placed in institutions very early in life and stay there until after the age of 3 may be in danger of never developing affectional bonds, the long-term effects of which can be severe in terms of emotional and social maladjustment. This situation will be at its most serious when the effects of lack of stimulation and attention are compounded with lack of a bond. In these cases social and emotional inadequacies will be exacerbated by intellectual retardation.

Even if an attachment is formed, lack of social and/or sensory stimulation can still lead to retarded intellectual and language development. This may be ameliorated if special attention is provided soon enough.

The mother-child attachment bond may be successfully replaced by bonds with a mother substitute, or even with several people. Strong peer group attachments may provide the necessary support for adequate development in the absence of a suitable adult.

Deprivation is an unclear term and covers the interaction of several factors, separation not only from a parent, but also from the family context, removal to a strange environment, lack of stimulation, malnutrition, inconsistent learning experiences, lack of love, lack of continuity and absence of individual care. All or any combination of these may be present at the same time.

The outcome of individual experiences will differ according to the prior and subsequent experience of the child, its age at separation, the availability of alternative bonds, the type of institution, the previous relationship with the mother figure and the constitution of the child. The role of the father as a provider of attention and stimulation and as a preferred figure has been neglected, but is likely to be just as important in its formative influence on the child.

To study the effects of loss of or separation from one parent alone seems to open the danger of losing sight of the whole context within which the child develops, the physical, social and emotional climate of the home and the child's position in it. One aspect of the latter which has implications for development is the order in which the child comes into the family.

BIRTH ORDER

A hundred years ago Francis Galton studied his fellow members of the Royal Society and found that more of them were first-born children than one would expect to find by chance.[50] Since then a lot of evidence has been gathered which shows a relation between being a first-born child and achieving some measure of success in life. A study of people listed in *Who's Who* showed that 64 per cent of those coming from two-child families were first-born (instead of a chance expectation of 50 per cent) and so were 52 per cent of those who came from three-child families (instead of a chance figure of 33·3 per cent.[20] First-born children have been said to show 'more conscience development' and to be more co-operative and curious whilst later-born children have been said to be more aggressive and affectionate.[51] Schachter reported of his sample that first-born children were more dependent upon the company and liking of other people.[52]

It seems that the sex of the other children in the family can also affect the consequences of birth order. Altus[53] found that first-born students of both sexes from two-child families scored higher on a test of ability if their siblings were boys than if they were girls. Boys with sisters not much older than themselves scored lower on 'masculinity' scales. Girls from a two-child family with an older brother were found to be more disparaging of themselves and more critical of their fathers than were girls with older sisters.

Most of these findings can be explained in terms of parental behaviour. Parents can spare more time and attention for their first-born children but also tend to be more anxious and stricter with them. If, in consequence, first-born children become more conformist and curious (their questioning behaviour having been reinforced by parents' interest), this may contribute to their success at school since they are also likely to win the approval of teachers, and so later eminence.

Hilton carried out an investigation involving the differences in behaviour shown by sixty mothers towards their first and later-born children.[54] Mothers and children were observed in two situations. Firstly, where the child appeared to fail badly on a test of 'creativity', and secondly, where the child appeared to succeed, both outcomes being manipulated by the experimenter and independent of the child's actual performance. The first-born children were more likely to ask for help and reassurance and were more likely to receive it from their mothers than were later-born children. Even when asked not to help, eighteen of the mothers did and of these fifteen instances were to help first-born children. The mothers were more demonstrative to their first-born when they were successful, with a noticeable withdrawal of love when they appeared to be failing. The later-born children received more evenly distributed demonstrations of love, less related to their success or failure. These findings suggest that mothers are more anxious about the abilities of their first-born children, but feel freer with later-born children and more able to express affection independent of the child's behaviour.

Thus one might expect the first-born child to be more dependent upon the approval of his parents, an attitude that is likely to make him somewhat conformist in his behaviour in an attempt to live up to parental values.

One must, however, make a distinction between physical and psychological dependence. A child may willingly go to the shops or travel on a bus alone but may be more psychologically dependent than another child who refuses to go out because there is something else he prefers to do. The dependent first-born may be more dependent on his mother for love and reassurance and yet try hard to conform to her expectations that he should behave in a 'grown-up' and independent way. Later-born children, being free of this pressure, may be more easily able to develop a genuine psychological independence as they grow older. The greater parental interference with the activities of the first-born or only child means that he or she is less able to establish independent goals but will aim at those set by the parents, whether the goals be academic achievement or being polite. The chief satisfaction of these children is then likely to come from pleasing other people.

PARENTAL ATTITUDES

The development of a child's sense of identity is dependent partly on his mother's view of him which she reflects in her behaviour. She may regard him as an extension of her personality – a symbol of her own competence and intelligence – or as a separate being. If she reacts to independent behaviour on his part with discouragement, he is liable to become less spontaneous, explorative and curious than he might have been and perhaps to have difficulty in establishing his own autonomy.

The evidence suggests that parents with attitudes like over-domination, over-protection and valuing the child for the prestige he can bring rather than for himself or rejecting the child under a veneer of affection – what we may call 'un-favourable' attitudes – do little damage during the first two years of the child's life. Once the child reaches the age of 4 or 5 other people may ameliorate the effects of parental attitudes. It is between the ages of 2 and 4 that the greatest damage can be done. The child is now perceptive enough to be aware if he is rejected (or to feel rejected if his parents are undemonstrative). Rejected children are said to become either shy or aggressive, depending on their constitution, to lack self-esteem and to be unassertive in personal relationships. They may also suffer some retardation in cognitive and language development (due perhaps to lack of parental attention) which aggravates their lack of self-esteem.[55]

Both over-protected and over-dominated children will tend to lack self-assertion, the one because he has had no need of it, the other because it has been discouraged. They may then find, on mixing with other children, that the rough and tumble of peer group relationships is too much for them and they may withdraw in favour of the company of protective adults, thus becoming dependent, shy, compliant and inadequate under stress.

On the other hand, lack of parental domination to the point of over-indulgence encourages self-assertion but may go too far, in that, because all the demands of the child are met, he has no opportunity to learn to adjust to the demands of other people. This may lead him to an exaggerated sense of his own power and importance, so that he believes others will always capitulate to his wishes and he becomes domineering and capricious and unpopular with other children. The child himself suffers when he finds that peers and teachers are not as accommodating as his parents.[55]

Of course, these are very general statements. The child's reaction to his parents will depend to some extent on his basic disposition – a highly active child may react to over-domination by rebellion rather than submission.

Parental attitudes and behaviour do seem to set the pattern for the child's own social relationships. If there are friendly relationships within the home, then the child is likely to expect others to be friendly and behave accordingly outside the home. This, in turn, will determine the way in which he is approached by other children and adults. If, on the other hand, the family atmosphere is characterised by suspicion and hostility this will form the norm for the child's attitudes and he will treat new acquaintances with fear and distrust. The Newson's study of Nottingham mothers found clear social class differences in some parental attitudes, for example, lower-class mothers tend to be more indulgent than middle-class mothers in such areas as feeding and sleeping, whereas the middle-class mothers have a more liberal attitude to masturbation.[56]

The child's information about the world is filtered through the words, behaviour and attitudes of his parents, so that initially at any rate, he acquires their view of social reality. How efficient the parents are at imposing their view of the world upon the child will determine to a large extent whether he continues to accept, or later reject, their interpretation.

REFERENCES

1 M. M. Shirley, 'The first two years' in *Personality Manifestations,* Vol. III (Minneapolis, University of Minnesota Press, 1933).
2 R. W. Washburn, 'A study of the smiling and laughing of infants in the first year of life', *Genet. Psychol.* Monog., *6* (1929), 397–539.
3 N. Bayley, 'A study of the crying of infants during mental and physical tests', *J. Genet. Psychol., 40* (1932), 306–29.
4 J. Kagan and H. A. Moss, *Birth to Maturity: a study in psychological development* (New York, John Wiley, 1962).
5 J. Shields, *Monozygotic Twins* (London, Oxford University Press, 1962).
6 K. Z. Lorenz, 'Der Kumpan in der Umwelt des Vogels', *J. Ornith, 83* (1935), 137–213.
7 E. Hess, 'The relationship between imprinting and motivation' in *Nebraska Symposium on Motivation,* Vol. VII. (Ed. M. R. Jones), (University of Nebraska Press, 1959).
8 R. A. Hinde, 'Some recent trends in ethology' in *Psychology: a study of a science,* Vol. II (Ed. S. Koch), (New York, McGraw Hill, 1959).
9 H. Moss, 'Sex, age and state as determinants of mother-child interaction' in *Readings in Child Socialisation* (Ed. K. Danziger), (Oxford, Pergamon Press, 1970), 285–307.
10 W. Sluckin, *Early Learning in Man and Animal,* (London, Allen & Unwin, 1970).
11 J. Money, J. G. Hampson and J. L. Hampson, 'Imprinting and the establishment of gender role', *A.M.A. Archs. Neurol. and Psychiat.,* 77 (1957), 333–6.
12 J. Piaget, *The Construction of Reality in the Child* (New York, Basic Books, 1937).
13 S. Freud, *New Introductory Lectures on Psychoanalysis,* Int. Psychoanalytical Library (London, Hogarth Press, 1933).
14 H. F. Harlow, 'The nature of love', *Amer. Psychologist, 13* (1958), 673–85.
15 H. F. Harlow and M. K. Harlow, 'Social deprivation in monkeys', *Sci. American, 207* (1962), 136.
16 A. H. Riesen, 'Post-partum development of behaviour', *Chicago Med. Sch. Quart., 13* (1951), 17–24.
17 D. O. Hebb, *A Textbook of Psychology* (London, W. B. Saunders, 1964).

18 M. R. Rosenzweig, 'Environmental complexity, cerebral change and behaviour', *Amer. Psychologist, 21* (1966), 321–32.

19 V. H. Denenberg and J. R. C. Morton, 'Effects of environmental complexity and social groupings upon modification of emotional behaviour', *J. Comp. Physiol. Psychol., 55* (1962), 242–6.

20 S. Levine, 'Infantile experience and resistance to physical stress', *Science, 126* (1957), 405.

21 H. E. Jones, 'The environment and mental development', in *Handbook of Child Psychology* (Ed. L. Carmichael), (New York, John Wiley, 1954), Ch. 10.

22 M. Geber, 'The psychomotor development of African children in the first year and the influence of maternal behaviour', *J. Soc. Psychol., 47* 1958), 185–95.

23 C. J. Warden, *Animal motivation studies: the albino rat* (New York, Columbia University Press, 1931).

24 D. E. Berlyne, 'Curiosity and exploration', *Science, 153* (1966), 25–33.

25 M. L. K. Pringle and V. Bossio, 'Early prolonged separations and emotional adjustment', *J. Child Psychol. Psychiat., 1* (1960), 37–48.

26 J. Bowlby, *Child Care and the Growth of Love* (Harmondsworth, Penguin Books, 1953).

27 J. Bowlby, *Attachment and Loss*, Vol. 1: 'Attachment' (Harmondsworth, Penguin Books, 1971).

28 R. A. Spitz, 'Hospitalism: an enquiry into the genesis of psychiatric conditions in early childhood', *Psychoanalytic Studies of the Child, 1* (1945), 53–74.

29 W. Goldfarb, 'Variations in adolescent adjustment of institutionally reared children', *Amer. J. Orthopsychiat., 17* (1947), 449–57.

30 H. L. Rheingold and N. Bayley, 'The later effects of an experimental modification of mothering', *C. Devel., 30* (1959), 363–72.

31 H. F. Harlow, 'The heterosexual affection system in monkeys', *Amer. Psychologist, 17* (1962), 1–9.

32 W. A. Mason and R. R. Sponholz, 'Behaviour of rhesus monkeys raised in isolation', *J. Psychiat. Res., 1* (1963), 299–306.

33 H. L. Rheingold, 'The modification of social responsiveness in institutional babies', *Monog. Soc. Res. Ch. Devel., 21* (1956), Suppl. 63.

34 W. Dennis and P. Najarian, 'Infant development under environmental handicap', *Psychol. Monog., 71* (1957), 1–13.

35 H. R. Schaffer and W. M. Callender, 'Psychological effects of hospitalisation in infancy', *Pediatrics, 24* (1959), 528–39.

36 B. Bettleheim, *The Children of the Dream* (London, Thames & Hudson, 1969).

37 S. Freud and S. Dann, 'An experiment in group upbringing', *Psychoanalytic Studies of the Child, 6* (1951), 127–68.

38 H. F. Harlow, 'The maternal affectional system', in *Determinants of Infant Behaviour*, Vol. II (Ed. B. M. Foss), (London, Methuen, 1963).

39 H. F. Harlow and M. K. Harlow, 'Developmental aspects of emotional behaviour', in *Physiological Correlates of Emotion* (London, Academic Press, 1970).

40 D. B. Gardner, G. R. Hawkes and L. G. Burchinal, 'Non-continuous mothering in infancy and development in later childhood', *Ch. Devel., 32* (1961), 225–34.

41 H. R. Schaffer and P. E. Emerson, 'The development of social attachments in infancy', *Monog. Soc. Res. Ch. Devel.*, *29* (94), (1964).

42 H. R. Schaffer, *The Growth of Sociability* (Harmondsworth, Penguin Books, 1971).

43 R. Burton and J. W. M. Whiting, 'Childhood and mental health: the influence of the father in the family setting – a symposium', *Merrill-Palmer Quart.*, *1* (1961), 72–111.

44 D. Lynn and W. L. Sawrey, 'The effects of father absence on Norwegian boys and girls', *J. Abn. Soc. Psychol.*, *59* (1959), 258–262.

45 L. Ancona, 'An experimental contribution to the problem of identification with the father', *Readings in Child Socialisation* (Ed. K. Danziger), (Oxford, Pergamon Press, 1970), 187–218.

46 L. M. Stolz, *Father Relations of War-born Children* (California, Stanford University Press, 1954).

47 L. Eisenberg, 'The fathers of autistic children', *Amer. J. Orthopsychiat.*, *27* (1957), 715–25.

48 A. R. Crane, 'A note on pre-adolescent gangs', *Aust. J. Psychol.*, *3* (1951), 43–6.

49 R. G. Andry, 'Faulty paternal and maternal child relationships, affection and delinquency', *Brit. J. Delinq.*, *97* (1960), 329–40.

50 F. Galton, *Inquiries into human faculty: its development* (London, Dent, 1919), 2nd edition.

51 R. R. Sears, E. E. Maccoby and H. Levin, *Patterns of Child-rearing* (Evanston, Row, Peterson, 1957).

52 S. Schachter, 'Birth order, eminence and higher education', *Amer. Soc. Reg.*, *28* (1963), 757–68.

53 W. Altus, 'Birth order and its sequelae', *Int. J. Psychiat.*, *3* (1966), 23–32.

54 I. Hilton, 'Differences in the behaviour of mothers towards first and later-born children', *J. Pers. Soc. Psychol.*, *7* (1967), 282–90.

55 D. P. Ausubel and E. V. Sullivan, *Theory and Problems of Child Development* (New York, Grune & Stratton, 1970), 2nd edition.

56 J. Newson and E. Newson, *Infant Care in an Urban Community* (London, George Allen & Unwin, 1963).

5

Exploring and Understanding

The world is but a school of enquiry.
Montaigne, *Essays III*

The child's efforts to come to terms with reality, construct an internal model of the world and to achieve independence are greatly aided by two properties of the human brain. One, shared by the animal brain, is its need for stimulation; the other is the ability to recognise, interpret and construct language – a uniquely human attribute.

EXPLORATION AND CURIOSITY

We have seen that the build-up of schemata takes place through exposure to events. Where there is discrepancy between events the individual is alerted by means of the orienting response and the novel information either leads to accommodation or is assimilated by the existing model. This stream of new information leads to the restructuring of thought and behaviour as the child progresses to higher levels of cognitive ability. The individual is, thus, an active participant in his own growth – a view in contrast to the Behaviourist view of Man as a passive organism motivated by the need to restore physiological equilibrium.

Studies of exploration in animals and Man have illustrated the inadequacy of the Behaviourists' simple push/pull, reward/punishment model. Although a great deal of rudimentary behaviour is probably learned as a consequence of reinforcement, other complex activities take place spontaneously in the apparent absence of reward.

Well-fed, dry and comfortable babies will pay close attention to their environment and begin visual and tactile explorations at a very early age. This aspect of Piaget's 'need to know' has also been labelled as 'curiosity' or 'exploratory' drive, implying that the quest for information can in itself be rewarding or drive-reducing. This may well be a consequence of the stimulating and arousing effect that information input has on the brain.

There are many examples of exploratory behaviour in animals. Harlow[1] found that well-fed monkeys would undo and reassemble a complex puzzle without any kind of reward, other than the activity itself. They kept this up for as long as ten hours. Chimpanzees have been observed to prefer the stimulation of a learning task to available food.[2] An episode has been recounted concerning a female chimpanzee who was learning to do problems for the reward of banana slices. One day the chimpanzee arranged the slices, as she received them, in a row instead of eating them. It was not, therefore, the food reward primarily which had kept her working at the puzzles. She was then presented with a further problem which involved opening a particular box. She solved the puzzle and put one of her stored banana slices inside it and gave it back to the experimenter who subsequently ended up with 30 slices of banana.[3] This kind of behaviour is a very long way from responses contingent upon material reinforcement.

A rat offered a simple or a more complex path through a maze to food will often choose the longer path provided it is not too difficult and retains its novelty value by being changed frequently. The longer pathway will be ignored if it is too simple and, therefore, presumably unstimulating.[4] A male rat will stop copulation with a particular female after prolonged sexual activity, but not apparently because of physical satiation. If offered a fresh partner he will continue mating with undiminished vigour.[5]

It has been suggested that exploratory behaviour can be explained on the basis that it has been rewarded in the past and so has tended to persist. In an experiment to test this hypothesis, kittens were reared by hand, so that they never had to forage for food and did not have the opportunity to associate exploration with reward. They still learned to choose the arm of a T-maze that contained a ball of paper, with which they could play, in preference to the other arm of the maze which was empty.[6] The evidence suggests that most animals prefer activity to idleness, unless sleeping.

Piaget described the behaviour of his two-month-old son thus : '. . . he systematically explores (visually) the hood of his bassinet which I shake slightly, he begins by the edge, then little by little looks backwards at the lowest part of the roof. . . . Four days later he resumes this exploration in the opposite direction.'[7] This kind of simple early curiosity develops a more complex nature as the child matures, until in adult life it gives rise to such self-imposed activity as growing orchids, mountain-climbing, voyages to the moon and the scientist's search for facts.

PLAY

The child's main exploration of the world is through play. No one forces him to do this, nor is he necessarily rewarded for it, indeed, he may persist with play behaviour in the face of scolding. The activity arises spontaneously and, initially, it is simple and solitary. Up to the age of 2 years play largely consists of using movement and sensation as a means of discovery, but slowly symbolic elements enter into it as the child develops language ability. Bricks can stand for cars or trains, a chair can become a horse, toys are transformed into characters in stories. From the age of 2 onwards children play increasingly in the company of other children, although at first the play is egocentric and self-centred, showing little genuine interaction between the children. Gradually there is an increase in communication between playmates and shared use of symbols.

By the age of 3 or 4 the child has learned to play with other children as part of his social and intellectual development, aided by his improving command of language. From the age of 5 onwards, play takes place mostly in groups and gangs, a situation which involves the child in recognising the needs of others, the sharing of common rules and co-operation. Interlocking roles are adopted such as leader/follower, doctor/patient, teacher/pupil, mother/father and the appropriate behaviour is allocated to each child. In this way the child begins to learn that there is a point of view other than his own, new ideas and possibilities for behaviour open up to him, and he learns that other children have needs that are not always compatible with his own. Rivalry over toys, for example, can challenge his natural egocentricity and be a salutary lesson in his social education. Conflicts of this kind occur frequently amongst pre-school children. Jersild and Markey[8] found that the average rate of conflicts in such a group was one per child every five minutes, but they were generally brief (thirty seconds or less), resolved without lingering resentment, and greatly exceeded by friendly encounters. As the children grew older, conflicts became less frequent but lasted longer and had more painful after-effects. This change no doubt represents the growing child's increasing gain of control over the expression of emotion; the concomitant of this being that when emotion becomes too strong for control the effects are more upsetting.

Play is essential for the normal development of intellectual, social, motor and imaginative skills. Space, companions and a minimum of interference are all that is necessary. What to adults may appear to be purposeless activity is often the precursor to more serious behaviour. Not only are the rules of games learned, but also the moral rules of a culture. Self-knowledge is acquired through observation of the reactions of others and the boundaries to the possible are established by the operations performed on the environment.

Role-playing is an important aspect of play, as the child takes the part of different figures in his experience – father, a cowboy, the milkman. In this kind of imaginative play the child learns to look at the world from the point of view of others and is preparing himself for adult roles, by early imitation. Another kind of imaginative play, involving fantasy and make-believe, can be seen as a step towards the freeing of meaning from the concrete here and now in which young children exist.[9] Ideas can be tested and abandoned, the child can behave 'as if' something were the case and play it out in imagination. It has been suggested that this propensity for 'scientific' investigation, the constant establishment and testing out of hypotheses about the world, is the distinguishing characteristic of Man.[10]

In imaginative play children may work out conflicts which they experience in real life. There is less tension, anxiety and guilt centred in play activities than in contact with the 'real' world, so that the child can use the occasion to explore and learn to cope with his feelings. In play children exhibit 'animism', in which the child gives a toy characteristics and feelings derived from his own ego. Thus the object is animated by the emotions and experiences belonging to the child. This is the underlying rationale of using play therapy and 'psycho-drama' to provide sanctioned situations where disturbed children and adults can express strong emotions and learn to cope with them. During play therapy a child may relive painful experiences, but also be able to work out a solution for himself. Axline[11] describes a child 'Dibs' whose father was very strict, demanding and emotionally cold. Dibs was initially withdrawn, referring to himself in the second or third person, never as 'I'. He crawled about the floor and hid under tables. Playing with a sand box he always hid one doll (his father) deep in the sand, but gradually during succeeding sessions he built up a friendly world of dolls for himself and so moved towards a solution he could use in the outside world.

A paradox of exploratory behaviour is that the same situation may evoke curiosity and advance, or alarm and retreat. This approach/avoidance conflict may be seen in young children when exposed to a strange situation, e.g. seeing Santa Claus for the first time. Inspection at a distance will be followed by a cautious approach with increasing confidence, but a sudden movement or a gruff question may send the child rapidly back to his mother. At all ages, stimulating behaviour by the mother, such as pulling faces or adopting strange postures, causing the child to laugh, is also likely to produce crying and withdrawal if performed by a stranger. King has put forward the idea that the presence of the mother, or other familiar figure, reduces the fear of novel stimuli and acts as a kind of buffer for exploratory behaviour.[12]

We have already noted some of the deleterious effects of a lack of adequate stimulation in infancy. One of the results of exploratory behaviour is that it stimulates the brain with a continual flow of sensory input. To be deprived of this input can be very distressing for adults as well.

Sensory Deprivation

American college students were paid twenty dollars per day to do nothing.[13] They lay for twenty-four hours per day on a comfortable bed with cushions over their ears, shields over their eyes which admitted light but no patterns, and cuffs over their hands. In consequence a large proportion of the normal information intake of the brain was cut off. A microphone was suspended in front of the volunteers to record their remarks and so that they could ask to be let out when they wished. They were allowed to get up to eat and to go to the lavatory. Few of the students could stand this regime for more than two or three days. No one endured it for longer than six days and one stood it for only eight hours, even though all the students needed the money. The subjects of this experiment found it disturbing in several ways. Sleep became impossible and attempts to pass the time by day-dreaming or mental problem-solving were increasingly disrupted by incoherent thoughts, anxiety attacks and even panic. Some of the subjects found that symptoms of lack of concentration, poor memory and mild hallucinations persisted for twenty-hour hours or more after they had left the experimental situation.

An experiment by Vernon[14] showed that even a boring, neutral stimulus will be preferred to none in these circumstances. Subjects were placed in a sensory deprivation cubicle, soundproof, dark and visually bare except for some apparatus. Pressing a button on the equipment would turn on a dim light that illuminated a drawing of two circles, one large, one small and connected by a diagonal line. The button (unknown to the subject) activated a clock in the experimenter's room and recorded how long and how often subjects looked at the drawing. The results were that the longer they stayed in the cubicle the more they looked at the drawing. The amount of viewing also differentiated those who wanted to be released early (average 37·6 hours) from those who completed seventy-two hours in the room. The first group spent ten times as long looking at the drawing as did the second group. It would seem that people differ in the amount of stimulation they need, possibly as a consequence of inherited differences in random activity in the central nervous system. Vernon also describes people in a similar deprivation condition as requesting over and over again to hear a temperance society talk for 6-year olds on the evils of drink.

Thus one of the functions of exploratory behaviour would seem to be to keep the brain in a state of arousal conducive to its efficient working. In the lower part of the brain there is a structure known as the reticular formation or the reticular activating system which sends messages up to the higher parts of the brain when a stimulus is received which is sufficiently novel. These messages arrive in advance of that conveyed by the specific stimulus and act as a kind of advance warning of the information to come, rousing the brain to activity.

Continuous stimulation of a particular kind, for example, the stimulation of one's skin by one's clothes, the odour of perfume worn by oneself, ceases to provoke a response in the reticular formation as the nervous equipment adapts to the same type of stimulation constantly present. The orienting response ensures that novel stimuli will be noticed and stimuli which are within the focus of attention and constantly changing also get through. The function of the reticular activating system seems to be to tune up the cortex and prepare it for the incoming information.[15]

Arousal

It has been suggested by several writers that there is some optimal level of arousal at which the brain works best.[16][17] Boredom and monotony give an arousal level that is too low, whereas anxiety and anger can produce an arousal level that is too high. In either case the brain's performance is impaired. It must be made clear that the terms 'arousal' and 'activity' in this context refer to physiological activity in the brain and not to mental processes such as thought.

The degree of arousal is also related to efficiency in solving problems. This is expressed by the Yerkes-Dodson law which says that moderate degrees of anxiety or arousal can facilitate

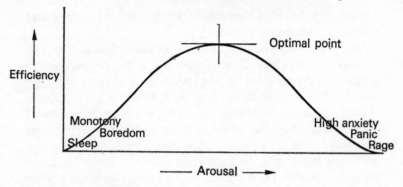

Figure 8   Arousal level and brain efficiency

the learning of simple tasks, but will tend to disrupt the learning of more complex tasks.[18] Since people differ in their need for stimulation, the optimal level of arousal will tend to vary from one person to another and also with the level of difficulty of the task, which will not be the same for everyone. Arousal often has the effect of enhancing what is happening already so that an efficient performance may improve somewhat up to a limiting point, but a poor performance will become even worse.

The effects of arousal on efficiency have been studied in a number of real-life situations involving stress. Some obervers have reported that under attack no more than 15 to 25 per cent of soldiers even fire their rifles, let alone shoot accurately.[19] In disasters such as fires or floods only between 12 per cent and 25 per cent of people behave at all adaptively. About the same number panic or become paralysed with fear and the remainder show a variety of behaviours which are less than intelligent and effective.[20]

The wide, but popular, classification of people into introverts and extroverts, first proposed by Jung,[21] and now adopted by Eysenck,[22] has introduced the idea that extroverts are people who have a naturally low state of physiological arousal and thus a high need for external stimulation which impels them to search for bright lights, noise, the company of others and a lot of change. Introverts, on the other hand, are said to have a naturally high level of physiological arousal and are thus inclined to shun further high levels of stimulation, tending to prefer quiet and relatively unchanging pursuits.

There are two main implications of the different effects of arousal for the child. Firstly, whether or not he experiences a situation as pleasant or unpleasant may depend upon his own level of arousal at the time. If it is low, a game such as 'Murder' may be enjoyable, but if he is already in a state of high arousal then the game is likely to become frightening. Secondly, there are educational implications. Mild arousal is a stimulant to learning, thus the child will learn best when faced with an interesting and challenging situation that is not beyond his comprehension. On the other hand a child will learn little in the presence of a feared or hated teacher.

Arousal theory implies that excitement is positively attractive and that the satisfaction of material needs is not enough to make an individual contented. Social planners would do well to take note of this since ensuring a plentiful supply of food, clothing, housing and physical benefits, although desirable, is not going to be sufficient to ensure universal happiness. The need for exploration and stimulation also requires outlets. Risk-taking is enjoyable as the proliferation of betting shops and the popularity of sports like rock-climbing and pot-holing show.

Another function of exploratory behaviour, related to the foregoing, is to provide extra information for the organism. A great deal of learning is needed to equip an individual with a basic framework for coping with the environment. He needs information from which he can construct a model of the external world, not only as it is, but also as it might become. Thus events can be anticipated and this increases the chances of survival. The attention that Man gives to novelty is a defence against unknown dangers. The evolution of Man was probably aided by his capacity to store scraps of information not directly related to the task in hand at the time but which came in handy for future planning.

The idea has been put forward that some of the apparently ghoulish curiosity at the scene of disasters is a universal expression of the need to assimilate happenings outside the present frame of reference.[23] Expectations and fantasies can thus be aligned with reality.

Opportunities for exploration and the expression of curiosity are fundamental to a child's development. These opportunities increase enormously with the development of speech.

SPEECH

The development of language in the individual is dependent upon a combination of maturation and encouragement. Speech is primarily a social function which replaces events and objects, experiences and actions, by symbols. It is the quality that distinguishes Man most from other animals. Written down it enables the transmission of the accumulated knowledge of the centuries to be passed on from one generation to the next, accelerating the rate of achievement enormously. Even cultures without a written language are able to pass information down the years by prodigious feats of memory, so that whole histories are encapsulated in the folktales of the people. Speech, moreover, aids the co-operation of individuals on a large scale and the build-up of complex organisations – sometimes with not wholly desirable side-effects.

As already noted, babies of all nationalities and even the congenitally deaf have pre-language repertoires of noises that cover very much the same range from any one baby to another. It seems, therefore, that these noises are not learned. It has been reported that by the age of two months an infant is babbling all the possible phonemes of any language.[24] Selective reinforcement of the sounds appropriate to his own language by the adults in his life encourages the repetition of certain phonemes whilst others tend to fall away. English parents repeating the coos and gurgles of their baby are teaching him an English accent.

By the age of five months, deaf babies no longer babble, whilst normal babies appear to enjoy hearing the sound of their own voice and this self-stimulation is reinforcing and persists. Towards the end of his first year the average baby can say some words to which he attaches meaning, but this stage is preceded by one in which 'echolalia' occurs, i.e. the baby will repeat words in 'parrot fashion' without understanding to what they refer. Initially the child's production of words

H

depends upon association and imitation and the more parents repeat and respond to their child's attempts to talk, the more frequent will be his use of words.

Retarded adults can be encouraged to talk by being given rewards, using a form of operant conditioning. Giving candy to sub-normal female patients as a reward for speech was found to be effective in increasing their utterances by 13 per cent. Giving them tokens which could be used to buy a variety of desirable goods increased their output of words by 39 per cent.[25]

Although reinforcement plays an important part in the early development of language it is not sufficient to account for the several aspects that speech behaviour can assume. Children use language in its early stages as a form of play and as a commentary on their actions, but the fact that they often receive parental attention as a consequence of talking makes them see speech as part of a social relationship and as a means of satisfying their needs, because they can now ask for what they want. Talking in itself seems to hold some intrinsic interest for a child, since there is evidence that children practise talking even when alone. A tape-recording taken of a two-year-old as he lay in bed at night revealed that he tried out various sentences substituting different nouns as subject or object and using different kinds of verbs within the same basic construction.[26]

Early language is embedded in action. Speech is learned at the same time as various aspects of social behaviour – drinking, getting dressed, sitting round the table, etc. As time goes by and the vocabulary grows, meaning is learned through its context and language becomes increasingly freed from action and more abstract. Things not present can be referred to, plans made and hypotheses about the world can be constructed.

Retarded language development may occur for a variety of reasons. One of these is brain damage and another is lack of stimulation and feedback such as has been shown to occur in some institutions. If a child is continually told to 'Shut up' or 'Be quiet' whenever he asks a question, not only does this stifle his curiosity, it may also be a barrier to the achievement of adequate language skills, since the opportunity for practice in the ordinary give-and-take of conversation is being denied him. Over-solicitude in the form of continually anticipating the child's every need and what he is about to say can also discourage a child from adding to his speech ability. Both bilingualism and being a twin can produce a degree of backwardness in speaking, although normally this is not very serious. Two Russian investigators, Luria and Yudovich,[27] found in their study of twins that the children had evolved a form of private language, which was interfering with the development of abstract thought. Both children improved when they were separated and given special training. Mittler[28] studied 200 4-year-old twins for linguistic ability and compared them to 100 single children, matched for age and social background. The twins were found to be retarded by an average of six months in language ability. Middle-class twins were at a relatively greater disadvantage than working-class twins who came in any case from a background of poor linguistic skill. Only children tend to show accelerated speech development, using longer sentences and a wider vocabulary than their peers from families with more than one child.[29]

Speech accelerates socialisation and enables parents to present children with their view of reality more effectively since behaviour can now be labelled as 'good' or 'bad' and the child learns conditioned responses to particularly emotive words. Russian work on verbal conditioning has illustrated the way in which words can become conditioned stimuli for internal reactions. Markosyan, for example, conditioned the salivary response to food to the words 'right' or 'wrong'. It was found that the response generalised to right and wrong sentences, correct and incorrect calculations.[30] Thus words in themselves can evoke emotional reactions via the conditioning process.

Bernstein has suggested that different language 'codes' may be used by different groups in society. The 'restricted code' may be used in adolescent groups, families, working-class subcultures and amongst close friends. It is likely to be dislocated in form, narrative and descriptive, with frequent repetitions and terminal questions such as 'innit?', 'you know?' and 'right?'. The 'elaborated code' is more explicit, abstract and analytical with logical sequences of sentences linked by conjunctions such as 'because', 'however' and 'although'. Bernstein suggests that these codes are also linked to social class, so that the elaborated code is more common in middle-class households. Children brought up in circumstances where the restricted code is the only one they hear may be at a disadvantage in a classroom situation where the teacher talks in elaborated code and schoolwork demands logical analysis.[31]

Speech is vital in the development of the secondary process, the capacity for active memorisation, and interpretive and integrative cognitive skills. Deaf-mutes have difficulty in abstracting the attributes of objects since without speech it is impossible to separate an object from its attributes. Speech facilitates social interaction and adaptation to others. Speech therapy given to subnormal people aids their social adjustment.[32]

Early speech in children, that is between the ages of 3 and 7 years tends to be egocentric. It is not directed at a listener, but is often a monologue or an accompaniment to activity. No answers are expected even if someone else is present. Piaget[33] considered this private speech to be an external manifestation of inner thought, which the child eventually realises he can share so that it becomes social speech. This view has been challenged by Vygotsky[34] who suggested the contrary – that the earliest speech is social speech which become egocentric and eventually internalised into private inner speech. This notion is supported by an experiment[35] which showed that pre-school children of high popularity have highly developed social and private speech. Older children who do tasks in silence will, if questioned about their thoughts, give answers that have the form of egocentric speech. More private speech is observed when children are alone together than when they are with adults. This is consistent with Vygotsky's observation that more private speech takes place in situations that are similar to talking to oneself.

Although early investigators tended to assume that all language was learned by a combination of imitation and association, there is increasing interest in evidence which suggests that each human being has innate cognitive structures that are rule-seeking and anticipate the underlying 'deep' grammar of language.[36] When talking to a child, an adult tends to expand the rudimentary remarks of the child. This is one of the ways in which a child may induce the general rules that are implicit in the language he hears.[37] The idea is that there is some 'pre-wired' structure in the brain that is organised to handle the acquisition of language – an inherited feature of the human brain. This view gains support from the fact that all known languages share certain common features, 'linguistic universals'.[38] Besides this, children do seem to expect that language should have regular rules – so that they render the irregular past tense of English words into a regular form, saying 'I fighted' or ' I falled down' and many of the rudimentary sentences uttered by children cannot have been learned by imitation, for example, truncated sentences like 'Birdie gone', 'Da-da comes'. Formations of this type are never used by adults (except in imitation of their infants), although the individual words may be. So it is possible that there is an in-built propensity for us to talk in particular ways.

The use of speech also aids the child in his exploratory quest as can be seen from the interminable 'why' questions that children ask. It also speeds up the process of intellectual and emotional development, as the child is no longer confined to the 'here and now', nor so dependent upon the ability of others to recognise his needs from his behaviour.

Speech and exploration are also intimately involved in the child's social development as he learns to recognise and label the values and standards by which other people live.

REFERENCES

1 H. F. Harlow, 'Learning and satiation of response in intrinsically motivated complex puzzle performance by monkeys', *J. Comp. Physiol. Psychol.*, *43* (1950) 289–94.

2 D. O. Hebb, *A Textbook of Psychology* (Philadelphia and London, W. B. Saunders, 1958).

3 O. M. Rumbaugh, 'Learning skills of anthropoids', *Primate Behaviour*, Vol. I (New York, Academic Press, 1970).

4 J. Havelka, 'Problem-seeking behaviour in rats', *Canad. J. Psychol.*, *10* (1956), 91–7.

5 A. E. Fisher, 'Effects of the stimulus variation on sexual motivation in the male rat', *J. Comp. Physiol. Psychol.*, *55* (1962), 614–20.

6 R. C. Miles, 'Learning in kittens with manipulatory, exploratory and food incentives', *J. Comp. Physiol. Psychol.*, *51* (1958), 39–42.

7 J. Piaget, *The Child's Conception of the World* (London, Routledge & Kegan Paul, 1929; Paladin, 1973).

8 A. T. Jersild and F. V. Markey, *Conflicts between Pre-school Children* (New York, Teachers College Press, 1935).

9 S. Isaacs, *Social Development in Young Children* (London, Routledge & Kegan Paul, 1933).

10 G. Kelley, *The Psychology of Personal Constructs*, Vols. 1 and II (New York, Norton, 1955).

11 V. Axline, *Dibs, In Search of Self* (Harmondsworth, Penguin Books, 1964).

12 D. L. King, 'A review and interpretation of some aspects of the infant-mother relationship in mammals and birds', *Psychol. Bull.*, *65* (1966), 143–5.

13 J. C. Lilly, 'Mental effects of reduction of ordinary levels of physical stimuli on intact healthy persons', *Psychiat. Res. Reps.*, *5* (1956), Amer. Psychiat. Ass. 1–9.

14 J. D. Vernon, *Inside the Black Room* (Harmondsworth, Penguin Books, 1966).

15 G. Moruzzi and H. V. Magoun, 'Brain stem reticular formation and activation of the EEG', *EEG Clin. Neurophysiol.*, *1* (1949), 455–73.

16 H. Schlosberg, 'Three dimensions of emotion', *Psychol. Rev.*, *61* (1954), 81–6.

17 D. O. Hebb, 'Drives and the CNS (conceptual nervous system)', *Psychol. Rev.*, *62* (1955), 243–54.

18 R. M. Yerkes and J. D. Dodson, 'The relation of strength of stimulus to rapidity of habit formation', *J. Comp. Neurol. Psychol.*, *18* (1908), 459–82.

19 S. L. A. Marshall, *Men Against Fire: the problem of battle command in future war* (New York, Apollo, 1946).

20 L. Tyhurst, 'Individual reactions to community disaster : the natural history of psychiatric phenomena', *Amer. J. Psychiat.*, *107*, 764–9.

21 C. G. Jung, *Psychological Types or the Psychology of Individuation* (trans. H. G. Baynes), (London, International Library of Psychology, Philosophy and Scientific Method, 1923; Routledge, 1971).

22 H. J. Eysenck, *Fact and Fiction in Psychology* (Harmondsworth, Penguin Books, 1965).

23 R. S. Lazarus, *Psychological Stress and the Coping Process* (New York, McGraw Hill, 1966).

24 C. E. Osgood, *Method and Theory in Experimental Psychology* (London, Oxford University Press, 1953).

25 E. S. Barton, 'Operant conditioning of social speech in the severely subnormal and the use of different reinforcers', *Brit. J. Soc. Clin. Psychol.*, *11* (1972), 387–96.

26 R. H. Weir, *Language in the Crib* (The Hague, Mouton, 1962).

27 A. R. Luria and F. Ia. Yudovich, *Speech and the Development of Mental Processes in the Child* (Ed. J. Simon, transl. O. Kovasc and J. Simon), (London, Staples Press, 1959).

28 P. Mittler, 'Biological and social aspects of development in twins', *Devel. Med. Child. Neurol., 12* (1970), 741–57.

29 E. Davis, 'The development of linguistic skills in twins and singletons with siblings and only children from 5–10 years', *Inst. Child Welfare Res. Monog.*, Series No. 14 (1937).

30 A. A. Markosyan, 'The interaction of signal systems in the process of blood coagulation', *Zh. Vyssh. Nervn. Deyatel., 8* (1958), 161–7.

31 B. Bernstein, 'Social class, linguistic codes and grammatical elements', *Lang. and Speech, 5* (1962), 221–40.

32 B. G. Schmidt, 'Language development as an aid to the social adjustment of mental defectives', *Ment. Hyg. N.Y., 25* (1941), 402–13.

33 J. Piaget, *Le Langage et le pensée chez l'enfant* (Neuchatel-Paris, Delachaux & Niestle, 1923).

34 L. S. Vygotsky, *Thought and Language* (Massachusetts, Inst. Tech. Press, 1962).

35 L. Kohlberg, J. Yaeger and E. Hjertholm, 'Private speech: four studies and a review of theories', *Child. Dev., 39* (1968), 691–736.

36 N. Chomsky, *Syntactic Structures* (New York, Morton, 1957).

37 R. Brown and U. Bellugi, 'Three processes in the child's acquisition of syntax', *Harvard Educ. Rev., 34* (1964), 133–51.

38 E. H. Lennenberg, *Biological Foundations of Languages* (New York, John Wiley, 1967).

6

Developing Morality

There is nothing good or bad, But thinking makes it so.
Shakespeare, *Hamlet*

All known societies have rules by which their members are supposed to live. These include legal, religious and traditional observances. Within the society the interpretation of these rules will differ and some individuals will have a relatively idiosyncratic system of values. Within any individual the system of morality he has will be a product of many learning experiences, within the family and among peers and others.

As the child grows he is exposed to value judgements, both explicit and implicit, emanating from his parents, teachers and friends. Some of these judgements may well be incompatible with each other. When parents deliberately try to transmit standards of behaviour they may unwittingly contradict themselves ('Don't swear at me you little bastard'), so that two mutually exclusive messages are being conveyed to the child, one a verbal stricture and the other a behavioural model. Parental standards are usually reinforced by rewards and punishments of some kind, but parents reward and punish in the belief that the child knows to which of his actions their reactions refer. This is not always the case, especially when the reinforcement occurs after a time lapse and the child may have little idea for what he is being praised or blamed.

These conflicts and contrasts between moral ideologies and between professed belief and action can be confusing for a child, but they are also the source of moral growth.

By the time adulthood is reached the vast majority of people have developed some internal moral code, an ideology which governs their behaviour to a lesser or greater extent. There are often large gaps between thought and action. The fact that someone believes a certain action to be wrong is no guarantee that they will refrain from performing that action.

The external standards of a society become internalised as the child becomes socialised. External sanctions of approval and disapproval become internal emotions of pleasure or fear which effectively control individual behaviour in the interests of society. Total conformity, however, is attended by the dangers of inflexibility and totalitarianism. Obeying the dictates of society without question, moreover, cannot be an expression of a moral belief since the element of choice is not present. Fortunately the inconsistencies inherent in the socialisation process guard against complete transmission of moral systems from one generation to the next and adolescent rebellion also represents a safeguard against slavish conformity.

Psychologists are little concerned with the content of moral beliefs which will, after all, differ according to time and place, with history and culture. Instead, they concentrate on the learning of moral values, the nature of moral emotions, the development of moral judgement and the relation of these to actual behaviour. Morality may be regarded as having three components: emotional, feelings of guilt or shame; behavioural, what the person actually does in a situation involving a moral decision; and judgemental, how the person believes he and others should behave and his knowledge of morality.

EMOTION AND MORALITY

Freud was most concerned with the emotional constituents of morality such as anxiety and guilt.[1] His model suggests that there develops within the child a moral arbiter – the Super Ego – derived from the Ego as a result of parental praise and blame and the child's identification with a loved parent. Those things which a parent has praised as being good are said to give rise to the Ego Ideal which involves such qualities as unselfishness, tolerance, kindness, etc. Those actions to which parental blame and punishment is attached lead to the establishment of the conscience which is concerned with such things as aggression, tabooed forms of sex, disliking one's parents and so on. The function of the Super Ego is, then, to control the impulses of the Id. This it does by the use of unpleasant guilt feelings, the moral equivalent of the child's anxiety that he may lose the love of his parents.

Freud was pessimistic about human beings, implying that they are somehow born anti-social, containing within them seeds of destruction, which uncontained would lead to the derangement of whole societies. He believed that a civilisation must literally 'civilise' its members. In his energy model of personality, energy that would have been used by the Id to fulfil its forbidden wishes becomes diverted to the Super Ego which uses it to 'punish' the Ego, for example, by making the person feel uncomfortable or even by making him have an accident. The Super Ego like the Id is not ruled by reality and may impose excessive punishments on the Ego, causing painful feelings of guilt merely for thinking something 'naughty'. According to the system, the stronger the impulse that is repressed the more energy will be directed to the conscience and the more powerful it will become. Quite harmless people may, said Freud, be repressing strong emotions and so may be tortured by guilt even though they have not committed any undesirable act. Other people who give violent expression to their emotions may, conversely, feel little or no guilt. The Ego Ideal does not appear to be a very powerful influence on behaviour since the standards it upholds are not related to the child's fear of losing parental love. It thus represents standards which may be passed from generation to generation without ever being put fully into practice by anyone.

Freud pointed out that the strength of the Super Ego was not in any way related to the severity of the punishment that a child had received for wrongdoing. This is borne out by evidence from studies of delinquents who often have a history of physical beatings from the father. The idea that the conscience develops out of the child's dread of losing love implies that where the child has no love to lose a conscience will not develop, a notion that is supported by the studies of deprivation of maternal care where those children who fail to develop attachments are in danger of growing into 'affectionless characters'. The importance of Freud's model is that it emphasises the role of attachment and aggression in the development of moral feeling, but many of his ideas are hard to test by experiment because of their vagueness and generality.

Punishments that play upon a child's fear of losing his parents' love – coldness, withdrawal of affect, expressions of hurt, however, do seem to be more effective in conscience development than physical punishment.[2] Bandura and Walters[3] compared the attitudes of the parents of twenty-six 'highly aggressive' boys with those of the parents of 'normal' boys, matched for social class and I.Q. score. The aggressive boys were said to experience less guilt than the other boys and their fathers were more rejecting and likely to rely on physical punishment as a means of control. This is not necessarily a case of the fathers' attitude causing the boys' aggressiveness. It is a possibility that it was the aggression in the boys which led to the attitudes of the fathers. However, studies on the imitative behaviour of children do suggest that aggressive models will be copied, especially if the aggression achieves the desired result.

Groups of children were exposed, either to the sight of an adult behaving aggressively towards a large plastic doll, or to the sight of an adult sitting quietly ignoring the doll. The children in both groups were subsequently frustrated by having their play continually interrupted. They were then left alone with the plastic doll. Those children who had observed the aggression of the adult to the doll were themselves much more likely to behave aggressively towards the doll than were the children who had seen the adult sitting quietly.[4] Parents do act as models for their children and it is what they do rather than what they say which is likely to be the more formative. The use of aggression for dealing with conflict is likely to be emulated by children, though possibly not when in the presence of their parents.

Seeing the consequences of someone else's actions may also encourage or discourage imitation. Children seeing aggression rewarded, e.g. where snatching and bullying succeed in getting a toy, are more likely to use it themselves in a similar situation than children who have seen the same behaviour fail in its objective.[5]

Psychological forms of punishment give rise to feelings of anxiety in the child which he then associates with the particular misdeed. Thus a conditioned emotional response is established to a particular situation. This conditioning process becomes more effective after the development of language since the child now associates a particular label, say, stealing, with the situation. Because of this the emotional response can become anticipatory, so that the contemplation of an act which has the label 'stealing' gives rise to the emotional response of anxiety well before the act is committed and may well prevent it from being so. A conditioned emotional response of this kind can be established also from observing others. If a person sees someone else given an electric shock every time a buzzer has sounded the observer, too, begins to show a reaction to the buzzer, what we may call 'vicarious conditioning'.[6] This only appears to work if the person actually sees the punishment, not if he only knows about it. The arousal of anxiety in response to an intended transgression has a two-fold outcome. The anxiety inhibits the intended response, but it also provides a motive for doing something else, i.e. to get rid of the anxiety. It is thus a particularly effective method for ensuring obedience.

MORAL JUDGEMENT

The ability to make a moral judgement depends to a large extent on the maturity of the cognitive processes. In order to study the developmental aspects of children's moral beliefs and knowledge Piaget[7] told stories to children of differing ages, which concerned a variety of 'naughty' acts and asked them to tell him which was the naughtiest. One example contrasts the story of a little girl called Marie who wanted to give her mother a nice surprise and cut out some sewing for her, but by mistake cuts a big hole in her dress, with the tale of a child called Margaret who took some scissors one day whilst her mother was out and cut a small hole in her dress. Younger children tend to judge Marie as being naughtier than Margaret, whilst for older children the judgement is reversed. It seems that young children (between the ages of about 4 and 8) tend to judge actions by the sheer size of the resultant disaster : to cut a big hole is naughtier than to cut a small one. Similarly, in another set of stories, a child who broke a large number of cups by accident was judged naughtier than one who smashed one cup on purpose. Older children are more inclined to be influenced by the intention of the wrongdoer and to feel that little or no blame should be attached to accidental damage.

Another difference between age groups is that for the older children an action is wrong whether or not someone catches the miscreant, whereas at the younger ages, wrong is seen as related to being caught – to tell a serious lie and get away with it is not so bad as to tell a trivial lie and be found out. This seems to be because younger children judge wrongdoing in terms of what their parents punish. It follows that if a child has successfully deceived them he will not have been punished – hence the deed is blameless.

In relation to lying, children under 8 years of age, according to Piaget, thought that any deviation from the truth, including tall stories and white lies, was bad. Children in the older age group judge lying to be wrong when there is intent to deceive, believing the outcome to be irrelevant.

From the results of his researches Piaget distinguished two main stages in the development of the child's concept of morality :

1. *Heteronomous morality:* At this stage which lasts from about the age of 4 years until 8, children believe themselves to be completely subject to the laws of other people, especially parents. These laws are for the child paramount, unquestioned, sacred and eternal. The child feels inferior and powerless in the face of parental justice and sees his duty as being to obey those in authority over him (although he may not do so). Since the parents are omnipotent in the child's eyes he believes that they know what he is doing even when not present. From this derives the idea that if he does something his parents don't punish then it isn't wrong (although in reality it could be that they don't know about it). There is also at this stage a belief in divine retribution. Nature, God, Fate are all on the side

of the parents and have the power to punish with floods, lightning, thunder, and with cuts and bruises. If some accident occurs to a child after he believes himself to have been naughty then this is seen as a retributive event, even although, logically, there is no connection between the two occurrences.

These attitudes also show up in the child's reactions to the rules of games. Piaget watched children playing marbles and noted their reactions. Up to the age of 3 years, marbles are used as free-play materials. Between 3 and 5 there is imitation of older children playing the game, but the rules are not fully understood and so they are violated. By the age of 5, knowledge and acceptance of the rules are established and they are regarded as binding and immutable.

By approximately the age of 8 years the child's concepts of morality have undergone a change, a change which, Piaget believes, takes place largely independently of adult teaching, to the stage of :

2. *Autonomous morality:* After the age of 8 years children focus more upon intent than the deed and begin to recognise their parents as fallible beings. The rights of others come to be conceded and ideas of justice and fairness become important aspects of judgement. Co-operation with peers, mutual respect and empathy are now present and it is recognised that since rules are reached by consensus they can be changed.

The two types of morality were contrasted by Piaget as being initially a 'morality of constraint' and finally a 'morality of co-operation'.

Whereas Freud believed that children incorporated into themselves their parents' system of values, Piaget maintains that parental intervention is relatively ineffective in bringing about the change from heteronomous to autonomous morality. Instead he attributes it to two associated processes. One is the change that is taking place in the child's cognitive abilities and the other is the changes that have taken place in social relationships. There is a decline in egocentricity as the child grows older and he is less reliant on parents for support and information. As the child moves out into a wider social circle of peers, he begins to understand that there are other points of view than his own and his parents. Through clashes of interest and attitude, mutual respect develops in the peer group, leading to the idea of individual rights.

Piaget's findings have been validated in other societies[8] insofar as the change over from one morality to another is present. However, the relationship predicted between respect for authority and heteronomy and between respect for peers and autonomy does not always appear.[9]

There are people who see rules as being sacred and unchangeable although they have little respect for authority and some individuals agree on the subjective and arbitrary nature of rules without necessarily having respect for their fellow human beings. Many adults do not seem to have moved on from the stage of heteronomous morality and still see wrongdoing in terms of whether or not one gets caught ('It's all right if you can get away with it'). Piaget did recognise that some individuals may not progress beyond a stage of unilateral respect for authority and considered that where a person was bound by social constraint and deference to authority rather than by principles based upon social interchange between equals, that person was an adult behaving as a child.

Piaget's formulation does seem a little too simple to encompass the variety of moral judgements that people make, but there is another developmental view of morality which considerably enlarges upon Piaget's theory of a two-stage development.

The method of Kohlberg[9][10][11] is also to tell stories to children, but they are of a more sophisticated kind than those told by Piaget. They involve moral dilemmas of a kind which involve conflicts between legality and humanity, between authority and the individual. In one study[9] Kohlberg presented a set of ten such moral dilemmas to seventy-two boys divided into age groups of 7, 10, 13 and 16 years. In one story a man whose wife is dying of cancer hears that a certain chemist has developed a new drug which might help her. But the chemist will only sell the drug for ten times what it cost him to manufacture and the man does not have sufficient money, so one night he breaks into the chemist's shop and steals the drug. The boys were asked was the man right to do what he did or not? and why was he right or wrong? Kohlberg is not so much interested in whether or not the man was justified in his action, rather he is concerned with the reasons the boys give for their judgements.

Another story concerns a man who leaves a civil defence post in the middle of an air raid to see if his family are safe, thus presenting a conflict between duty and love for one's family. Considering the level at which Kohlberg's stories are pitched, it is not surprising that he emerges with results that present a far more complex picture of development than that of Piaget. He suggests that there are three levels of moral development, each of which can be divided into two types.

1. *Pre-moral:* This type of morality was prevalent among the 7- and 10-year-olds, but less common in the older age groups.

Type I: A person behaves so as to avoid punishment. Thus one will refrain from wrongdoing for fear of being found out.

Type II: Acts are motivated by the desire to receive some kind of reward. Thus a person would be dissuaded from some action by offering a material incentive.

Both these types feel powerless in the face of authority and are motivated not by any internal feelings but by the external reaction to their behaviour.

2. *Conventional:* Less common in the younger age groups, but increasing in incidence as the boys get older.

Type III: A person conforms to the laws or rules in order to avoid parental disapproval and to retain the affection of parents. They thus refrain from doing things because 'Mother wouldn't like it'. Kohlberg calls this the 'good girl/boy' morality.

Type IV: By this stage the good child has grown into a good citizen. Morality of this type is based upon the social order and what Society says is good or bad is a basis for individual behaviour. The focus is upon the duties, obligations and responsibilities of the person as a member of the wider social group and there is respect for authority as the representatives of the state. A person behaves as he does in order to retain the respect and esteem of his fellow citizens and to avoid breaking the law of the land.

3. *Principled:* This type of morality was not found at all in the 7- and 10-year-olds, was extremely rare at age 13 and shown by about 10 per cent of the 16-year-olds.

Type V: This involves a concern with reciprocity in social relationships, with human interaction seen as a form of social contract. All individuals are seen as having equal rights, regardless of their station in life. The welfare of all men is what is important, so that one should act so as not to violate the rights of other people.

Type VI: This stage involves the possession of self-imposed individual principles, which are independent of the moral rules and strictures of other individuals and of the society. There is an awareness of the arbitrary nature of rules and this morality, unlike the conventional, defines what the social order should be and is not based upon what it is. A person behaves so as to avoid violating his own standards. Kohlberg suggests that this final stage is not attained by more than a minority of individuals and certainly cannot appear prior to adolescence, since it is only then that the child becomes capable of the degree of abstraction involved in this kind of moral judgement, which embodies an awareness that, whilst rules are man-made and arbitrary, there should also be universal and absolute standards of morality. One should not imagine that this type of morality is inevitably on the side of the angels, since the individual principles might contain elements regarded as undesirable in, say, a democratic society.

Kohlberg's levels of morality have a higher association with age than they do with I.Q. score. This suggests that they are not just the result of the verbal learning of the kinds of morality available, but are, rather, a consequence of life experience and maturity.

The ten moral dilemmas were also used to explore the idea that people at level 3 are more inclined to accept individual responsibility. They were given to two groups of young men matched in age, I.Q., education and social background. One group consisted of army cadets and the others were draft-resisters. The cadets were mainly at the conventional stage, whilst the resisters were mostly of Type V and VI. The cadets tended to believe that the solution to problems lay in the hands of society, whilst the resisters thought that it was up to the individual to do something.

A study by Haan and his associates included the gathering of biographies and the administration of personality tests along with the Kohlberg stories.[12] They found that young people at level 3 tended to be independent of their parents, politically active, rebellious and agnostic or atheist. Those at level 2 were, in the main, politically conservative and inactive, religious and conformist, while those at level 1 had, interestingly enough, quite a lot in common with the level 3 people, being rebellious, radical and non-conformist. The authors concluded, however, that the rebelliousness of the latter group grew out of personality problems rather than springing from idealism.

Kohlberg, like Piaget, believes that moral development proceeds independently of adult teaching, but results from the restructuring of experience to take account of the words, deeds, feelings and expressed attitudes of other people. It has been found that progression through the stages that Kohlberg suggests is positively related to the extent of social participation by adolescents.[13] Thus the more varied experience a person has of himself and others the more likely is he to develop some kind of principled morality. The laws of society, the standards that parents profess, their behaviour, the values of the peer group and other adults all present the growing child with different facets of belief and action. It is his efforts to fit these into a coherent framework which lead to his moral growth. There will, it follows, be conditions that militate against this development such as highly authoritarian systems that stifle dissent, a narrow experience of life, a family background that encourages dependence, the imposition of completely arbitrary rewards and punishments.

The first level of Kohlberg's formulation has much in common with the Behaviourist view of motivation as being related to the reinforcement, either negative or positive, of the child's actions. It would precede the development of the Super Ego in Freudian psychology and has much in common with Piaget's heteronomous stage where it is the regard for external consequences that governs behaviour. If we accept the evidence of Bowlby, Freud, Sears and others, then progression beyond this stage would entail a loving relationship with some significant figure and the use of psychological, rather than physical, forms of punishment.

Kohlberg's second level is akin to Freud's notion of Super Ego development, where the child has internalised the external sanctions of his parents because of the fear of losing their affection and support. This regard for the respect and admiration of others then generalises to the society as a whole. The Type V morality resembles Piaget's autonomous stage, where regard for 'fairness' and equal rights prevails. Type VI morality does seem to involve elements of Super Ego, but not in the Freudian sense since the standards of the individual are derived not from parental values but from the totality of experience and they may develop quite late in life. Type VI morality nevertheless implies the presence of a conscience, albeit idiosyncratic, which has the power to condemn the self for transgressions against the principles of the individual.

The work of Kohlberg does suggest that there is a certain consistency between the moral judgements made by a person and their willingness to act upon them. Other studies, however, indicate relatively little association between moral belief, moral feeling and moral behaviour.

MORAL BEHAVIOUR

Between 1928 and 1930 a massive and by now classic study of 11,000 schoolchildren was carried out by Hartshorne and May.[14] [15] The investigations were conducted both at home and in school and involved giving the children opportunities to lie, cheat and steal. The results indicated that the behaviour of any one child was highly specific to the situation it was in and that there was little correspondence between their feeling guilty, knowing what was said to be right and wrong, and the way they behaved. A later study on resistance to temptation has, however, suggested that there may be a general trait of honesty in children[16] but, in any situation, a personality trait is only one of a multiplicity of factors which interact to bring about an action. One must take into account also the incentive to commit the act, the enormity of the offence, the risk of detection, the level of emotional arousal and the social context of the behaviour, for example, whether or not it has the support of other people. Self-esteem can also influence the propensity to commit certain acts. In one experiment,[17] high or low self-esteem was induced in subjects by giving flattering or derogatory remarks concerning their performance on personality tests. In comparison with a control group who did the tests but got no feedback, the subjects in the low self-esteem condition were more likely to exhibit dishonest behaviour in a subsequent test, whilst the high self-esteem group showed more resistance to temptation.

We must remember that morality is developed within society. Perhaps the low association between professed beliefs, guilt and action is not too surprising in a society such as our own where conflicting values and shifting standards are the norm. Children are praised for being unselfish and honest, whereas it must often appear that it is the unscrupulous and dishonest who succeed in life.

Although there is evidence to support Freud in his belief that the development of conscience requires the existence of a love-tie to the parents, Kohlberg holds the view that a good parent–child relationship is only necessary in so far as it forms a basis for other social relationships. Some institutionalised children and those from very unhappy homes are in danger of growing up 'defective' in moral behaviour, but they have been deprived of other things than love. Children brought up on the Israeli kibbutzim, whose main contacts are with other children, show about the same maturity of moral judgement as Israeli children of the same age brought up by their own parents. An intense parent–child relationship may thus not be necessary for adequate moral development.[11]

As children grow up the peer group takes over some of the power of the parents as an enforcer of the moral code and may supplant them entirely at the time of adolescence. Since children normally belong to more than one group they will have opportunities to explore several standards and roles.

Of course, there are also individual differences to be taken into account. An over-indulged child may feel exempt from all moral rules, a rejected child may acquire a harsh conscience because his parents have been primarily punishing by the non-display of affection, or he may rebel and reject all parental and authoritarian values. Inconsistent and capricious parental discipline is found to be related to a lack of self-discipline in children.[18]

Intelligence appears to have little effect on moral behaviour, unless it is so low that the child has difficulty in grasping any kind of rules at all. If high it may help wrongdoers to escape detection, but it may also mean that there is no need to cheat or steal in order to achieve one's aims. There are sex differences in moral behaviour : fewer girls than boys become delinquent and girls are more likely to go along with the wishes of their parents. There are, however, greater pressures on girls to be conformists and 'nicely behaved'.

The whole area of research into morality is drenched in value judgements as to what constitutes 'good' and 'bad' behaviour on the part of parents or children. Generally it is accepted that mere obedience to a feared parent or other authority does not constitute moral behaviour, since the element of choice is ruled out. Adult advice and comments should certainly be adjusted to the level of development at which the child is. It is no good trying to reason with a child of Kohlberg's Type V morality by using Type II incentives. Adults provide guidance, example and support (or lack of it) but the evidence suggests that the formation of moral beliefs depends more upon the child's opportunities to explore a variety of ideas and experiences from a basis of security than upon the utterances of their parents and teachers.

REFERENCES

1 S. Freud, *The Ego and the Id* (London, Hogarth Press, 1927).
2 R. R. Sears, E. E. Maccoby and H. Levin, *Patterns of Child-rearing* (Evanston, Row, Peterson, 1957).
3 A. Bandura and R. H. Walters, *Adolescent Aggression* (New York, Ronald Press, 1959).
4 A. Bandura, D. Ross and S. A. Ross, 'Transmission of aggression through imitation of aggressive models', *J. Abn. Soc. Psychol.*, *63* (1965), 575–82.
5 A. Bandura, D. Ross and S. A. Ross, 'Vicarious reinforcement and imitative learning', *J. Abn. Soc. Psychol.*, *67* (1963), 601–7.
6 S. M. Berger, 'Conditioning through vicarious instigation', *Psychol. Rev.*, *57* (1962), 450–66.
7 J. Piaget, *The Moral Judgement of the Child* (London, Routledge & Kegan Paul, 1932).
8 D. Macrae, 'A test of Piaget's theories of moral development', *J. Abn. Soc. Psychol.*, *49* (1954), 14–18.
9 L. Kohlberg, 'The development of children's orientations towards a moral order. I: Sequence in the development of moral thought', *Vita Humana*, *6* (1963), 11–33.
10 L. Kohlberg, 'Development of moral character and ideology', in *Review of Child Development Research* (Eds M. L. Hoffman and M. Hoffman), (New York, Russell Sage Foundation, 1964), 383–432.
11 L. Kohlberg, 'State and sequence: the cognitive-developmental approach to socialisation', in *Handbook of Socialisation: theory and research* (Ed. D. A. Goslin), (Chicago, Rand, McNally, 1969).
12 N. Haan, M. B. Smith and J. Block, 'The moral reasoning of young adults', *J. Pers. Soc. Psychol.*, *10* (1968), 183–201.
13 C. B. Kensey, 'Social participation as a factor in the moral development of pre-adolescents', *Devel. Psychol.*, *5* (1971), 216–20.
14 H. Hartshorne and M. A. May, *Studies in Deceit* (New York, Macmillan, 1928).
15 H. Hartshorne and M. A. May, *Studies in Service and Self-control* (New York, Macmillan, 1929).
16 E. A. Nelson, R. E. Grinder and M. L. Mutterer, 'Sources of variance in behavioural measures of honesty in temptation situations', *Devel. Psychol.*, *1* (1969), 265–79.
17 E. Aronson and D. R. Metter, 'Dishonest behaviour as a function of different levels of induced self-esteem', *J. Pers. Soc. Psychol*, *9* (1968), 121–7.
18 D. E. Hunt and R. H. Hardt, 'Developmental stage, delinquency and differential treatment', *J. Res. Crime and Delinqu.*, *2* (1965), 20–31.

7

School Life

'Tis education forms the common mind,
As the twig is bent, the tree's inclined.
Alexander Pope, *Moral Essays*

The child's first years at school coincide with what Freud called 'the latency period'.[1] Between the emotional lability of early childhood and the onset of puberty Freud believed that there was a period when the emotional side of the child's life was less in evidence. There does appear to be less emotional conflict in some children at this time, but this may not be a built-in aspect of development; it may merely reflect the fact that the child is at school all day and has reduced contact with parents.

The years between infancy and puberty do show, in general, a concentration on the cultivation of cognitive skills and mark the beginning of the child's psychological movement away from parents as moral and social arbiters, and towards the peer group.

This stage has been labelled as one of 'industry', when the child has the opportunity for extending his competence in technical and intellectual skills, but involving the attendant danger that through adverse experiences he will develop instead a sense of 'inferiority'.[2] Provided a child has developed a sense of trust and initiative he will look forward eagerly to going to school. This is, however, also a time of vulnerability to failure, when feeling competent in relation to friends and peers is important for the growth of self-confidence and self-respect.

IN THE CLASSROOM

A need for acceptance means that the child will try to conform to the expectations of his teachers and the rules of his peer group, although these are not always compatible, and the child may experience a clash between the values mediated by the school and those encountered in the street and at home.

The attitudes of teachers have been shown to be very important in influencing the behaviour of their pupils. If, for example, a teacher rewards conventional thinkers his pupils will do their best to oblige.[3] The expectation by a teacher that his pupils will perform badly (or well) may subtly influence his behaviour and bring about a self-fulfilling prophecy.[4] A child's performance at school does not depend only on his intellectual capacity. Teacher proficiency and attitudes, home life, friends and the school regime are all significant in determining the outcome of the educational process.

It has been suggested that there are three aspects to a child's life in the classroom. These are emotional acceptance, feelings of competence, and social power.[5] Part of the learning environment of the child involves the particular system of praise and criticism favoured by a teacher. In one study it was found that children subjected to disapproving comments learned more slowly and made more errors than children who merely had their errors corrected (this was especially marked for younger boys). These effects were still in evidence eight days later.[6] On the other hand, children who are praised by a teacher tend to be seen by the other children as more competent even where praise is randomly distributed and without relation to performance.[7] Where teachers feel confident enough to delegate part of their power to their pupils there tends to be more interaction and less tension and conflict in the classroom. Pupils express more liking for each other and the teacher and are said to be more tolerant, responsible and independent.[7]

A study of boy scout groups varying in size indicated that in large groups individuals feel less powerful and that power tends to be concentrated in the hands of the more aggressive or skilled boys.[8] Classes of different sizes may similarly bring out different norms of behaviour and so be more or less supportive of the individual.

Whether a group is constructive or destructive may depend upon whether desired goals, such as the teacher's approval or being sent on errands, are open to all or only a few.[9] A teacher who concentrates on his favourite pupils may destroy friendly co-operation and establish hostile rivalry in his class. The relation between pupil and teacher has been found to affect academic performance and to be more important in this respect than parental attitudes.[10] Pupils who are well accepted by teachers and peers and have social power tend to be more accurate in their picture of themselves than do those children who are rejected by others or who have low status.[11] When rejection results from physical defect, however, the child so affected is often accurate in perception of his low status. Since those who feel themselves to be of low status are inclined to underachieve academically,[12] [13] those children who suffer some physical defect are likely to labour under a double disadvantage. Mentally retarded children are especially likely to be rejected by their peer group,[14] an apparent fact that has been used in argument against those who maintain that special schools for the mentally handicapped increase social isolation[15] – the retarded, it seems are already socially isolated.

The academic performance of girls is more closely linked to their acceptance by other children than is that of boys.[16] Boys are more affected by their position in the hierarchy of power. Girls, more than boys, are perhaps demoralised by not being liked, and boys, more than girls, by feeling powerless. Boys and girls who are rejected by other children have been found to be more aggressive and unco-operative,[17] although in working-class schools aggression and hostility to authority tend to be associated with leadership.[18] The effects of school are, in general, to perpetuate and exaggerate existing social beliefs, norms and status. Strong, healthy, middle-class, socially skilled children are preferred by teachers and, if they conform, acquire self-esteem and status. Unhealthy, poor, aggressive children, lacking in the social graces, tend to be rejected by teachers and other children and are caught in a vicious circle of poverty and inadequate education, a process which is exacerbated by equating potential ability with score on an I.Q. test.

THE CONCEPT OF INTELLIGENCE

'Intelligence' is, arguably, one of the most overworked words in the English language, but has little uniformity of meaning. Nevertheless, psychologists have not hesitated to construct instruments for the measurement of this elusive concept on the grounds that, like electricity, we may not know what it is exactly, but we can devise instruments for its measurement. Whilst most psychologists are trained to recognise the drawbacks and limitations of I.Q. tests, it is unfortunate that many of those who come into contact with the tests, whether as parents or as representatives of social agencies, are not fully conversant with the many factors which can affect the score or the assumptions upon which the testing rests.

Intelligence has been described as judgement, good sense, practical reasoning and the ability to adapt to circumstances,[19] the ability to relate concepts to one another in a constructive way in order to achieve some goal,[20] insight,[21] and as many other things. The important thing to remember is that the content of an I.Q. test will reflect the compiler's definition of intelligence. The tendency to split off cognition from emotion in these definitions is particularly unfortunate in view of the fact that, as we have tried to show in earlier chapters, most learning takes places in an emotional context, for example, in association with reward or punishment.

Vernon distinguishes three common approaches to intelligence:[22]

1 The operational, which defines intelligence as that which is measured by the test. Thus the results of such a test need bear no relationship to success in a real-life situation. In practice, tests based on this principle are heavily loaded with scholastic items such as vocabulary and comprehension, mental arithmetic and rote memory.

2 The biological, which views intelligence as the flexibility and adaptability which is found increasingly as one goes up the evolutionary scale and which appears to be related to the ability to profit from experience. I.Q. tests do not measure this aspect of functioning.

3 The psychological approach, which is implicit in the other two types of definition. Here the concern is with particular

mental abilities such as grasping relationships, problem-solving, language and mental agility.

Attempts to study intelligence have been bedevilled by the belief that it is like a possession which one might have or not have. Intellectual ability, however, is probably less like an unchanging object which can be owned, like a double-bed, and more like a fluid process which analyses and organises the world outside us. If this is so it is likely to fluctuate with emotional state and time of day and there will be many interacting factors – physical, social and psychological – which will affect the intellectual performance of any individual.

The Operational Approach to Intelligence

The first intelligence tests were developed in France around the turn of the century when it was realised that some people were not able to cope with the complexities of an industrial society. Series of tests were designed for primary school children which compared them with others of the same age. A child who was more than two years behind the average score of his peers was deemed to need special education.[19] Although more modern tests tap a wider range of skills, they are still based upon the principle of comparing the performance of one child with that of others of the same age.

The construction of a test is a complex task and can take more than five years. Tests are not, therefore, replaced very rapidly and tend often to have an old-fashioned air in appearance and wording. There are six stages in the construction of a test :

1 Defining the purpose – for example, to try and predict scholastic achievement or to provide vocational guidance.

2 Choosing or inventing items to be included in the test – a fairly arbitrary process which depends upon precedent and the preferences of those compiling the items.

3 Trying out the items on a sample that is representative of the population to whom the test will finally be given, in terms of age, sex, class, nationality, geographical location, income group and so on.

4 Analysing the answers obtained at the third stage and rejecting those that show evidence that the item has been misunderstood, those that give rise to confusing results, and those that show sex differences.

5 Trying out the remaining items on a further representative sample.

6 Obtaining separate scores for each age group, so that each individual taking the test can be compared with the average score of his age group.

In practice it is rarely possible to obtain a truly representative sample of an age group on which to standardise a test (say, all 8-year-olds in Britain) because of the number of children who play truant, those who are chronically ill, and those who have travelling parents like gypsies, actors and bargees. All these and similar categories are likely to be under-represented. This is important since it is an invalid procedure to give an I.Q. test to someone who was not represented in the original sample. Thus the Wechsler Intelligence Scale for Children[23] was standardised on white American children and so will give inaccurate results if used to test black Americans or white or black British children and will be wholly inappropriate for use with children from a totally different culture such as Nigeria or Pakistan.

Ideally a test, whether of 'intelligence' or 'creativity' or vocational aptitude, should be reliable, that is, if given to the same person twice it should yield the same result. In practice, it is not possible to do this, since actually to repeat the test would mean that the results would be affected by the child's recollection of his first performance or, if a relatively long interval was allowed to elapse, by maturation and learning. It is possible to produce two tests which are supposed to be 'parallel' in the items they present so that the results of one test can be compared with the results of the other. Again, in practice, it is difficult to achieve the necessary degree of similarity. The more usual method of checking reliability is a statistical one whereby the results from one half of the test are compared with the results of the other half. Theoretically there should be a high degree of agreement.

The validity of a test is also important – is it really measuring what it set out to measure? Practically there are difficulties in deciding on criteria of the validity of an intelligence test. Often, testers settle for such external signs as examination results, but since these tend to reflect the same kind of conformity to school standards as do I.Q. tests it is not valid to assume, in the event of high agreement between I.Q. scores and examination results, that the I.Q. test therefore measures 'intelligence'.

Most intelligence tests aim at assessing such things as reasoning ability, memory, abstract thought, concentration, perceptual-motor ability and pattern matching speed. There are two ways of scoring; in both the number of items correctly completed by a child (his raw score) is related to the average scores of the children of his own age. The first method of scoring, which produces the familiar I.Q. score, converts the raw score into a mental age (using the tables and instructions that are supplied with each test). This mental age is then divided by his actual age and multiplied by a hundred to give the I.Q. score :

$$\frac{\text{Mental Age (M.A.)}}{\text{Chronological Age (C.A.)}} \times 100 = \text{I.Q.}$$

Where mental age and chronological age are the same the child's I.Q. will be the average of 100 .

For example, a 5-year-old who passes the average number of items for his age will have a mental age of 5 and, therefore, an I.Q. of 100 :

$$\frac{\text{M.A. (5)}}{\text{C.A. (5)}} \times 100 = 100 \text{ I.Q.}$$

If, however, a 5-year-old passes the average number of items for 6-year-old he will have a mental age of 6 and, therefore, an I.Q. of 120 :

$$\frac{\text{M.A. (6)}}{\text{C.A. (5)}} \times 100 = 120 \text{ I.Q.}$$

Since I.Q. scores are always relative to the average of a particular group they are really only rankings and, therefore, although an I.Q. of 120 may be said to be higher than an I.Q. of 60, it cannot be said to be double. It is also arbitrarily assumed by many I.Q. tests that a person's score will not increase after age 15, so adults taking such a test will be shown as having a chronological age of 15 for the purposes of calculation.

The second way of scoring intelligence is by percentiles so that instead of saying a child has an I.Q. of 100 he may be said to lie at the 50th percentile – that is that he is more intelligent than 50 per cent of the age group to which he belongs. It is assumed that scores on a test are 'normally' distributed in a population – that is, that half will score above average and half below, that most people will score about the average and that as the test scores tend towards the extremes of the scale so progressively fewer people will be represented at each level of intelligence (see Figure 9). The tests are constructed so that the scores will tend to form a normal distribution, but this does not necessarily mean that 'intelligence' is spread through the population in this neat and balanced fashion.

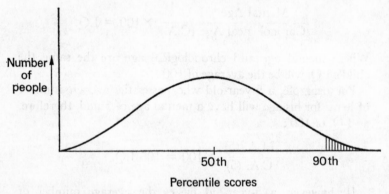

Figure 9   Normal distribution of percentile scores

The 90th percentile represents the score which will be exceeded by only the top 10 per cent of the population, and the advantage of this method of scoring is that it discourages the idea that 'intelligence' is something precise and unchangeable.

Whatever score a child gets has no meaning in itself but only reflects that child's level of scoring in comparison with others of the same age on the same test. All I.Q. tests should be accompanied by a booklet which gives details of the standardisation sample and the reliability and validity scores of the test, and no test should be given without taking these into account.

Heredity and Environment

Intelligence has been a topic in the centre of the Nature/Nurture debate since Francis Galton studied 400 'geniuses' in 1892 and found that many of them were related to one another and had other distinguished relatives.[24] He concluded that their abilities were the result of heredity and failed to note that they all sprang from the privileged stratum of society in terms of money, status and education.

Studies of identical twins, who may be assumed to have a similar genetic inheritance, reveal that these twins show a high agreement in I.Q. score, higher than either non-identical twins or siblings. If identical twins are brought up separately, the agreement between their scores is less, but still higher than for siblings brought up apart. The number of twins who can be studied in this way is, however, very small since efforts are usually made to keep them together in the event of adoption or fostering. One must also consider that the pre-natal and post-natal environments of identical twins will be more alike than for any other pairs.

The idea that 'Nature' is the main influence in determining intellectual ability implies that a person's capacity will remain fixed throughout life. There are many studies which suggest that this is far from being the case. Skeels[25] reports a study on thirteen children who were diagnosed as mentally retarded when they were less than 3 years old. They were transferred from their adequate, but impersonal, orphanage to a State school for the mentally handicapped where they were placed with older girls and women who gave them plenty of attention and affection. Stimulation in the form of toys and outings was also provided by the attendants. After six months for some children and fifty-two months for the slowest their scores on tests were no longer at the sub-normal level and they were sent out for adoption, or returned to the orphanage. Another group of twelve children who were initially said to be brighter than the first group and who acted as a control group for the study remained in the orphanage throughout.

Those who had been moved gained, in two years, an average of 28·5 I.Q. points whilst the control group lost an average of 26·2 points. Twenty-one years later the entire experimental group were self-supporting and had completed twelve years of schooling whilst the control group had completed, on average, less than three years of schooling and eight of them were in institutions for the mentally handicapped.[26] A case has been reported where two children diagnosed as 'feeble-minded' were fostered by a woman regarded as sub-normal. In spite of this not very promising placement the children showed large gains in intellectual and motor development due, presumably, to the extra attention and stimulation they were receiving.[27]

Thus there can be no doubt, as pointed out also in earlier chapters, that the environment within which a child develops plays a most important part in determining the direction and extent of that development. It is not, however, in the early years of life only that intellectual ability is affected by environment. It has been found that in a sample of university-educated people matched with early school-leavers, the average of the university-educated was twelve points higher than the average of the others, although at 15 years old all of them had had the same score.[28] Vernon and Parry showed that by comparison with people in intellectual jobs, the I.Q. scores of people in manual jobs decline more rapidly and start to decline earlier in life.[29] One must beware of taking this as evidence that those who have jobs requiring some mental ability become somehow 'cleverer'. It could be that they are better motivated to co-operate in such tests and more conversant with the kind of answers expected.

There is a widespread tendency to assume that early measures of academic success like I.Q. score or degree class will predict later achievement, but above a certain level, say, a score of 120 on the commonest kind of test, I.Q. is not predictive of later excellence, and it has been shown that a large proportion of Doctors of Science at Oxford and Cambridge did only moderately on their first degree.[30] A study of outstanding architects, mathematicians, scientists, engineers and writers suggested that many of them were no better than average at college.[31] Getting a high I.Q. score, like getting good marks at school, college or university requires a willingness to play the education game, which is not necessarily related to the possession of any creative talent or originality.

It is possible that heredity sets limits to intellectual potential, but the environment throughout life determines whether or not this limit is reached. A useful distinction has been made by Hebb[32] between what he calls 'Intelligence A' which refers to the potential with which a person may be born and 'Intelligence B' which is the present level of functioning of the individual as brought out by environmental factors. Vernon has suggested that to these one can add 'Intelligence C' which is the sample of present functioning that is tapped by an intelligence test.[22] Although A, B and C will be related at some level it is obviously quite mistaken to assume that an intelligence test measures all aspects of cognitive functioning or that I.Q. scores reflect the built-in capacities of the individual.

The assumptions behind intelligence tests and the way in which they are constructed means that they automatically discriminate against some of the people to whom they are given. Most of the tests depend upon a child's understanding of written or spoken instructions, so that the results depend upon command of language, which is in turn affected by culture, social class, family environment, size of family and opportunities for certain kinds of stimulation, reading and the availability of books, for example. The home background, if disrupted in some way, may lead to emotional upset in the child which will affect his performance on tests and at school. Anxiety is known to be a disrupter of intellectual performance above a certain level. For example, children of 9, 11 and 13 years of age were tested on their creative and intellectual ability under two conditions: 1. moderate stress, where a time limit of three minutes for each item was ostentatiously imposed; 2. reduced stress, where a relaxed attitude was adopted by the tester and little emphasis put on the time limit. Some children, said to be of 'low arousal' did better under the first condition, whilst other children were disturbed by the stress imposed and did better in the relaxed condition.[33] It seems that the same testing situation does not provide all children with the same conditions; it favours some and discriminates against others.

Numerous aspects of the child's family background may increase the stress under which he performs, his parents' ambitions (whether very high or very low), the level of literacy in the home, his physical well-being and his parents' health. The extent to which parents support the school will also influence how well he gets on there, although we must bear in mind that support can range from attending parent/teacher meetings and helping with homework to instructing the teacher to give little Johnny 'a good belting' if he steps out of line.

Middle-class children, in general, have a better start, the values of home and school tend to be the same, and their parents stress the importance of success. In lower-class households, however, there is a danger of children coming to see themselves as inferior and through repeated failures at school becoming completely discouraged, especially if they see school values as being the 'correct' ones. As we have noted, the school environment can encourage or discourage intellectual development by its effects on self-esteem and the rewards it offers for particular skills. A democratic home may ill prepare a child for an autocratic school and vice versa. There is a deep-rooted and self-protective tendency for school authorities to see a child who plays truant, or who is apathetic or disruptive, as being at fault. Instead of attempting to make school less frightening or more interesting, the child may be 'treated', 'counselled' or 'tested'.

The emphasis in most schools on competition and on passing exams means that inevitably some children will be classified by themselves and by others as failures. School may then become a place of anxiety and unhappiness and these feelings can generalise to all school activities, including reading and learning. The emphasis on academic abilities may devalue other skills such as craftsmanship, originality and leisure pursuits. The top streams may concentrate on Latin and physics, whilst the bottom streams do woodwork and art.

The majority of teachers still tend to be drawn from or aspire to the middle strata of society. Quite unwittingly this may affect their attitude to their pupils. In a three-year study of one class in a primary school it was found that even in the first two weeks middle-class children were perceived as the keenest and most able by the teacher who thereafter concentrated most on these pupils.[34] Douglas demonstrated that there were more working-class children in the lower streams of primary schools than would have been predicted from their I.Q. scores.[35] Student teachers especially tend to prefer passive and conforming children because they are easier to control.[36] It has been pointed out, however, that the attitude of the pupil to the teacher affects the extent to which he can be influenced. If the pupil's attitude is one of indifference or dislike then the teacher's praise is less rewarding and his blame less punishing.[37]

All teachers bring their own opinions to the classroom which may be subtly, but non-deliberately, conveyed to the pupils so as to affect their approach to history, politics, social class and other nationalities. The very seating arrangements can determine social relationships. Teachers try to disperse disruptive elements by putting them at the end of a row or between two 'good' children. Children judged more attentive are given front row seats (where they provide positive reinforcement for the teacher).

In one study it was found that teachers label some children as disruptive even without prior experience of the child's behaviour and if asked to justify their judgement ascribed it to 'instinct' or 'chemistry'.[38] Seating arrangements can affect friendship patterns, questioning, learning and the self image of the pupils.

Although the exponents of the operational approach to intelligence would by no means deny the profound effects of environment on ability and I.Q. score, the subtle and debilitating effects of home and school or the advantages conveyed by class and conformity are not always recognised by those whose job it is to take assessments of intelligence into account in deciding the future of a child.

The Biological Approach to Intelligence

In earlier chapters we have talked about Piaget's analysis of intellectual development in terms of the growth and interaction of schemata. His theory can account for the fact that learning may not take place in what appears to the observer to be adequate circumstances, that is, because the necessary antecedent conditions for the growth of underlying schemata are not present. According to Piaget, intellectual growth arises out of the child's attempts to understand increasingly complex experiences by assimilation and accommodation, processes which are biologically given. Although Piaget has not specially concerned himself with environmental factors, it follows from his theory that a poor and unstimulating situation will retard cognitive development. Piaget has made a considerable contribution to educational theory, especially in supplying the rationale for 'discovery' methods of teaching in which the child first handles materials that demonstrate some principle rather than being taught the principles by rote. He suggests that there are stages of development through which children pass at rates which vary from individual to individual, but which they must complete before they can take in concepts appropriate to the next stage.[39] [40]

Piaget maintains that the first period of development through which the child passes is the sensori-motor which lasts until about the age of 2 years and with which we have already dealt. Between the ages of 2 and 7 years is the period when language and symbolic thought are developing. At first, the child's concepts tend to be rudimentary and either too specific, so that 'dog' may be used to refer only to the family dog, or too general so that the word 'Daddy' may be applied indiscriminately to all men. For this reason the period is sometimes known as the 'pre-conceptual stage'. Next comes a time called by Piaget 'concrete operational', between the ages of, say, 7 to 11, when although the range and stability of the child's concepts has increased enormously he is still tied to the concrete here and now. Finally come the development of abstract thought, ability to follow logical argument and notions of objectivity, probability and hypothesis-testing.

During the pre-conceptual period children find it difficult to focus on more than one dimension of an object or problem at any one time. Width and height, for example, are considered separately, so that if water is poured from one container into a taller, thinner container, the child who focuses on the height of the liquid will say that there is more in the second jar, whilst the child who focuses on width will say that there is less liquid in it. Similarly, changes in shape are assumed to involve changes in amount, so that a fat round ball of plasticine which is rolled into a long thin sausage may be seen as having gained materials if the child focuses on the length, or as having lost something if he focuses on the width. The mental operations at this stage seem to be strongly influenced by the child's perceptions. What he can see tends to dominate over the symbolic processes which tell us that things are not always what they seem. If one asks a child to give a description in the absence of the thing to be described, there is less likelihood of what he sees dominating what he, in a sense, knows. For example, if water is poured into a differently shaped container, but the level of the water is hidden from the child, he is much more likely to say that the amount of water remains the same.[41]

Although young children often give the appearance of possessing certain concepts, closer investigation shows that this is more apparent than real. At about 5 years of age, for instance, a child can quite easily count two rows of marbles and say that there is the same number in each row. If one, however, condenses one row of marbles so that they take up less space, he will say that there are now fewer marbles in the shorter row. It is not until about the age of 7, on average, that children develop notions of reversibility and compensation, that is, when they realise that certain operations like changes in shape can be reversed and that density may compensate for length and height for width and they begin to understand that weight, number and volume are conserved regardless of their appearance. In the pre-conceptual stage children are said to be 'egocentric', unable to see things from any point of view but their own. This shows up particularly in language where a child explaining or describing something will assume information in the listener that is possessed only by the child. When a child asks a question such as 'Mummy, what was that thing we saw at the seaside?' he assumes that his mother can pinpoint the exact time and place when the object was sighted because he himself knows exactly what he means.

During this period children find it difficult to distinguish between the external and internal worlds, between images and reality, so that they may be accused of lying when they are merely confusing some mental picture or narrative with an event in the physical world.

The child in the period of concrete operations has now developed such concepts as constancy, conservation and reversibility. He is able to distinguish between physical, social and mental realities and can deal with several points of view at once. There are limits to this, however. If, for example, three objects in a row, A, B and C are shown to a child it is not until about 11 years of age that he grasps that B can simultaneously be to the right of A and to the left of C. During this period the child may be capable of a number of mathematical and classificatory activities, but they tend to be linked with a particular content. Thus he may realise that the same number of bricks can build a low, spread structure or a tall tower, but still fail to understand the general rule that objects may be equivalent in number or volume without necessarily taking the same form.

The following experiment demonstrates differences in cognitive ability at different ages.[42] A child is shown four flasks containing colourless, odourless liquids, and a small bottle. The liquids are : 1 dilute sulphuric acid; 2 water; 3 oxygenated water; 4 thiosulphate. The small bottle contains potassium. The experimenter shows the child two glasses containing colourless liquids and adds some drops from the small bottle to each. One turns yellow. The child is given the flasks, bottle and glasses and asked to make yellow. (The combination of 1 and 3 plus potassium will make yellow, with or without 2.) A child at the preconceptual stage makes no attempt at planning combinations of the liquids. He may make yellow but will not be able to say how he did it. At about 7 years of age a child will combine one liquid at a time with drops from the small bottle. He may even try all four liquids at once, but will not try more complex arrangements. A 9-year-old may combine two liquids at a time but has no systematic order and does not understand that it is the combination that makes yellow. He seems to believe that yellow is somehow contained in one of the liquids. By the age of 12, however, a child can verbalise all possible combinations and will go about the task systematically.

Although Piaget's work has been criticised on methodological grounds (many of his experiments depend, for example, on the child's understanding of his questions) it represents the largest existing body of data on the cognitive development of children and many of his findings have been verified by other investigators using more rigorous methods, although the age ranges which Piaget postulated for the development of certain concepts have been found to be much more variable than he suggested.[43] Attempts have been made in America and elsewhere to speed up the rate at which children develop cognitively, but the effects appear to have been marginal and probably successful only where the children were almost ready for such development to a higher stage.[44]

Although Piaget implies that passage through the periods of development is inevitable, there is evidence that some people never enter the stage of formal operations. A comparison of rural and urban dwellers in Mexico showed the rural group to be poorer at tasks involving abstract thought, an ability scarcely required by poor farmers whose lives depend upon concrete and observable events such as rain, sun and the growth of animals and crops. The urban dwellers, on the other hand, had developed that distancing from their environment which is a necessity for coming to terms with the complexities of an industrial environment.[45] Although biology may well form the basis of cognitive structures, environment still plays a vital role in determining the content and the extent to which those structures will develop. One might infer from the work of Piaget that each further stage of intellectual development replaces the preceding one. However, observation suggests that each of the stages he proposes may exist at the same time in any individual. An alternative approach which does not involve this assumption is that taken by J. S. Bruner.

Bruner[46] suggests that a person is capable of processing information about the world in three different ways. These are the enactive, which involves taking some action in relation to the environment, the iconic, which is concerned with imagery, and the symbolic, which involves the use of verbal signs and propositions. Each of these processes emerges in the course of development, but one does not necessarily supersede the other.

The enactive process takes place at the level of sensory and motor transactions with the world, for example, using tools and manipulating objects. The iconic process is intimately related to the internal representation of perceptions of the world, whilst the symbolic process refers to the reflective abilities and the capacity to perform abstract mental operations.

Although there are obvious similarities between Piaget and Bruner, the latter makes greater allowance for a variety of mental processes within the one individual, so that the development of symbolic thought may alter the extent to which enactive and iconic processes are used, but it does not necessarily replace them.[47]

In view of the wide range of ages across which any concept may arise, the idea of grouping children by age, as in school classes or in I.Q. tests, may be inefficient in terms of providing the best possible chance for any child.

The child's life in school and with the peer group outside both continue the socialisation process which began in the family. The child's self-image becomes stronger in interaction with others of his own age and his performance at school depends upon a complex of interacting physical, social and emotional factors. Children do not soak up information automatically like sponges taking in water. Whilst at school they are developing socially and as individuals, as well as intellectually. They can be profoundly influenced, for good or ill, by the expectations and behaviour of parents, teachers and friends.

REFERENCES

1 S. Freud, 'Three Essays on the Theory of Sexuality' (1st edition, 1905), *The Complete Psychological Works of Sigmund Freud*, Vol. VII (London, Hogarth Press, 1953).

2 E. Erickson, *Childhood and Society* (Harmondsworth, Penguin Books, 1965).

3 J. Henry, 'Attitude organisation in elementary school classrooms', *Amer. J. Orthopsychiat.*, *27* (1957), 117–33.

4 R. Rosenthal and L. Jacobson, 'Teachers' expectations: determinants of pupils' I.Q. gains', *Psychol. Reps.*, *19* (1966), 113–18.

5 S. A. Allen, P. S. Spear and J. R. Lucke, 'Effects of social reinforcement on learning and retention in children', *Develop. Psychol.*, *5* (1971), 73–80.

6 N. A. Flanders and S. Havumaki, 'The effect of teacher-pupil contacts involving praise on the sociometric choices of students', *J. Educ. Psychol.*, *51* (1960), 65–8.

7 J. C. Glidewell, M. B. Kantor, L. M. Smith and L. A. Stringer, 'Socialisation and social structure in the classroom', in *Review of Child Development Research* (Eds L. W. Hoffman and M. L. Hoffman), (New York, Russell Sage Foundation, 1966), 221–56.

8 A. P. Hare, 'A study of interaction and consensus in different sized groups', *Amer. Sociol. Rev.*, *17* (1952), 261–7.

9 M. Sherif, O. J. Harvey, B. J. White, W. R. Hood and C. W. Sherif, *Intergroup Conflict and Co-operation: the robbers' cave experiment* (Oklahoma, Norman University Oklahoma Press, 1961).

10 R. A. Schmuck and E. Van Egmond, 'Sex differences in the relationship of interpersonal perceptions to academic performance', *Psychology in the Schools*, *2* (1965), 32–40.

11 D. A. Goslin, 'Accuracy of self-perception and social acceptance', *Sociometry*, *25* (1962), 283–96.

12 R. A. Schmuck, 'Sociometric status and utilisation of academic abilities', *Merrill-Palmer Quart.*, *8* (1962), 165–72.

13 R. A. Schmuck, 'Some relationships of peer liking patterns in the classroom to pupil attitudes and achievement', *School Rev.*, *71* (1963), 337–59.

14 D. G. Force, Jr, 'A comparison of physically handicapped children and normal children in the same elementary school classes with reference to social status and self-perceived status', *Dissert. Abstr.*, *14* (1954), 1046.

15 T. E. Jordan, *The Mentally Retarded Child* (Ohio, Merrill Books, 1961).

16 R. A. Schmuck and E. Van Egmond, 'Sex differences in the relationship of interpersonal perceptions to academic performance', *Psychology in the Schools*, *2* (1965), 32–40.

17 B. A. Schmidt, *The relationship between social status and classroom behavior*, unpublished study (St Louis, Washington University, 1958).

18 B. Pope, 'Prestige values in contrasting socio-economic groups of children', *Psychiatry*, *16* (1953), 381–5.

19 A. Binet and Th. Simon, 'Méthodes nouvelles pour le diagnostic du niveau intellectuel des anormaux', *L'année psychologique*, *2* (1905), 163–91.

20 R. Knight, *Intelligence and Intelligence Tests*, 2nd edition (London, Methuen, 1943).

21 W. Köhler, *The Mentality of Apes* (London, Routledge & Kegan Paul, 1925).

22 P. E. Vernon, *Intelligence and Attainment Tests* (London, University of London Press, 1960).

23 D. Wechsler, *Wechsler Intelligence Scale for Children Manual* (New York, The Psychological Corporation, 1949).

24 F. Galton, *Hereditary Genius*, 2nd edition (London, Macmillan, 1892).

25 H. M. Skeels, 'Adult status of children with contrasting early life experiences – a follow-up study', *Monog. Soc. Res. Child Dev., 31* (3), (1966), Series No. 105.

26 H. M. Skeels and I. E. Harms, 'Children with inferior social histories: their mental development in adoptive homes', *J. Genet. Psychol., 72* (1948), 283–94.

27 H. M. Skeels and H. B. Dye, 'A study of the effect of differential stimulation on mentally retarded children', *Proc. Amer. Ass. Ment. Def., 44* (1), (1939), 114–36.

28 T. Husen, 'The influence of schooling on I.Q.', *Theoria, 17* (1951), 61–8.

29 P. E. Vernon and J. B. Parry, *Personnel Selection in the British Forces* (London, University of London Press, 1949).

30 L. Hudson, 'Degree class and attainment in scientific research', *Brit. J. Psychol., 51* (1960), 67–73.

31 D. W. MacKinnon, 'The nature and nurture of creative talent', *Amer. Psychologist, 17* (1962), 484–95.

32 D. O. Hebb, *The Organisation of Behaviour* (New York, John Wiley, 1948).

33 G. Leith, 'The relationships between intelligence, personality and creativity under two conditions of stress', *Brit. J. Educ. Psychol., 42* (1972), 240–7.

34 R. C. Rist, 'Student social class and teacher expectations: the self-fulfilling, prophecy in ghetto education', *Harvard Educ. Rev., 40* (1970), 411–51.

35 J. W. B. Douglas, *The Home and the School* (London, MacGibbon & Kee, 1964).

36 N. Feshback, 'Student teacher preferences for elementary school pupils varying in personality characteristics', *J. Educ. Psychol., 60* (1969), 126–32.

37 D. C. Davidson, 'Perceived reward value of teacher reinforcement and attitude towards teacher: an application of Newcomb's balance theory', *J. Educ. Psychol., 63* (1972), 418–22.

38 A. I. Schwebel and D. L. Cherlin, 'Physical and social distancing in pupil-teacher relationships', *J. Educ. Psychol., 63* (1972), 543–50.

39 J. Piaget, *Judgement and Reasoning in the Child* (New York, Harcourt Brace, 1928).

40 J. Piaget, *The Origins of Intelligence in Children* (New York, International University Press, 1952).

41 F. Frank, 'Perception and language in conservation', in *Studies in Cognitive Growth* (Ed. J. S. Bruner), (New York, Wiley, 1972).

42 B. Inhelder and J. Piaget, *The Growth of Logical Thinking* (New York, Basic Books, 1958).

43 M. Laurendeau and A. Pinard, *Causal Thinking in the Child: a genetic and experimental approach* (New York, International University Press, 1962).

44 J. Smedslund, 'The acquisition of conservation of substance and weight in children', *Scand. J. Psychol.*, 2 (1961), 11–20.
45 M. Maccoby and N. Modiano, 'On culture and equivalence', in *Studies in Cognitive Growth* (Eds J. S. Bruner, R. R. Oliver and P. M. Greenfield), (New York, John Wiley, 1966), 257–69.
46 J. S. Bruner, 'The course of cognitive growth', *Amer. Psychologist, 19* (1964).
47 J. S. Bruner, 'Education as a social invention', in *Contemporary Educational Psychology* (Ed. R. M. Jones), (New York, Harper & Row, 1967).

8
Identity and Autonomy

Our earth is degenerate ... children no longer obey their parents.
Egyptian inscription about 4000 B.C.

Adolescence and young adulthood are times when, according to Erickson,[1] a developing sense of personal identity is opposed by doubts about sexual and social roles in life, and when the capacity for intimate relationships alternates with feelings of isolation. It is also a time when the whole future seems to depend upon making the right choice of job. To achieve independence the adolescents in our society have to rebel against the standards and beliefs of their parents and establish separate identities for themselves. This necessary rebellion, Freud suggested, reawakens childhood fears of being unloved, rejected and inferior.[2]

Not all societies experience these difficulties with the transition from child to adult. In some cultures the change is clearly marked by an initiation ceremony so that neither the individual nor the society has any doubt about his role. In some undemanding societies little differentiation may be made between the roles of adult and child. In our highly complex society far more responsibility and competence is expected from adults than from children. Our prolonged formal education often arbitrarily denies responsibility for too long to individuals quite capable of assuming it. The situation is complicated because parents, teachers and adolescents themselves often display ambivalent attitudes to vocational choice and to social and sexual behaviour.

Adolescence can be a time of intense emotional relationships. Freud[2] saw it mainly in terms of biological development and the changeover from 'immature' (auto-erotic) to 'mature' (heterosexual) sexual activity, so that procreation becomes possible. Adolescents, however, are concerned with the acquisition of a whole range of social skills and not only with the specifically sexual. As we have noted in the previous chapter, this is also a time of cognitive development to the stage of abstract thought.[3] This may, in certain circles, lead to an interest in political theories and philosophical doctrines which lead some young people to question the values of their society. Piaget suggested that this awakening of interest in abstract speculation can mean that the ideas of the adolescent have little relation to things as they really are. Intellectual attempts to understand society are not, of course, confined to adolescents, but their involvement is likely to be more dramatic at this period.

PHYSIOLOGICAL CHANGES AND SELF-IMAGES

The onset of puberty, which usually takes place between the ages of 11 and 15 years, is normally dated from the first menstruation in girls and from the emergence of pigmented pubic hair in boys. There are accompanying hormonal changes which lead to the production of mature sex cells. There occurs a growth spurt in bone and muscle, but increases in height and weight vary in duration and onset from child to child. In boys this growth spurt normally occurs between 13 and 15 years with the average boy growing about eight inches in two years. In girls it occurs between the ages of 11 and 13 years, giving an average increase of five or six inches in height. After this, growth slows down and usually ceases about three years later, although boys, especially, may go on growing until the age of 21. The popular idea that girls mature earlier than boys may derive from the fact that they do attain their adult body weight and height, body hair and adult voice about two years earlier than boys.[4] There has been a trend towards earlier onset of menstruation over the past couple of centuries, perhaps a consequence of better health and nourishment. The onset is usually earlier than average in blind girls and later than average in those who are subnormal.[4] Of interest is the fact that menstruation occurs for the first time with a statistically greater frequency near a girl's birthday and during the two-week period round about Christmas and New Year.[5] It may be that excitement acts as a kind of hormonal trigger.

A study of New York males found big variations in the age at which puberty was completed. Three stages were distinguished: 1 pre-puberty; 2 puberty, accompanied by growth of the genital organs and pubic hair; and 3 full maturity, when growth processes were completed. Seventeen per cent of 20- to 21-year-olds in this sample were said to be still at the pubertal stage whilst 7 per cent of the 14-year-olds and 4 per cent of the 10-year-olds were fully mature. Of the 14-year-olds only 6 per cent were pre-pubertal.[6]

Sudden changes in size and weight and hair growth affect the self-image of the adolescent and often make him or her anxious about appearance. Every culture tends to have an ideal physical image for each sex which is used as a model. If an individual feels that he or she bears no resemblance to this ideal it may lead to fears of sexual unattractiveness and rejection. Adolescents often spend a lot of time on their hair, face and clothes, even if the final result is the apparently casual unkempt appearance currently in fashion.

Whilst girls are most concerned with their beauty, boys focus on their strength, size and growth of facial hair.[7][8] Certain characteristics are popularly supposed to be essential for attracting a member of the opposite sex which may have no basis in fact other than that the opposite sex may share the same stereotyped assumptions, for example, in a year when big breasts are 'in' padded brassieres will be worn by the poorly endowed. The typical 16-year-old boy may wish to be six feet tall, broad-shouldered and deep-voiced, with plenty of hair on chest and chin.

Physical changes often make adolescents clumsy since they have to learn to handle changes in centre of gravity and adjust to their new dimensions. This usually leads to self-consciousness, often aggravated by adult teasing. Because changes in appearance are in conflict with the pre-existing self-image, strange postures and gestures may be observed, some girls may hunch their shoulders to hide their developing breasts, whilst others may try to emphasise theirs.

Boys who fall short of the ideal image to which they aspire may suffer blows to their self-esteem and either withdraw from social activities or attempt to gain the admiration of their fellows by feats of skill or daring.[9] Boys whose physical development is behind that of their peers are likely to feel inadequate and may become either exceedingly dependent or rebellious, depending upon previous personality.[10] Adults are also likely to react on the basis of physical appearance, so that a big 14-year-old may be treated as more mature than an under-sized 16-year-old. Late maturing does constitute something of a handicap, but the early developer who has disadvantages such as skin eruptions, physical weakness or an inadequate home may have even greater difficulties.

Girls may welcome menstruation as a sign of womanhood or see it as a 'curse', an attitude highly dependent upon how the event has been presented to them by their mothers or teachers. The initial discomfort, embarrassment and association with ordinary bleeding may suggest illness. Where a girl has not fully identified with her femaleness, menstruation may be resented as a sign that she is no longer 'one of the boys'.

SEXUAL BEHAVIOUR AND ATTITUDES

Among the typical sexual anxieties of adolescents are, first, that they will not be able to attract a member of the opposite sex and, secondly, that, having found a partner, they will not know how to behave. In spite of sex education in some schools there is still a surprising amount of ignorance about the anatomy and mechanics of sex. In our culture, which has such high romantic expectations of sex, and which supplies the maximum of titillation with a minimum of permitted outlet, it is particularly difficult for adolescents to know what course of conduct to adopt. Adolescents are ambivalent in their sexual attitudes. Boys tend to be admired for the amount of their avowed sexual experience, but girls have been found to reject socially other girls who are sexually experienced or who show an excessive interest in boys. In one study only 2 per cent of girls thought that 'fast' girls were popular with boys[11] – a belief which seems to have some basis at least. In a study of adolescent boys in the East End, Willmott[12] quotes one as saying: 'But that sort of thing turns you off after a while – you realise that if you can get it so can anyone else.' In a study by Schofield it was found that although 64 per cent of boys wanted to marry a virgin, 51 per cent were in favour of pre-marital sexual experience.[13]

Conflicting standards such as these mean that the social reality of the adolescent demands that boys should try to get what they can, whilst 'good' girls attempt to fight them off. This still appears to be a widely shared norm in spite of alleged changes in sexual morality. Western morality tends to emphasise that sex should be accompanied by love. Casual sexual relationships, therefore, can give rise to guilt and remorse, and girls especially may be persuaded that they are in love with the first boy they have intercourse with or even merely kiss (a harmless enough illusion unless it leads to a life-long misalliance). Schofield suggests that commercial interests have fostered the myth of the sexually sophisticated adolescent. In his sample, 36 per cent of boys and 54 per cent of girls reported that they had not enjoyed their first sexual experience but had continued because they wanted to appear sophisticated and, for the boys, to prove their masculinity; for the girls, often to keep the boy.

Parental teachings about sexual behaviour are riddled with contradictions. Throughout childhood and adolescence there is a prohibition on all forms of sexual behaviour (at least overtly). As a child one is taught that handling one's own or another's genital organs is wrong, and this activity, if indulged in, may become associated with anxiety and guilt. Cultural convention has it that as a result of the marriage ceremony this lesson will be forgotten overnight (literally) and a happy and mutually satisfying sexual relationship will ensue. Women in particular are taught to be anxious about sex (presumably because of parental fears about pregnancy and lingering doubts about whether it is a suitable activity for a lady) and a few have permanent difficulty in viewing sexual behaviour with other than revulsion. The role of learning and culture in this is demonstrated by the fact that among the Manus of New Guinea there is a strong taboo on sexual behaviour before marriage and both sexes have difficulties in adjustment to a sexual relationship, whereas, in contrast, the Hopi Indians are highly tolerant of sexual play throughout childhood and there is a gradual development in activities to intercourse without adjustment difficulties.[14]

INDEPENDENCE

The desire of the adolescent for independence conflicts with his fear of freedom. Society exerts pressures for him to conform to adult standards. Parents complicate the situation by having ambiguous expectations, for example, encouraging a boy to leave school and earn his own living, but insisting that he is home by 10 o'clock at night, or by demanding that he 'stand on his own feet' and then objecting when he does so. He may contribute to the family budget and be treated as an adult at work, but have to depend upon his parents for pocket money, food and shelter. Those who prolong their education may have even greater difficulty in staking out areas of independence.

Some cultures ease the path to independence by having clear demarcation lines between adult and child-like activities, for example, initiation ceremonies which endow full adult status which is recognised by all – a boy becomes a man and a girl a woman almost overnight. The social climate creates, as it were, the emotional readiness. In our culture dependence in childhood is often rewarded ('Our Johnny has never been any trouble'), which may make it all the harder for an individual to establish adult autonomy. If a child has been over-dominated he will find it hard to relinquish the support of his parents. If the reward for dependent behaviour has been high and the punishment for rebellion harsh, it can prove difficult for the child to escape psychologically and, as an adult, he will remain tied to his parents forever. Parents, however, can never win, since it is also suggested that if they are too tolerant they will fail to provide standards against which the adolescent can rebel. Perhaps the best equipped for a smooth transition from child to adult is the child who has been respected and loved by his parents from the beginning as an independent individual and not as an extension of themselves. Some children may become independent early, not because they have the respect of their parents, but perhaps because they feel rejected and so resent their parents' continuing attempts to dominate them. This resentment may generalise to the whole of the adult order and be expressed in violation of adult law and order, or in demands for a revolution.

Where there is marital discord one parent or both may invest a great deal of emotion in the children and so delay their emancipation. A mother who uses her child as a *raison d'être* can scarcely afford to let him or her go. It has been said that it is more difficult for parents to allow their children adult independence when they satisfy their own needs for love and control through the child.[15] The child may be needed as an ally against the marriage partner or by a solitary parent as a substitute spouse. This possessiveness may be expressed in remarks like 'No man is good enough for my daughter'.

PEER GROUPS

An adolescent is helped in the establishment of independence from his parents by identification with others of his own age. Knowing that he has the support of his friends gives him the strength to oppose adult authority. Many of the external attributes of youth symbolise and emphasise this need to place a psychological distance between self and parents : cult heroes such as pop stars and footballers, fashions in slang, music, hair styles and clothes. Winning the approval and acceptance of his peers gives an adolescent self-esteem and a sense of being himself and not just part of a family. The peer group provides a frame of reference where the young person has a chance to test himself against equals instead of the power of parents. In this way the peer group is essential in resolving the anxieties which accompany the ambiguous status of being half-child, half-adult.[16]

REBELLION

One of the recent phenomena associated with youth culture among the educated middle classes has been the growing opposition to material success and what is seen as adult hypocrisy over politics, money and sex. Marriage, for example, may be seen as a selfish relationship which narrows personality. A recent book has suggested that in the United States (and increasingly in Britain) there is a move towards a personal philosophy which lays emphasis on the self as the primary reality, rather than upon the group or society.[17] Self-expression, spontaneity, love and inner experiences are seen as more important than material success or power. The feeling generally is said to be a-political and the central concern is with individual worth, brotherhood, sharing and truthfulness. One manifestation of this movement towards the search for inner experience and one's 'true self' is the taking of drugs, especially cannabis and the hallucinogens. Drugs also have symbolic value as a rejection of adult values, which is one of the more potent arguments against the legalising of cannabis, a step which could lead to the substitution of more harmful symbols of revolt. Since alcohol and tobacco are drugs which parents themselves have held up as 'adult' symbols, adolescents may use these as signs of adult status.

Student demonstrations, those well-known occasions for outpourings of adult scorn and self-righteousness, have sometimes been approached by those who have studied them with preconceived ideas. One book on student strikes and sit-ins, for example, attempted to explain them in terms of the emotional needs of students.[18] It was argued that because many students are away from home for the first time they are lonely and therefore predisposed to gain security in group action, that guilt over the middle-class privileges they are receiving makes them espouse the causes of the deprived of all nations, and that demonstrations provide an outlet for the energy of maturing males. It is further argued that the anxiety of being without a clearly defined role in society makes attractive the feelings of certainty, courage and immunity that are gained from being in a mass movement. This type of explanation may have its attractions for some, but it assumes that the espousal of a cause is an unthinking act and ignores the element of choice which decides which cause should be supported. It is a fact, moreover, that only a tiny minority of students engages in political activity and these are often the ones who work hardest and who obtain the highest degrees.[19] They also tend to come from departments which examine and compare the basic structures and assumptions of societies, such as sociology, anthropology and politics. A potent factor in student unrest could be that the university itself often confronts students with conflicting values.[20] Students are taught the value of an open mind, to examine, doubt and criticise the content of their studies. The university as a body may, however, resent any examination or criticism of its teaching methods, staff, syllabus or rules. Students are expected to subscribe to the ethic of intellectual excellence and knowledge for its own sake (an ethic not always adhered to by their mentors) and yet to confine their studies within the straitjacket of the examination system. These ambiguities inevitably lead to criticism of the university and the society within which it operates.

Another form of rebellion is, of course, delinquency. There is some evidence that adolescent boys find it easier than girls to achieve independenc. The sex role of women is still strongly stereotyped and does not, as yet, include independence or nonconformity. In fact the adolescent girl often finds herself subjected to increased parental control and anxiety after puberty. It has been suggested that the stronger pressures on girls to conform are one reason why fewer girls than boys are delinquent, although the absolute numbers of both are increasing[21] (another reason may be greater reluctance to prosecute girls). It has also been stated that deviance in women is more likely to take covert forms such as habitual lying or sexual offences rather than overt criminality.[22]

Offences committed by adolescent boys are most often against property, or involve theft,[23] and those youths who appear before the Juvenile Court are a selected sample. The more offences a boy commits the greater his chances of going to court, but the actions of other people such as parents, policemen, teachers, shopkeepers and friends may well affect the outcome of an offence, for example, whether it is regarded as a natural bit of high spirits, a crime against society or a heroic act. People may decide not to report an offence, not to charge the boy, or to deal with the matter informally by means of a clip round the ear.

Adolescent reaction against authority may transiently take a criminal form. For instance, most of us have probably stolen apples at some time, but this rarely extends to adult life. Adolescent gangs with a stable membership seem to be largely an American phenomenon. In England, small groups of three or four boys may commit offences together, but they do not have the cohesion which would constitute a gang. Not surprisingly boys are more likely to become delinquent if they have a large number of contacts with adult and juvenile law-breakers which exceed their contacts with the law-abiding.[24]

Environmental factors and family relationships play a major role in anti-social behaviour. Urban slums and new housing estates where there is little community cohesion and few recreational facilities produce a disproportionate amount of delinquency. Children from homes broken by divorce or separation of the parents are particularly at risk[25] as are those who are exposed to erratic discipline, rejection and parental disharmony.[26] [27]

It has been suggested that the discrepancy in our society between ends seen as desirable, such as power and success, and the legitimate means of achieving them, forces some people to pursue illegitimate means of becoming rich or at least obtaining material goods.[28] Those at the top of the social pyramid are not only already affluent, but also have access without difficulty, through better education, good credit ratings and powerful connections, to more money and status. Those at the bottom of the ladder have the same culturally determined ambitions but are less able to satisfy them and so may turn to crime. This theory predicts correctly that proportionately more working-class people are prosecuted for criminal offences, but it cannot account for such 'white-collar' crimes as tax fiddles, large-scale fraud and corruption in high places. Moreover, the delinquent behaviour of boys is often destructive rather than acquisitive[29] – they may break into property without stealing or often rapidly abandon articles they have stolen. This suggests that they reject both means and ends.

No explanation of delinquency is entirely satisfactory. It

seems to be a consequence of a variety of interacting factors among which social disadvantage, conformity to subcultural norms, rejection of adult rules and emotional disturbance are certainly important. One should not forget, however, that there is something of the delinquent in all of us, but it is those who get caught who have to bear the label.

The generation gap between adult society and youth has existed at most times, but is exacerbated today by the 'knowledge explosion', especially in technology. Standards of behaviour are also changing more rapidly than of old, so that youth today may not be merely reacting against old values, but establishing a new set of values which emphasise individual freedom, pleasure and responsibility rather than conformity, self-denial and obedience.

Many textbooks on human development imply that after adolescence the individual's struggle to comprehend his environment and his experience is at an end, but it may be closer to the truth to see the conflicts of adolescence as continuing throughout life in an attenuated form. Change and development continue throughout adulthood. The integration of intellectual imaginings, emotional upheavals, social conflicts and vocational demands into an individual philosophy is a lifetime's task.

REFERENCES

1 E. Erickson, *Childhood and Society* (Harmondsworth, Penguin Books, 1965).
2 S. Freud, 'Three essays on the theory of sexuality', in *The Complete Psychological Works of Sigmund Freud*, Vol. VII (London, Hogarth Press, 1953).
3 J. Piaget, *The Origins of Intelligence in Children* (New York, International University Press, 1952).
4 D. P. Ausubel, *Theory and Problems of Adolescent Adjustment* (New York, Grune & Stratton, 1954).
5 A. Jewisson, 'Mois de naissance et puberté chez les filles', *Biométrie Humaine, 5* (1970), 1–16.
6 D. H. Eichorn, 'Variations in growth rate', *Childhood Education, 44* (1968), 286–91.

7 S. S. Silverman, *Clothing and Appearance: their psychological implications for teenage girls* (New York, Teachers College, Columbia University, 1945).

8 D. P. Ausubel, 'Problems of adolescent adjustment', *Bull. Nat. Ass. Secondary School Principles, 34* (1950), 1–84.

9 W. A. Schonfeld, 'Inadequate masculine physique as a factor in personality development of adolescent boys', *Psychosom. Med., 12* (1950), 49–54.

10 M. Peters and W. W. Waltenberg, 'Adolescence: behaviour disorders and guidance', *Rev. of Educ. Res., 36* (1966), 474–84.

11 E. Douvan and E. Kaye, *Adolescent Girls* (Ann Arbor, University of Michigan, Survey Research Centre, 1957).

12 P. Willmott, *Adolescent Boys of East London* (Harmondsworth, Penguin Books, 1966), revised edition.

13 M. Schofield, *The Sexual Behaviour of Young People* (Harmondsworth, Penguin Books, 1965).

14 M. Mead, *Male and Female* (Harmondsworth, Penguin Books, 1962).

15 C. E. Meyers, 'Emancipation of adolescents from parental control', *Nervous Child, 5* (1946), 25–62.

16 D. P. Ausubel, *Theory and Problems of Adolescent Adjustment* (New York, Grune & Stratton, 1954).

17 C. A. Reich, *The Greening of America* (London, Allen Lane, The Penguin Press, 1971).

18 M. Rooke, *Anarchy and Apathy: student unrest, 1968–1970* (London, Hamish Hamilton, 1971).

19 K. Keniston, *Young Radicals: notes on committed youth* (New York, Harcourt, Brace, 1968).

20 G. S. Jones, 'The meaning of the student revolt', in *Student Power* (Eds A. Cockburn and R. Blackburn), (Harmondsworth, Penguin Books, 1969), 25–58.

21 *Criminal Statistics (England and Wales)*, (HMSO, 1972).

22 H. Jones, *Crime and the Penal System* (London, University Tutorial Press Ltd, 1956).

23 W. Belson, *Causal Factors in Juvenile Stealing* (London School of Economics and Political Science, Survey Research Centre, unpublished research, 1970).

24 E. H. Sutherland and D. R. Cressey, *Principles of Criminology* (Chicago, Lippincott, 1939).

25 H. B. Gibson, 'Early delinquency in relation to broken homes', *J. Child Psychol. Psychiat., 10* (1969), 195–204.

26 S. Glueck and E. Glueck, *Unravelling Juvenile Delinquency* (Harvard, University Press, 1950).

27 M. Rutter, 'Parent-child separation: psychological effects on the children', *J. Child Psychol. Psychiat., 12* (1971), 233–60.

28 R. Merton, *Social Theory and Social Structure* (Glencoe, The Free Press, 1957), 2nd revised edition.

29 J. B. Mays, *Growing Up in the City: a study of juvenile delinquency in an urban neighbourhood*, Soc. Res. Series (Liverpool University Press, 1964).

9

Man at Work

. . . a person who dislikes work will be very sorry he was born.
W. H. Auden, *Vespers*

One important factor in the search for identity engaged in by
the adolescent is his choice of job or profession. Freud maintained that to love and to work were the two essentials of a
well-adjusted life.[1] Many adults define their own identity and
that of other people in terms of occupations. Men, in particular, are first described as doctors, miners, policemen or dockers
before being called honest, reliable, arrogant or selfish. The
need for self-esteem can be satisfied or frustrated by the status
which a society attaches to a particular job, and prolonged
unemployment can lead to feelings of hopelessness and apathy.
The work we do to some extent determines our choice of
friends, our leisure pursuits and our life style. It thus has widespread repercussions upon adult psychological development.

One legacy of Puritanism that still lingers is the high
spiritual value that we attach to work and the correspond-
ingly low one with which we invest idleness. Times of rest are
seen as having been 'earned', and someone who has worked
consistently over a long period may be described as having
'deserved' a holiday. As we move towards shorter working
hours we may have difficulty in adjusting our attitudes to
work and leisure. As has been pointed out, whereas a hundred
years ago a man worked on average for seventy hours a week
and lived to be 40, he now lives to be 70 and works forty
hours a week. This raises the prospect of large amounts of
time which will have to be filled other than by structured
work.[2] There are manual as well as white-collar workers who
see work as more important in 'general life adjustment' than

recreation, education or social life.[3] Of a random sample of 401 employees in the United States, 80 per cent said they were satisfied with their jobs although this could have been acceptance of the unavoidable, and 80 per cent also added that they would continue to work even if they became financially independent (older men and those in unskilled occupations were less likely to agree with this). Reasons given for working, apart from the financial, were both positive, such as seeing work as supplying occupation, interest, enjoyment and health, and negative, describing work as an escape from boredom or loneliness.[4]

The educational experience of adolescents and their job aspirations are inevitably related. Boys and girls who are going on to further education can not only hope for a better job, but can defer their career choice for several years. Social class, insofar as it is a determinant of past opportunities and present expectations, also affects job choice. Working-class children tend to have less interest in the nature of the job they will perform and to be more interested in the immediate monetary rewards.[5] Discontentment with the level of job secured may arise because ambition has outrun ability or because, as for some black adolescents and those living in areas of high unemployment, no job commensurate with their ability is available. It has been suggested that there are three categories of those going into work for the first time : those who are eager to leave school, although happy there, enthusiastic about starting work and ready for adult life; those who are less enthusiastic about work and school and who are easy to please in choice of job since they are largely indifferent to what they will do, believing themselves to be of limited capacity and resigned to their place in the social structure; and those who actively dislike the restrictions of school and see work as a mark of independent status with financial rewards. This last group is the most likely to enter dead-end jobs and to change them frequently.[5] Different social classes have different opportunities for finding their jobs satisfying. White-collar and professional occupations are more likely to involve the use of verbal and intellectual skills and to supply means of establishing social relationships. Working-class jobs are more likely to involve the exercise of bodily skills and to involve relationships with machines. It tends to be only at professional and managerial level that work means interest and achievement. To the unskilled worker, it is mainly a means of occupying time for financial ends.[6]

There is undoubtedly a complex inter-relationship between cultural, social, educational, financial and personality factors in the meaning that an individual assigns to his job and in the expectations he has of it in regard to satisfaction, ambition and reward. A worker is, for example, more likely to feel satisfied with his job if he considers that his abilities match up to the requirements of the post. In one study, nurses were asked to list their own personality traits and those they thought were required of a nurse. It was found that the greater the discrepancy between the two lists the greater was the individual's dissatisfaction at work.[7]

WORK AND HUMAN NATURE

Views in the western world of the underlying motives that men have for working have changed with increasing prosperity and with changes in conception of the nature of Man. Varying definitions of Man as an economic being, a mechanical device, a social animal, and as exploratory and self-determining, have meant that employees have sought, and bosses attempted to supply, the varying characteristics of the work situation which those descriptions imply are important for increasing productivity and keeping the workers happy.

After the Industrial Revolution three notions about Man were current and coalesced to give a picture of human beings as primarily materialistic. One of these was the idea of 'Social Darwinism', that is that people who were successful financially were somehow 'fitter' than the poor who were seen as naturally undeserving. Another philosophy was that of the virtuous nature of work for its own sake which has been attributed to the 'Protestant ethic'. Combined with these two was the conception of Man's physiology and psychology as working very much in a mechanical way.

Thus not only was Man seen as rational, motivated largely

by self-interest and economic incentives, but human performance also was regarded as if it had a machine-like nature.
This point of view was exemplified during the 1920s by the
idea attributed to Frederick Taylor that men, like machines,
can be managed scientifically and treated in a standardised
fashion.[8] The manager's job was seen as trying to find the most
efficient way of performing a task, to choose men to fit the
task, and to provide money incentives to keep them working.
This view ignores the fact of individual differences and complex motivation. It also implies a distinction between self-
motivating managers and machine-like workers. This concept
of human nature did, however, have a valuable pay-off in
that it directed research towards the physical and psychological aspects of work performance, such as the effects of noise,
heat and fatigue on human responses.

Human performance
The mechanistic view of Man implies that he works at a single
steady pace which can be maintained throughout the day,
provided a break is given for refuelling purposes. It is now
known that fatigue has two aspects; physiological when low
blood-sugar levels, bio-chemical changes in the muscles and a
build-up of lactic acid produce aching limbs and a weakened
response; and psychological, where the nature of brain functioning leads to missed signals and errors in performance.

Where an operator must make constant choices, say between
four alternative responses to some stimulus, for example,
where a lever must be moved into one of four alternative positions according to the signal given, it has been found that the
more often the response has to be made the longer does the
decision time become.[9] In inspection and monitoring tasks
where an operator has to watch for the occurrence of a signal,
vigilance may decline within twenty minutes. In one experiment where the subject's task was to watch the hand of a clock
which moved in jumps and to signal when a double jump
occurred, 12 per cent of double jumps were missed in the
first ten minutes of the task, 20 per cent were missed in the
second ten minutes and about 25 per cent in the next ten
minutes.[10]

In actual work situations where workers are required to perform repetitive and monotonous tasks, such as inspecting products on an assembly line for faults, there is usually a warming-up period before maximum efficiency is reached and thereafter vigilance usually improves slightly after any change such as a lunch or tea break. Performance also tends to improve towards the end of the day as workers anticipate release from the job. Vigilance also tends to rise after a worker realises that a lapse has occurred. There are thus fluctuations in performance throughout a day, even though daily output tends to remain constant.[11]

Human performance is characterised by variations in pacing, so that repetitive tasks, such as assembly line work set at a constant speed are not consonant with natural human tendencies. Variations in speed and complexity increase arousal and attention, so that efficiency and interest can be maintained for longer periods of time.[12]

These findings have important implications for jobs where continual vigilance is essential but little physical effort is required, such as radar scanning, driving, piloting an aircraft and inspecting products for faults, and are consistent with the theory that the brain needs a certain level of activity in order to work effectively and that this activity is largely dependent upon external stimulation. People who have to monitor apparatus such as radar screens, and heart-beat tracers, watching for rare and irregular signals, are likely to make more errors the longer their tour of duty lasts, response times will increase and some signals will be missed whilst non-existent signals may be reacted to as if they were really there. The monotony inherent in such jobs means that alertness and attention tend to fluctuate and decline with time although frequent rest-pauses can reduce this psychological fatigue.

Over-simplification of work tasks also tends to reduce arousal and may result in inefficiency and reduce the satisfaction of the employee. It has been suggested that different individuals have different optimal levels of arousal and that any variation from this, whether up or down, is felt to be unpleasant or disturbing.[13] These adult differences in arousal level may be related to early variations in the amount of environmental stimulation received in childhood.[14] Monotonous, repetitive tasks may also lead to a high incidence of psychosomatic and nervous complaints in those performing them, and these kinds of jobs tend to have high labour turnover and high absenteeism rates.[15] Some car manufacturers, as at the Volvo works in Sweden, have recognised the effects of the 'rationalisation' of work and have adopted a system whereby teams of men assemble large components and even whole cars, swapping tasks as they feel like it and all have responsibility for the finished product. This kind of 'job enlargement' has been found to improve morale and the quality of the finished product, although productivity may decline somewhat.[16] [17]

As might be expected, however, since individuals differ in their tolerance of monotony, some studies have found that repetitive tasks are preferred by some workers who have no wish to participate in decision-making and who prefer straightforward tasks where they are told exactly what to do.[18] [19] Among mass-production workers who report enjoying their work, one reason given has been that the job is without responsibility and easy to perform.[20] One might also hypothesise that where the social structure teaches certain sections of the public that it is not their 'place' to make decisions about the work situation, many will come to see this state of affairs as 'natural'.

THE SOCIAL CONTEXT OF WORK

One of the best-known studies in industrial psychology, carried out over forty years ago, started out to investigate the effects of variations in the physical environment on productivity and finished by triggering off a new phase in the examination of worker motivation. In a factory making electrical components several experiments were carried out of which we shall mention only one which epitomises the kind of results obtained. Two girls were picked out and asked to choose four more girls with whom to work on the task of assembling telephone relays. Various changes were made in their working conditions and the effects on productivity were observed. Initially the girls were put on piece-work instead of a fixed wage; five-minute rest periods were introduced; these were extended to ten-minute periods. Next, a free hot meal was provided; then the girls were sent home half an hour early. After each of these changes output was found to increase, even though in the final stages the girls were working shorter hours. The last change instituted by the investigators was to remove all the previous improvements. The workers went back to a fixed wage, had the rest periods stopped and the free meal and went home at the usual time. Astonishingly, the result of this step was that output rose to its highest ever level, to the confusion of the experimenters whose donkey and carrot hypothesis had just been disproved. The most popular explanation for these results is that the physical changes were in fact irrelevant to the productivity of the group. What seemed to play a more important part was the fact that for the first time in their working lives the girls had been made to feel important and had been involved in the study, had been asked for their comments and co-operation. In short, they had been transformed from indifferent and disregarded units to a highly integrated and interested work group.[21] Since that time many studies have been conducted which show the importance of social relationships in the work situation. Girls working on an assembly line who were allowed to control its speed by mutual consent reported less fatigue and more enjoyment at work.[22] The social solidarity of a work group has been found to play a more significant part in the satisfaction of workers than incentive schemes. For example, one study of semi-skilled machine-minders who were paid on a piece-work basis found that although individuals were capable of greater output, the group had agreed upon a self-imposed ceiling. Among the reasons given for this limitation of output were that the men doubted whether they could maintain a continuously higher level of productivity and feared losing their jobs if production fell, that working flat out could have caused disparities in pay as some men had better machines and this could have led to dissension in the group, and that working below their capacity gave them some minimum control over their job and provided opportunities for social satisfactions, such as talking and helping each other out.[23]

There is some evidence that the satisfaction workers feel in their jobs is related to their opportunities for social interaction. Isolated workers tend to dislike their work and report this as being due to the paucity of social contacts.[24] The morale of clerks in an insurance company was greatly lowered by a change which restricted their social contact[25] and a large-scale study of several types of American workers found that few rated incentives as more important than group loyalties.[26]

Again, however, we must take individual differences into account. Some people do enjoy working alone and some are primarily interested in financial rewards. A study of piece-workers distinguished between 'restricters', that is those who held their output down and who tended to lead active social lives both inside and outside the factory, and 'rate-busters' who disregarded group norms about output and who were unsociable at work and believers in economic individualism.[26] Neither of these types are likely to be disturbed by the existence of incentive schemes designed to raise productivity, for the restricters ignore the incentives and rate-busters ignore group standards. Those to whom both money and social ties are important are those most likely to find themselves in some conflict under incentive schemes.

Both the economic and social views of man at work tend to focus on the individual as a passive being almost totally concerned with the avoidance of unpleasant stimuli, whether these are material lack or the disapproval of one's mates. The self-initiated aspects of human motivation, needs for exploration, discovery and psychological growth, have only lately begun to receive attention from psychologists.

WORK AND INDIVIDUAL DEVELOPMENT

In the 1950s research on job satisfaction entered a new era, following the investigations of Frederick Herzberg and his associates.[27] [28] Instead of focusing upon material and social conditions at work, Herzberg maintained that an occupation only became satisfying when the individual was able to derive from it a sense of personal growth. By personal growth Herzberg appears to mean a feeling in the person that he or she is developing in wisdom and experience, becoming more autonomous and competent and having the opportunity to exercise and expand whatever potential he or she has. Herzberg has made an attempt to define the elements of experience which may be conditions for such growth and has discussed the extent to which these may be available in the work situation.[29]

He believes that any job, to cater to the need for psychological growth, should provide new information so that the worker has the feeling of knowing more one day than he did the last. Some jobs may be so governed by routine procedures that this is impossible. Knowing more is not enough, however; being able to relate old material to the new is essential for increasing mental flexibility and enlarging schemata. Work that is fragmented into small isolated processes makes it difficult for the individual to relate his task to the whole process and so constitutes a barrier to creativity and novel solutions. Herzberg has said that modern industry tends to cut work procedures down to the lowest common denominator of ability, literally making jobs into 'child's play'; which fosters dependence and stifles growth. Another precondition for adult development is said to be 'individuation', that is, the movement towards personal integrity and autonomy which may be blocked by social pressures emanating from the company and work mates, so that the individual draws status from the fact that he works for a particular company rather than from his own competence. Finally, Herzberg suggests that a job should allow the individual opportunties for facing up to the truth and not encourage fantasies of personal growth and power by supplying such external props as the key to the executive washroom, larger carpets as one advances, badges of rank or grander uniform, behind which uncertainty and incompetence can hide.

Herzberg bases his comments upon research carried out by himself and others on the sources of satisfaction and dissatisfaction at work. One such study was carried out on 200 engineers and accountants in Pittsburgh and asked the men to tell the interviewers about good times and bad times at work.[26] From the replies five factors were extracted which appeared to determine job satisfaction and which were called 'motivators'. These were individual achievement, recognition, the job itself, having responsibility and getting promotion. The absence of these factors was, however, rarely mentioned as a source of dissatisfaction. This tended to emerge in what were called 'hygiene factors' – company policy, social relationships, supervision, salary and working conditions. Where hygiene factors are good it is suggested that they will only briefly give rise to feelings of comfort whereas workers may be quite happy to operate in unpleasant conditions, provided that the job supplies them with opportunities for personal growth. If a job, on the other hand, provided no 'motivators' then people would be likely to become highly sensitive to the absence of the hygiene factors and complaints and strikes would focus around wages, poor toilet facilities and physical surroundings. Thus constant demands for shorter hours and better pay may disguise deeper discontents which are a consequence of the stifling of individual endeavour and potential.

The work of Herzberg does provide a refreshing orientation in the history of industrial psychology, allowing a worker to be more than a passive cog in the factory wheel, motivated solely by the need to avoid unpleasantness. His theory can also supply us with an explanation for the well-known fact that high pay and excellent facilities are no guarantee of industrial peace. There are, however, a number of criticisms that have been made of his formulation. Firstly, the idea of personal growth and need for autonomy, although currently fashionable and emotionally appealing, remains, as Gross has pointed out,[30] a belief rather than an established conclusion. Many people may value security and predictability at work rather than personal fulfilment. It has been found that dissatisfied workers are no less hard-working than satisfied ones, although one would not predict this from Herzberg's theory[31] and at least one study has resulted in the finding that workers do sometimes cite lack of achievement and responsibility as sources of dissatisfaction, and company policy and salary as sources of satisfaction.[32] Possibly the way in which the research of Herzberg was carried out affected the kind of replies he got. For example people may prefer to ascribe 'good' times to their own efforts, whilst 'bad' times are more comfortingly assigned to external conditions.

It may be, moreover, that 'motivators' are elicited as part of a middle-class expectation that work should be interesting and offer advancement. A study of Luton car workers earning above average wages found that they did not expect to find satisfaction in their work, seeing it merely as a necessity and possible means to a higher standard of living. Their satisfactions were sought and found outside work.[33] The kind of factors which promote satisfaction or discontent are not absolute but depend upon the employee's frame of reference. There is evidence that white-collar workers value 'motivators' above 'hygiene' factors but that the reverse is true for blue-collar workers.[34]

Differences which are a consequence of the individual's past experience in a particular social structure, of educational opportunity, age and social class, will all affect the worker's perception of his job and the expectations he has of it. Whilst there is some support for Herzberg's dual-factor theory of job motivation it may be wiser to regard it as a stepping stone to further investigation of the more complex human needs which are not being met in the work situation, rather than as a basis for action.

Work as a source of conflict
It has been pointed out that conflicts between individual needs and the demands of organisations are not confined to the work situation.[35] A basic human adjustment is that which must be made between the individual and any group to which he belongs whether it is the family, the peer group, the work team or society as a whole. Organisations do tend, however, to have the balance of power heavily weighted in their direction and are able to exert overt or covert pressure on the individual which taxes his capacity to adapt to the requirements of his job. Opportunities for self-fulfilment at work, nevertheless, do not ensure mental health. Mental disturbance in the form of anxiety and depression and psychosomatic complaints are found throughout all occupations and most often among scientists, managers and the professional groups. Job-

changing, social mobility and constant challenge are often associated with a breakdown in the individual's ability to cope. The least vulnerable to these effects appear to be the dependent and conformist, who do as they are told and like it that way.[36]

In a survey of role conflict in seven industrial areas it was found that men in certain focal positions such as foremen and managers were often caught between groups with conflicting interests. The resulting conflict in the middle man was emotionally disturbing and such people tended to get little satisfaction from work.[37] The consequence of this kind of conflict can be an over-identification with one side (a foreman who always sides with the management) and the avoidance of those who aggravate the feeling of tension (ignoring the complaints of the workers). Although this may be adaptive for the individual it may exacerbate ill feeling and cut off important sources of information. Role ambiguity, that is, uncertainty about the scope of one's responsibilities and the expectations of fellow-workers, the standards by which one's work is judged and opportunities for promotion, can lead to unhappiness at work, lowered self-confidence, and high levels of tension.[37] This implies, in contradiction to Herzberg, that workers do need some structure and certainty in their working lives, although the contradiction may be resolved by examining the background of the workers involved. In a study of 470 workers which included one group of rural and small-town Protestants and another of urban-living Catholics, the rural workers tended to be more satisfied with and had lower absenteeism rates for jobs involving some complexity and skill, whilst the urban workers preferred more simple and undemanding jobs. The authors explain this in terms of the urban workers' greater alienation and insecurity which is a product of a highly industrialised environment and lack of community support.[37]

Unskilled workers tend to be less interested in their jobs (which are often not very interesting anyway), to be less concerned about having the opportunity to take independent action and to be more concerned with monetary return than are skilled workers.[38] This is hardly surprising since the only thing that the workers do get out of their jobs is the money. The task itself may supply little chance for innovation or responsibility and a man can take little pride in his job when he knows that it could probably be equally well performed by a chimpanzee. It has been suggested that unskilled and semi-skilled workers come to see themselves as passive instruments of production because the work is unsatisfying and without physical or psychological freedom.[39] In this situation it is more adaptive to keep expectations low and ask for nothing more than good wages and hygienic conditions. This kind of attitude may be a consequence not only of individual experience, but also of generations of deprivation.

People vary in their perception of their own needs for satisfaction at work, so that those who see themselves as having high needs are more likely to be disappointed, to feel alienated and to suffer conflict, than those who either never consider job satisfaction at all or see it as less essential to their self-image and self-esteem.

Where work does provide for the individual to develop and grow in competence and expertise and where the person regards work as an important part of his life-style, one would expect his horizons to widen and his personality to become more complex. If work is unimportant to the individual except as a necessary evil, then deeper satisfaction may be sought and found outside work, in the family and in leisure pursuits with little resultant harm, except that the individual's ability, energy and goodwill may be relatively unemployed for a large proportion of his day. If work and leisure are both undemanding and without meaning then the personality may become increasingly rigid and narrow.

Whilst our culture continues to place such a high premium upon work as a desirable and inevitable pursuit, and whilst we continue to use it as a means of labelling a man's worth, we can expect it to play a considerable part in the development of the adult personality and in providing a major part of life satisfaction or dissatisfaction.

REFERENCES

1 S. Freud, *Civilisation and its Discontents* (London, Hogarth Press, 1930).
2 J. Cohen, 'Leisure and the scientific revolution', *Nature, 198* (1965), 1028–33.
3 F. Friedlander, 'Importance of work versus non-work among socially and occupationally stratified groups', *J. Appl. Psychol., 50* (1966), 437–41.
4 N. C. Morse and R. S. Weiss, 'The function and meaning of work and the job', *Amer. Soc. Rev., 20* (1955), 191–8.
5 M. Carter, *Into Work* (Harmondsworth, Penguin Books, 1966).
6 N. C. Morse and R. S. Weiss, 'The function and meaning of work and the job', *Amer. Soc. Rev., 20* (1955), 191–8.
7 A. L. Brophy, 'Self, role and satisfaction', *Genet. Psychol. Monog., 59* (1959), 263–308.
8 F. W. Taylor, *Scientific Management* (London, Harper & Row, 1947).
9 W. T. Singleton, 'Deterioration of performance on a short-term perceptual-motor task', in *Fatigue* (Eds W. F. Floyd and A. T. Welford), (London, H. K. Lewis, 1953).
10 N. H. Mackworth, 'Researches on the measurement of human performance', in *Selected Papers on Human Factors in the Design and Use of Control Systems* (Ed. H. W. Sinaiko), (New York, Dover Publications, 1961), 174–331.
11 E. C. Poulton, *Environment and Human Efficiency* (Springfield, Illinois, C. C. Thomas, 1970).
12 J. P. Frankman and J. A. Adams, 'Theories of vigilance', *Psychol. Bull., 59* (1962), 257–72.
13 D. W. Fiske and S. R. Maddi (Eds) *Functions of Varied Experience* (Homewood, Illinois, Dorsey Press, 1967),
14 V. H. Denenberg, 'Critical periods, stimulus input and emotional reactivity: a theory of infantile stimulation', *Psychol. Rev., 71* (1964), 335–51.
15 G. Friedmann, *The Anatomy of Work* (New York, Free Press, 1961).
16 A. R. N. Marks, 'An investigation of modifications of job design in an industrial situation and their effects on some measures of economic productivity' (unpublished doctoral dissertation, University of California, summarised in L. E. Davis and R. R. Canter, 'Job Design Research', *J. Indust. Eng., 7* (1956), 275–82).
17 J. F. Biganne and P. A. Stewart, *Job Enlargement: a case study, Research Series No. 25* (State University of Iowa, Bureau of Labor and Management, 1963).
18 P. C. Smith and C. Lem, 'Positive aspects of motivation in repetitive work: effects of lot size upon spacing of voluntary rest periods', *J. Appl. Psychol., 39* (1955), 330–3.
19 V. H. Vroom, *Some Personality Determinants of the Effects of Participation* (New York, Prentice-Hall, 1960).
20 C. R. Walker and R. Marriott, 'A study of attitudes to factory work', *Occup. Psychol., 25* (1951), 181–91.

21 F. J. Roethlisberger and W. J. Dickson, *Management and the Worker* (Cambridge, Mass., Harvard University Press, 1939).
22 L. R. Sayles, *Behaviour of Industrial Work Groups: prediction and control* (New York, Wiley, 1958).
23 D. J. Hickson, 'Motives of work people who restrict their output', *Occup. Psychol., 35* (1961), 110–21.
24 C. R. Walker and R. H. Guest, *The Man on the Assembly Line* (Cambridge, Mass., Harvard University Press, 1952).
25 C. B. Richards and H. F. Dobryns, 'Topography and culture; the case of the changing cage', *Human Org., 16* (1957), 16–20.
26 W. F. Whyte, *Men at Work* (Homewood, Illinois, Dorsey & Irwin, 1961).
27 F. Herzberg, B. Mausner, R. O. Peterson and D. F. Capwell, *Job Attitudes: review of research and opinion* (Pittsburgh Research Series, 1957).
28 F. Herzberg, B. Mausner and B. Snyderman, *The Motivation to Work* (New York, John Wiley, 1959).
29 F. Herzberg, *Work and the Nature of Man* (Cleveland, World Publishing Co., 1966).
30 E. Gross, 'Work organisation and stress', in *Social Stress* (Eds S. Levine and N. H. Scotch), (Chicago, Aldine, 1970), 54–109.
31 V. H. Vroom, *Work and Motivation* (New York, John Wiley, 1964).
32 N. King, 'Clarification and evaluation of the two-factor theory of job satisfaction', *Psychol. Bull., 74*, 18–31.
33 J. H. Goldthorpe, D. Lockwood, F. Bechhoffer and J. Platt, *The Affluent Worker* (Cambridge University Press, 1968).
34 R. Centers and D. E. Bugenthal, 'Intrinsic and extrinsic job motivations among different segments of the working population', *J. Appl. Psychol., 60* (1966), 193–7.
35 G. Strauss, 'The personality versus organisation theory', in *Individualism and Big Business* (Ed. L. R. Sayles), (New York, McGraw Hill, 1963), Ch. 8.
36 L. E. Hinkle, Jr, 'Physical health, mental health and the corporate environment', in *Individualism and Big Business* (Ed. L. R. Sayles), (New York, McGraw Hill, 1963), Ch. 11.
37 R. L. Kahn, D. M. Wolfe, R. P. Quinn and J. D. Snoek, *Organisational Stress* (New York, John Wiley, 1964).
38 C. Argyris, *Personality and Organisation* (New York, Harper, 1957).
39 B. Gardell, 'Alienation and mental health in the modern industrial environment', in *Society, Stress and Disease*, Vol. 1 (Ed. L. Levi), (London, Oxford University Press, 1971), 148–80.

10

Sex, Marriage and the Family

Lay your sleeping head my love
Human on my faithless arm.
W. H. Auden, *Lay your sleeping head*

The achievement of sexual and marital relationships constitutes an important landmark in the lives of most individuals.
The quality of such relationships has implications for the
development of adults and, after the establishment of a family,
for the emotional environment in which the children are
brought up. The foundations for the adequate development
of a child are thus laid down long before his birth in the
familial, social and intimate relationships of his parents.

SEX

It is probably safe to say that most people have a deep and
abiding interest in sex, whether condemnatory, exploratory or
prurient. Since sexual feelings, thought and behaviour are
highly susceptible to learning, the kinds of interpretations available in a culture will obviously affect sexual attitudes. The
usefulness of sex as a sales device testifies to the uncertainties
and anxieties which some people have about their sexual experiences and attractiveness. Advertisers are able to create
sexual fantasies which imply that success or failure in bed
depends upon a particular make of soap, cigarette, deodorant
or car.

Social myths about sex may conflict with an individual's
subjective experience and cause anxiety by making him or her
feel in some way peculiar. Some commentators on the topic
manage to convey the impression that there is some optimal
amount, some ideal kind of sexual activity, although not sur-

prisingly they never specify what it is. Sexual experiences by
their very nature are personal and impossible to communicate.
Individuals vary tremendously in their needs and expectations
which are the consequence of a particular physical constitution overlaid with social learning, so that every day may not
be enough for some, whilst once a year is too much for others.

In our changing social climate people now feel freer to be
openly interested in sex and there has been a proliferation of
sex manuals that describe the gymnastics of the sex act. A detailed knowledge of how to achieve position 43 is, however,
no guarantee of a satisfactory sexual relationship, as disappointed readers have found. Intimate relationships are
primarily dependent upon social skills combined with the
ability to trust and abandon oneself to another person.
Although the capacity for sexual activity is largely physical,
sexual arousal, performance and preference are all susceptible
to a variety of psychological influences that are a consequence
of past experience and present atmosphere.

The evolutionary advantages of the variability produced by
sexual reproduction have already been noted. In the life of
man, sex is subject to complex social learning, for example, that
certain acts are permissible whilst others are taboo, which is
often unrelated to evolutionary or biological functions and not
paralleled in the behaviour of other animals. Nevertheless,
animal studies have recently been able to cast some light on
the subject. Whilst Freud, for example, was able, seventy years
ago, to contend that a sexual drive underlay, in generalised
form, all human attachments,[1] the Harlows' studies of monkeys
suggest that there may be an innate sensuality and need for
soft comforting contact that is separate from the drive towards sexual release.[2]

It is possible for sex to take on learned functions and forms
only when it is not entirely dependent upon the instinctual
triggers of sign stimuli, hormonal influences and season of the
year. In lower animals these automatically produce appropriate
sexual responses but higher up the evolutionary scale learning
becomes increasingly important so that experiences early in
life may disrupt later social and sexual behaviour.

Apes thus may show gross disturbances in sexual behaviour

if reared in isolation. Zoo-keepers often have difficulty in persuading animals to mate – an indication that for many species copulation is not solely governed by their internal state. Mating may also be inhibited by such factors as overcrowding[3] or failing to obtain a territory.[4] A case has been described of a male and a female chimpanzee who had been reared until one year old in virtual isolation. When brought together in Basel Zoo each preferred to masturbate rather than to mate with the other.[5] Similarly, Harlow's monkeys who were reared in isolation or without sufficient peer group experience did not know how to mate at maturity, and if mating was eventually achieved, became very bad mothers.[6]

The susceptibility of sex to learning can also be seen by the way in which activities which are essentially non-sexual come to take on sexual connotations. Thus small children may indulge in what most adults would regard as sexual activity, such as genital play, but it is only in adolescence that sexual feelings and acts begin to take on adult connotations. Prior to adolescence, adults tend to label certain childish acts as sexual in nature, and insist on their children behaving as if they had the sexual knowledge of an adult, teaching small girls to sit with their knees together for instance. In this way an early association may develop between certain activities, not yet explicitly sexual, and anxiety, which may later serve to control and direct sexual behaviour. In human beings successful sexual behaviour, rather than being an in-built propensity, is almost universally dependent upon learning to recognise the correct social signals.[7]

Social control of sexual activity is transmitted through parental anxiety aroused by children's questions concerning sex and about the exposure of some parts of the body. This anxiety is conveyed to the child through avoidance behaviour by parents and by prohibitions. Children may be encouraged to explore virtually every topic except that of sex and so come to learn that certain areas of inquiry are taboo.[8] Whether this has any later ill effects with regard to sexual adjustment will depend very much on the strength of the associations between anxiety and sexual curiosity and subsequent experience with peers and others.

Physiological factors such as fatigue, poor health, low calorie intake, or excessive drugs or alcohol, can affect sexual performance, as can recency of fulfilment. Sexual activity tends to decline as people get older, but this may be partly due to state of mind rather than loss of vigour – a feeling that 'we're too old for that sort of thing'. Some couples continue cheerfully well into their 80s. Keeping in practice seems to be an important element in their success.

The prolonged social conditioning which most people undergo in relation to sex means that few people are able to respond spontaneously to their first sexual experience, and it may take some time before couples are able to reach the peaks of delight which they expected to come naturally.

The importance of social learning in moulding sexual practices is well illustrated by cross-cultural studies. Different societies have different standards and different concepts as to what is 'normal', 'natural' or 'immoral'. In many societies there is a clearly defined age after which sexual intercourse is allowed. In some this age is marked by post-pubertal ceremonies. Amongst the Chagga of East Africa all boys, after circumcision, have intercourse with a barren woman, after which they are free to seek other partners, but must take precautions against getting them pregnant.

In the Chukchee society of Northern Asia, girls are allowed to have serious sexual relationships between the time of their first menstruation and marriage. There are many societies which, like our own, regard marriage as the proper time for the first intercourse (a custom which may be related to the inheritance of property so that it would not do for a man to unknowingly father another man's child). To ensure the virginity of brides a variety of precautions has been taken, ranging from sexual segregation, chaperonage and public disgrace to public execution. Except for the latter these sanctions are rarely fully effective.

There are societies which encourage sexual activity from a very early age. On Pouapee Island in the Pacific, instruction in sexual intercourse is given from the age of 4 or 5. The Chewa of West Africa believe that unless children get plenty of sex practice they will not be able to have children; play involving

trial matings is encouraged well before puberty and continues into adolescence with changes of partner from time to
time.[9]

Masculine and Feminine

The rise of the Women's Liberation Movement gave a new
interest to research concerning the relative contribution of
biology and learning in producing 'typical' masculine or
feminine behaviour. It is useful here to make a distinction between 'sex', that is the biologically given attributes of the individual in terms of reproductive system, genital organs, etc.,
and 'gender', that is, the psychological orientation of the
individual with respect to feelings of masculinity or femininity.
Thus although sex and gender are the same for most
individuals this is by no means necessarily true of everyone.

It has been suggested that there are distinct patterns of
child-rearing which result in masculine or feminine traits. A
permissive attitude by parents towards such things as genital
play has been found to be associated with masculinity in the
children's choice of toys and activities. A non-permissive attitude is said to produce non-masculine qualities in both girls
and boys.[10] Parents seem to encourage exploration and aggression more often in boys than they do in girls, and self-assertion
tends to be associated with masculinity in our society, whilst
passivity is associated with femininity.

An important element in learning the appropriate sex role
is identification with and imitation of the same sex parent.
Clinical evidence suggests that some male homosexuals tend
to identify with their mother. This may arise because of an
early rejection by the father so that the mother fulfils all the
boy's needs for love and security, or it may be that the mother
is seen as the more powerful and dominant partner in the
marriage.[11] [12]

Once a sex role has been assigned and language has
developed so that the child is increasingly aware of himself as
a boy, or of herself as a girl, it is very difficult to change this
role assignment.[13] Our whole perception of the world is inter-
meshed with our self-image and to change one's self-image involves a whole new mode of adjustment to the world.

Some writers have argued that at birth a state of 'psychosexual neutrality' exists.[14] By this is meant that the child, although biologically assignable to a particular sex, has no innate feeling of being of that sex, but has to learn through social interaction to think of himself as, and to prefer to be, a particular gender. It thus becomes possible for a biologically female person to think of herself as a man and for a person with male physiology to think of himself as a woman depending upon the particular type of learning experience the individual has undergone. Since normally children are socialised into a gender role appropriate to their overt physical characteristics there appears to be an automatic association between sex and gender, which is only questioned when for some reason the socialisation process is not fully effective. The evidence for psychosexual neutrality has been drawn exclusively from studies of hermaphrodites, that is, individuals who for a variety of reasons possess, in varying degrees, physiological attributes of both sexes. Hermaphrodites do appear to show a clear adherence to the gender role which was assigned to them during rearing regardless of the masculine or feminine characteristics they possess. In some cases where hormonal imbalances have begun to correct themselves at puberty and the individual has become, say, more 'masculine' (by growth of body hair, deepening of voice and genital development), the individual has preferred to retain the gender role to which he was assigned early in life, in spite of the very real difficulties involved.[14]

Against the theory of psychosexual neutrality it has been argued that where individuals do not suffer from physiological or chromosomal anomalies, gender role is not so malleable by experience. Normally-sexed individuals who have been reared in a sex role opposite to their biological sex are hard to find, so evidence on this point is scarce. A case was reported of two males reared from birth as females until both concerned refused to continue as girls. One adopted the male role at 14 years of age without apparent difficulty, as did the other at 20, in spite of having had a penis amputation at birth.[15] The opposite has been described in the case of a female reared as a male (because of an abnormality of the vagina). The mistake became apparent at puberty and at 17 the patient decided to become female. She was reported to be happily married at the age of 20.[16] Thus there is some evidence that hormonal influences acting at puberty may be sufficiently strong to overcome the assigned gender role, in some cases at least.[17]

Differences in behaviour between boys and girls do appear very early in life, but then, as described in an earlier chapter, they are treated differently almost from birth. Various writers have discerned more aggressive behaviour in boys, one as early as seventeen months.[18] Significant sex differences with regard to block-building behaviour were found in one study. Boys built more complex structures at the age of 2 years and more stable structures at 4 years, than did girls of the same ages, and at 6 years twice as many boys as girls built symmetrical structures. Girls were also more likely to destroy their buildings than were the boys.[19] Boys are generally allowed to show more interpersonal aggression than girls which might be why girls take it out on the building blocks. There do appear to be differences in the types of aggression displayed by boys and girls at certain ages. At the age of 5, male aggression is predominantly anti-social, that is, destructive and directed towards fighting, whilst female aggression is inclined to the pro-social, that is used as a means of maintaining order. By 8 years this difference has disappeared.[20]

Apparently aggressive behaviour in boys, such as horseplay and mock-wrestling, may indicate, not hostility, but merely a socially acceptable means of establishing friendly relations through physical contact. Because such behaviour is not so acceptable in girls, its appearance may signify genuine hostility.[21]

Girls in most cultures are subjected to greater pressure to be conformist and well-behaved, whilst boys are encouraged to be self-reliant and ambitious.[22] Sex roles are, however, less clear in some societies than they are in our own. Some languages have no gender forms, and so no distinction between male and female names. In the Iatmul tribe of New Guinea boys are classed with women until initiation, and among the Manus who live not far away the girls are classed with men until betrothal.[23]

Harlow[24] has reported distinct patterns of play and aggression in monkeys of each sex, even when reared in isolation, which suggests that there may be unlearned elements of gender roles.

Nevertheless, many of the ideas people have about sexual differences are socially acquired and unrelated to innate dispositions towards masculinity or femininity. The popular ideas that women are sexually more passive, need more security and are less easily aroused than men may be without foundation, except insofar as women may feel obliged to conform to this stereotype. Masters and Johnson have demonstrated the multi-orgasmic potential of some women.[25] In a study in which erotic pictures were shown to members of each sex, the women reported much less sexual arousal than the men. However, physiological measures taken at the time suggested that their arousal was just as high as that of the men.[26] Either the women failed to label their excitement correctly or were unwilling to admit to it, for fear of not being thought nice girls, and because they accepted the common notion that women are not interested in erotica.

Permissiveness

Although the mass media and various pundits continuously tell us that the Western world has become more 'permissive', the evidence, if the phrase refers to greater tolerance of the behaviour of others, is contradictory. A survey started in the United States in 1970 produced some rather surprising findings; 80 per cent of respondents regarded homosexuality as wrong and 60 per cent thought that there should be a law against it. Of those interviewed, 11 per cent thought that prostitution was never wrong whilst 72 per cent thought that it was always wrong. Premarital sex was regarded by 50 per cent as wrong, even when the couple were in love, and the rate of disapproval rose to 75 per cent if they were not in love. Of the sample 52 per cent wanted laws against adultery and 28 per cent thought there should be a law against unmarried adults having sexual intercourse.[27]

A survey carried out in Britain in 1970, however, supported the idea that we have become more permissive. Since a Gallup

Poll survey in 1963,[28] public opinion has moved towards a greater tolerance of forms of sexual behaviour previously condemned. There was, for example, an increase in support for the view that sex before marriage is acceptable if the couple are in love. Women have traditionally expressed less tolerance than men in the past, but this gap now appears to be narrowing,[29] possibly a consequence of greater sexual freedom for women.

There is some evidence that more people express permissive attitudes than actually put them into practice,[30] although people who report that they enjoy sex do seem to be more likely to be tolerant of the sexual behaviour of others,[30 31 32] although this is not necessarily a case of cause and effect. Anthropological studies suggest that attitudes to sex reflect general social attitudes. So the co-operative Zuni of North America regard sex without guilt or shame, as they do other aspects of their lives, whilst the Mungadumor, who continually squabble amongst themselves, are also repressive and intolerant in their attitudes to sex.[33] These, however, are small-scale societies where a common ethos may well affect all. In more complex societies common attitudes are less likely to be found.

MARRIAGE

It was only in Western Europe in about the eleventh century that 'love' became a fashionable experience and troubadours, so we are told, went about singing songs of hopeless love for ladies locked up behind castle walls. Romantic love was originally a concept separate from explicit sexual desire and marriage, but today all aspects have become fused in thought, so that many feel that it is wrong to have a sexual relationship without either love or marriage and preferably both. Young girls seem particularly prone to mistake a sexual relationship for a life-long love-match. Monogamy may be exalted as an ideal, but in most cultures people tend to have more than one sexual relationship whether sanctioned or not.[34]

Romantic love, as distinct from mutual respect and affection, seems to be by no means essential for a successful marriage.

Indeed, as Van der Haag pointed out, the legal contract of marriage testifies to the fact that something stronger and more constant is needed to keep a couple together.[35] Although some people, girls especially, have a stereotype of marriage as being a state of 'living happily ever after', the reality can be very different, as is recognised by at least some adolescents. In Schofield's survey, 28 per cent of adolescent boys and 27 per cent of the girls agreed with the statement : 'It is best to have a good time before you are married because after that life is pretty dreary.'[36] Research on children between the ages of 10 and 17, however, showed most of them to approve of the married state : 67 per cent of 10- to 11-year-old boys and 79 per cent of the girls wanted to get married some day, and by the age of 17 the percentages had gone up to 78 per cent and 94 per cent respectively.[37]

During the last century marriage was an economic necessity, not only for women but also for men since an increase in family size added to family income in times when 4- and 5-year-olds were put to work. Marriage then also formed part of the framework of the larger family group in which aunts, cousins and in-laws were important and the wider range of relationships helped to spread emotional conflict. Today people tend to see marriage primarily as a relationship between two people only. This may be potentially more rewarding. It is also more vulnerable to upset. Married partners require from each other now a wider range of roles – lover, confidant, friend, tension-releaser, playmate, decision-maker and so on. The requirements will vary somewhat within individual marriages but some versatility and reciprocity is necessary if the marriage is to be a happy one.

Although theoretically a person has a wider choice of partners now than in the past, people are marrying younger and so reducing their opportunities to meet others from a wider social setting. They still choose from a rather narrow range determined principally by geography. There are pressures towards choosing a 'suitable' partner, and non-conformity in mate selection has been pinpointed as the greatest source of dissension between parents and daughters.[38] Although those who marry before the age of 20 are more likely to undergo marital breakdown, early marriage may have some positive aspects. Those who married before the age of 20 have been found to have higher scholastic attainment[39][40] and to show greater improvements in personal adjustment[41] than the unmarried, although which is cause and which is effect is uncertain.

A study of marriage in Britain carried out in 1971 suggested that there has been a change in the kind of characteristics partners expected in each other.[42] Up to about 1950 it seems that men and women wanted their spouses to have complementary traits to their own. So husbands were expected to be providers and decision-makers, wives were expected to be home-makers and to be submissive and loving. Husbands did not help in the home except in tasks where physical strength was required. Men who didn't fit this pattern were in danger of being derided as being 'hen-pecked' and letting the wife 'wear the trousers'. Since then, however, expectations have changed; both husbands and wives now see the sharing of household tasks and leisure pursuits as natural. The emphasis is on doing things together which may contribute to a closer relationship, but also imposes great strains, as husband and wife will spend little time apart and have a greater emotional investment in each other. Prior to marriage couples tend to minimise differences and points of disagreement, which later become inescapable. There thus comes a feeling that the partner has changed whereas the fact is that he or she comes to be seen more clearly and continuously. The changing status of women in society is also affecting marriage. Women need no longer be wholly dependent on men, but neither sex has fully adjusted to the concept of equality of opportunity and there is considerable uncertainty on both sides as to how to adjust. Men, whilst paying lip service to the idea that women have an equal right to take decisions, have careers and run the country, may still harbour considerable resentment at the implied loss of their own power and authority. Women, whilst arguing for their rights and autonomy, still welcome the reassuring dominance and financial support of men.

Each married couple has its own idiosyncratic pattern of marriage which others might find intolerable. Working wives, continual bickering, living with in-laws, riches, poverty,

N

promiscuity, celibacy or drunkenness may be disastrous to some marriages but the support of others. There is no universal prescription for a happy marriage. However, in a sample of over 5,000 couples it was found that certain factors were associated with dissatisfaction. These were minority group status, low income, poor education, physical illness or disability, social isolation and heavy drinking by one or both partners.[43] All these factors will, of course, pose an extra strain on the partnership. Where differences exist between partners in class, ethnic and religious background, marital break-up is somewhat more common, but this may be a reflection of the strong individuality of those who are willing to withstand the forces of convention in their particular social group.

Support, flexibility and recognition of the other's individuality are important constituents of most relationships, although in some marriages one partner may be perfectly content to be subjugated by the other. Marriages that are based upon a complementary relationship of dominance and submission may become unstable if the submissive partner matures emotionally and is no longer willing to take orders, or if the dominance needs of the other are satisfied elsewhere, for example, by gaining promotion at work.

Many unsuccessful marriages perpetuate unhappy childhood experiences, and those who lacked attention and affection as children may make impossible demands on the partner. Continual requests for attention, time, money or sex may be made which are manifestations of the need to be loved. Eventually the partner may be able to give no more and the marriage breaks up. One unhappy marriage of this sort may be followed by another where the pattern is repeated.

It has been estimated that more than 50 per cent of marriages have serious adjustment difficulties.[44] Most of these are resolved and only about 14 per cent of the marriages in Britain end in separation or divorce. The first and second years of a marriage are the most vulnerable as both try to establish new images and new roles. Old groupings of family and friends have to be redefined or even abandoned, and new relationships with in-laws must be cemented. Some societies ritualise the likely conflicts with in-laws into 'joking' relation-

ships where tension and hostility may be released in the form
of socially sanctioned 'jokes'. Another crisis point in marriage
is reached when the children are grown up and leave home
and the parents confront each other alone perhaps for the
first time in twenty years. A common interest in the children
can disguise an accelerating growing apart.

A common cause of marital discord is where either partner
has failed to achieve emancipation in adolescence and is still
emotionally dependent on his or her parents. This will be
exacerbated where the parents live close by and a coalition
may be formed against the other partner.[45]

Ideas of what marriage is like tend to be related to what
the person experienced as a child *vis-à-vis* his own parents.
Different patterns of behaviour can thus come into conflict.
One partner, for example, may have learned to make up
quarrels quickly, or uses humour to reduce tension, whilst the
other may resort to long periods of punishing silence and resent
levity. Some people have learned to give affection uncondi-
tionally, whilst others use it as a means of barter. Generally,
husbands expect their wives to be somewhat like their own
mothers and wives expect husbands to behave somewhat in
the way their own fathers did. These misconceptions become
very important because of the isolation of most modern
marriages, and because people have high expectations of perpetual bliss. Research has shown that even in the happiest
marriages quite radical differences in the meaning and interpretation of events can occur. If asked, for example, what they
talk about, each spouse tends to claim that they talk most
about the other's interests and that the other talks most about
him or herself.[46] If asked such a straightforward question as
who does what in the house and who is responsible for family
budgeting, a high level of discrepancy in the answers of the
two is often apparent.[47]

Sexual maladjustment as a cause of marital breakdown is
said to be comparatively rare.[48] Where a good relationship
exists, some accommodation to sexual difficulties can be
achieved by the partners co-operating or by their deciding to
seek advice. If the underlying relationship is poor, however,
and they are unable to discuss their problems with each other,

then sexual problems can become a focus for discontentment and later a ground for separation or divorce. Sexual difficulties are more likely to occur where both partners are inexperienced prior to marriage, so that taboos on sexual behaviour have to be abandoned (literally overnight) with high expectations of success which may well be disappointed.

THE FAMILY

The arrival of the first child always constitutes a crisis point for a married couple as they are required to transform their reciprocal roles as friends and lovers to include the roles of parents and to adapt to the idea of sharing their home and each other with another demanding human being. In addition, they may have fears of being unable to cope, financially, physically or psychologically. Neglected husbands who feel left out of the mother-child system are a common phenomenon.[49] The wife may resent what she sees as the husband's relative freedom from the demands of the child. There is evidence that the marital satisfactions of wives diminish with the arrival of children and pick up again when the children leave home.[50][51] It is obvious that the meaning of the pregnancy to the couple will affect their reactions to it, whether it comes as an unwelcome surprise or as a result of planning. The Newsons have indicated that clear social class differences may exist in relation to reactions to pregnancy. They suggest that there are culturally defined times at which motherhood is regarded as appropriate and that these are generally after the age of 20 and before 26. Earlier than 20 is considered too early and to have a baby after 26 is thought to be getting a bit late. However, working-class mothers are much more likely than middle-class ones to have become pregnant before the age of 21. Thus for the working-class woman her pregnancy may be regarded as somewhat less than a blessing and a large number of children may well have been unwanted insofar as they were conceived before marriage. For middle-class mothers, on the other hand, motherhood is likely to come at what is regarded as a more suitable time and thus be more welcome. Middle-class women are also more likely to seek expert information during pregnancy and to be less influenced by 'old wives' tales'. They are thus better prepared for the actual arrival of the child, both physically and psychologically.[52]

Pregnancy supplies an important social as well as a biological role for a woman. By proving that she is fertile she enhances her status and has a legitimate source of pride. New avenues of social contact are opened up to her. Pregnancy becomes a time of stress where the person is reluctant to become a mother, where the baby is unwanted or wanted only to prop up an ailing marriage and where the woman is ill-prepared.

The experience of childbirth itself will be affected by the woman's expectations and attitudes. In some cultures women pursue their daily routines right up to the moment of delivery, are unattended and start work again after a break of a few hours. In other cultures there is an expectation of pain and an atmosphere of illness surrounds the event.

It used to be claimed that women have a maternal instinct which springs into action at the moment of birth, but there is little evidence that this is the case, although there does seem to be a widespread human response of warmth towards all young animals with small round faces such as puppies and kittens as well as small babies.[53] Even in lower animals where instinctive patterns are more important as shapers of behaviour, maternal activities can be disrupted. Rats reared in isolation perform a variety of stereotyped activities associated with motherhood, such as collecting the young together and nest-building. Although these activities would appear to be genetically programmed they can be disrupted by depriving the rats of materials which they can manipulate.[54] It is customary for pregnant rats to lick their own genitalia, probably to obtain certain salts; if they are not permitted to do this, for instance, by fitting them with a rubber ruff, they eat a high proportion of their young at birth and no longer retrieve stray offspring.[55] The evidence from the Harlows' studies is also clear; female rhesus monkeys who are socially inadequate through being reared in isolation become inadequate, neglecting and cruel mothers. Similarly, there is no automatic bond between human mothers and their children and many mothers may feel guilty at their lack of enthusiasm as they gaze for the first time upon the unappealing and wrinkled face which they are told is that of their child. Babies cannot distinguish between adults for about the first three months of life and the maternal bond likewise needs time to develop.

The hormone pro-lactin that induces lactation twenty-four hours after the delivery of a baby does seem to produce a feeling of warmth and relaxation in the mother, and there are cultural and social pressures which channel this towards the dependent infant. Breast-feeding may enhance maternal responsiveness by mutual rewards which reduce the infant's hunger, relieve pressure on the mother's breasts and supply both with bodily contact and warmth.

Family tensions

Until this century almost the whole of life took place within the family circle, but now education, religious teaching, work, social gatherings and leisure activities are more likely to take place outside the family home. Nevertheless, the family continues to provide a stable environment which changes less rapidly than the complex society outside, and it is a place in which the individual can relax, drop his 'social mask' and be himself. 'Being oneself', however, may mean that one feels one can be unkind more readily than elsewhere, as well as being freer to express affection or eccentricity. Hostility which has to be kept in check at work may be discharged in the safer family environment, although, where the family is unstable, individuals may release hostile feelings, which are a consequence of family disputes, outside the home.

. The characteristics of unhappy families seem to be that roles are rigidly defined and adhered to even in a crisis, for example the mother will still be expected to cook and clean even if she is ill, a denial that problems exist and an inability to discuss them. Happy families seem to be more flexible, less intense and able to 'talk out' their problems, and individual members are willing to change roles occasionally.

The most frequent areas of disagreement within a family are money, child-rearing and leisure activities.[56] Members of families which have frequent quarrels or underlying discord which threatens the stability of the group may react by overstressing 'togetherness' on birthdays, anniversaries and holidays. Parents whose marriage is unsatisfactory are likely to find their biggest satisfaction in their children.[56]

Families develop their own norms and standards of permitted freedom of emotional outlet, behaviour and the extent to which outsiders are admitted to the family circle. Families may also have a collective image of themselves such as 'artistic', 'sports-loving', 'religious' or 'adventurous', up to which individual members are expected to live, perhaps whether they like it or not. This idea of a collective unity is expressed in remarks such as 'We're not that sort of a family', 'Nothing like that ever happens in our family'. Families may also be loosely classified as authoritarian or democratic. The authoritarian family restricts flexibility, has clearly defined roles and rules and discourages curiosity, imagination and close ties outside the family. The democratic family is more flexible in its recognition of individual needs, but may arouse feelings of guilt by setting a very high premium on love, tolerance and the suppression of overt hostility.

Ill-feeling between husband and wife may be expressed by attacks on the children. One child, in particular, may be selected as a scapegoat; parents who are very ambitious, for example, may 'choose' the child who is a poor achiever on whom to vent their hostility, or one child may be identified with the disliked partner – 'You're just like your Dad'. Children may also be used to goad the partner, so that one parent encourages a certain behaviour in the child whilst the other discourages it. A child may thus become a 'problem' which is symbolic of marital disharmony and provides a safety valve which keeps the family from disintegrating but which is naturally disturbing for the child.

Since the family is the usual environment within which a child's development takes place it has the potential to ensure the full flowering of its children, providing security, affectionate acceptance and opportunities to explore, or to disturb and disrupt through indifference, dislike and apathy. The adult personality too can be stimulated and enhanced by deep personal relationships whether these be purely sexual, marital or parental within an atmosphere of mutual trust and understanding. Where opportunities for these are lacking, an individual may find fulfilment elsewhere, or, if this too is unavailable, become bitter and self-centred.

REFERENCES

1 S. Freud, *New Introductory Lectures on Psychoanalysis* (London, Hogarth Press, 1933).
2 H. F. Harlow, 'The nature of love', *Amer. Psychologist, 13* (1958), 673–85.
3 D. Lack, *The Natural Regulation of Animal Numbers* (Oxford University Press, 1954).
4 V. C. Wynne-Edwards, *Animal Dispersion in Relation to Social Behaviour* (London, Oliver & Boyd, 1962).
5 H. Hediger, 'Environmental factors influencing the reproduction of zoo animals', in *Sex and Behaviour* (Ed. F. A. Beach), (New York, John Wiley, 1965), 319–54.
6 H. F. Harlow and M. K. Harlow, 'Social deprivation in monkeys', *Sci. American, 207* (1962), 136.
7 W. Simon and J. H. Gagnon, 'On psychosexual development', in *Handbook of Socialisation Theory and Research* (Ed. D. Goslin), (Chicago, Russell Sage Foundation, Rand McNally, 1969), 733–52.
8 A. Bandura and R. H. Walters, *Social Learning and Personality Development* (London, Holt, Rinehart & Winston, 1969).
9 C. S. Ford and F. A. Beach, *Patterns of Sexual Behaviour* (London, Methuen, 1965).
10 R. R. Sears, 'Development of gender role', in *Sex and Behaviour* (Ed. F. A. Beach), (New York, John Wiley, 1965), 133–63.
11 I. Bieber, H. J. Dain, P. R. Dince, M. G. Drellich, H. G. Grand, R. H. Grundlach, M. W. Kremer, A. H. Rifkin, C. B. Wilbur and T. B. Bieber, *Homosexuality* (New York, Basic Books, 1962).
12 J. Chang and J. Block, 'A study of identification in male homosexuals', *J. Consult. Psychol., 24* (1960), 307–10.
13 J. Money, J. G. Hampson and J. L. Hampson, 'Imprinting and the establishment of gender role', *A.M.A. Archs. Neurol. and Psychiat., 77* (1957), 333–6.
14 J. Hampson, 'Determinants of psychosexual orientation', in *Sex and Behaviour* (Ed. F. A. Beach), (New York, John Wiley, 1965), 108–32.
15 F. Ghabrial and S. M. Gingis, 'Reorientation of sex, report of two cases', *Int. J. Fertility, 7* (1962), 249–58.
16 A. S. Norris and W. C. Keetel, 'Change of sex during adolescence: a case study', *Amer. J. Obstet. Gynec., 84* (1962), 719–21.
17 M. Diamond, 'Genetic-endocrine interactions and human psychosexuality', in *Perspectives in Reproductive and Sexual Behaviour* (Ed. M. Diamond), (Bloomington and London, Indiana University Press, 1968), 417–43.

Sex, Marriage and the Family   201

18 F. L. Goodenough, 'Anger in young children', *Inst. Child Welfare Monog.*, Series No. 9 (Minneapolis, University of Minnesota Press, 1931).

19 L. B. Ames and J. Learned, 'Developmental trends in child kaleido-block responses', *J. Genet. Psychol.*, *84* (1954), 237–70.

20 R. R. Sears, 'Development of gender role', in *Sex and Behaviour* (Ed. F. A. Beach), (New York, John Wiley, 1965), 133–63.

21 J. Kagan and H. A. Moss, *Birth to Maturity: a study in psychological development* (New York, John Wiley, 1962).

22 H. Barry, M. Bacon and I. L. Child, 'A cross-cultural survey of some sex differences in socialisation', *J. Abn. Soc. Psychol.*, *55* (1957), 327–32.

23 M. Mead, 'Cultural determinants of sexual behaviour', in *Sex and Internal Secretions* (Ed. W. C. Young), (Baltimore, Williams and Wilkins, 1961), 3rd edition, 1433–79.

24 H. Harlow, 'The heterosexual affection system in monkeys', *Amer. Psychologist, 17* (1962), 1–9.

25 W. H. Masters and V. E. Johnson, 'The anatomy and physiology of human sexual response', in *Human Reproduction and Sexual Behaviour* (Ed. C. Lloyd), (Philadelphia, Lea & Febiger, 1964).

26 V. Sigusch, G. Schmidt, A. Reinfeld and I. Wiedermann-Sutor, 'Psychosexual stimulation: sex differences', *J. Sex. Res.*, *6* (1970), 10–24.

27 E. E. Levitt and A. D. Klassen Jr, 'Public attitudes towards sexual behaviour: the latest investigations of the Institute for Sex Research', *Amer. J. Orthopsychiat., 81* (1973), 285–6.

28 Social Surveys, Gallup Poll Ltd., *TV and Religion* (London University Press, 1964).

29 D. Wright and E. Cox, unpublished data, quoted in *The Psychology of Moral Behaviour* (D. Wright), (Harmondsworth, Penguin Books, 1970).

30 G. Gorer, *Sex and Marriage in England Today* (London, Nelson, 1971).

31 A. C. Kinsey, W. B. Pomeroy and C. E. Martin, *Sexual Behaviour* (London and Philadelphia, W. B. Saunders, 1948).

32 E. Erickson, *Childhood and Society* (Harmondsworth, Penguin Books, 1965).

33 R. Benedict, *Patterns of Culture* (Boston, Houghton Mifflin, 1934).

34 C. S. Ford and F. A. Beach, *Patterns of Sexual Behaviour* (London, Methuen, 1965).

35 E. Van den Haag, 'Love or marriage', in *The Family: its structure and functions* (Ed. R. L. Coser), (New York, St Martin's Press, 1964), 192–202.

36 M. Schofield, *The Sexual Behaviour of Young People* (Harmondsworth, Penguin Books, 1965).

37 C. B. Broderick, 'Social heterosexual development among urban negroes and whites', *J. Marr. Fam., 27* (1965), 200–3.

38 M. S. Wilson, 'Do college girls conform to the standards of their parents?', *Marr. and Fam. Living, 15* (1953), 207–8.

39 N. Z. Medalia, 'Marriage and adjustment: in college and out', *Personnel and Guid. J., 40* (1962), 545–50.

40 V. Jensen and M. Clark, 'Married and unmarried college students', *Personnel and Guid. J.*, *37* (1958), 123–5.
41 C. E. Vincent, 'Socialisation data in research on young marrieds', *Acta Sociologica*, *8* (1964), 118–28.
42 G. Gorer, *Sex and Marriage in England Today* (London, Nelson, 1971).
43 K. S. Renne, 'Correlates of dissatisfaction in marriage', *J. Marr. Fam.*, *32* (1970), 54–67.
44 G. Rowntree, *Population Studies*, *28* (1964), 147.
45 J. Dominion, *Marital Breakdown* (Harmondsworth, Penguin Books, 1969).
46 B. C. Rollins and H. Feldman, 'Marital satisfaction over the family life cycle', *J. Marr. Fam.*, *32* (1970), 24–32.
47 D. H. Granbois and R. P. Willett, 'Equivalence of family role measures based on husband and wife data', *J. Marr. Fam.*, *32* (1970), 33–8.
48 J. Dominion, *Marital Breakdown* (Harmondsworth, Penguin Books, 1969).
49 D. T. Dyer, 'Parenthood as a crisis: a re-study', *Marriage and Fam. Living*, *25* (1963), 196–201.
50 P. C. Pineo, 'Disenchantment in the later years of marriage', *Marr. and Fam. Living*, *23* (1961), 3–11.
51 R. O. Blood, Jr and D. M. Wolfe, *Husbands and Wives* (Glencoe, The Free Press, 1960).
52 J. Newson and E. Newson, *Infant Care in an Urban Community* (London, Allen & Unwin, 1963).
53 I. Eibl-Eibesfeldt, *Love and Hate* (London, Methuen, 1971).
54 B. P. Wiesner and N. M. Sheard, *Maternal Behaviour in the Rat* (Edinburgh and London, Oliver & Boyd, 1933).
55 H. G. Birch, 'Sources of order in the maternal behaviour of animals', *Amer. J. Orthopsychiat.*, *26* (1956), 279–84.
56 R. O. Blood, Jr and D. M. Wolfe, *Husbands and Wives* (Glencoe, The Free Press, 1960).

11

Man in Society

No more fiendish punishment could be devised ... than that one should be turned loose in society and remain absolutely unnoticed by all the members thereof.
William James, *Principles of Psychology*

From the time of birth the vast majority of individuals belong to a group. There is no choice about the first of these, the family, but other social relationships involve a greater degree of freedom. One fundamental human dilemma is that individual interests often conflict with group interests and yet we need the support and co-operation of other people. Some cultures minimise this conflict between individual and group by reducing the emphasis on individual needs. Small-scale hunting and agricultural communities may be wholly co-operative, or group thinking may be encouraged, so that, in a sense, there is little conflict between individual and group identity. Other cultures, such as are found in the western world, tend to exacerbate the conflict by placing a high premium on individualism.

Man is born as a biological organism, but he is formed by his experience of the social world. It is within a social context that language and thought develop, and where the person gains a sense of his or her unique identity. Such human attributes as empathy, sympathy and morality can only arise out of our interactions with other people.

Most human beings are ambivalent in their attitudes to others; fearing to acknowledge a mutual dependence which, whilst it brings security and support, also brings responsibility and restrictions. We seem both to need and, at times, to wish to avoid social contact. These contradictions may imply that there is some optimal amount of social contact which will vary between individuals and in the same individual from time to time.

As described in an earlier chapter, the tendency to form social attachments is present at an early age, and the ill-effects of the deprivation of stable relationships with others have been noted. For a child, the presence of other people is essential to his physical survival, but although this may occasionally be the case for adults, their tendency to form groups that have no protective, nourishing or occupational function, suggests a need for companionship which is basically psychological. Other people constitute sources of stimulation and are foci for our curiosity. Indeed the sheer presence of others, even where no interaction takes place, appears to have an arousing effect on the nervous system.

SOCIAL CONTACT

In a study where subjects had to track a moving target and learn to hit it by monitoring its trajectory and speed, it was found that the presence of a passive audience interfered with the learning of the task, insofar as subjects being watched made more errors, were less consistent and took longer to reach a criterion level of performance. After prolonged practice, when those taking part had attained a consistent level of proficiency, the presence of an audience was found to improve their performance.[1] These results match those found in other experiments where it has been shown that individuals who are being watched do better on well-learned tasks, but are worse at acquiring new skills, or solving complex problems, than are individuals working alone.[2][3][4]

These findings have implications for performance where the person is required to act in the presence of others. In an examination, for example, where the answers have been rote learned to a high degree of proficiency, the presence of others in the room should aid the examinee in his task. Where examination items demand complex thought, however, it seems likely that the performance of some individuals will suffer. Similarly, one might expect that the current fashion for 'open-plan' offices would encourage productivity and efficiency in routine affairs, but would have a disrupting effect on the training of new staff and the solution of novel or complex problems. Naturally there will be individual differences in the degree to which these effects show themselves, but it seems likely that they are related to the theory of the association between arousal level and efficiency discussed in Chapter 5.

It follows from that formulation that extremes of social contact, from very little to a great deal, might be experienced as disturbing in some way. Lack of social relationships has, for example, been implicated as a precipitating factor in suicide attempts.

Attempts at suicide seem to occur when the individual feels that he is alone and has no one to turn to. The incidence of suicide is lower in married people[5] and more common amongst the widowed and separated, whilst in some London districts where as many as one-third of the population live alone and are, therefore, vulnerable to isolation and loneliness, suicide rates are particularly high.[6] Those individuals who cannot accept their need for others and who expect to be disliked are particularly at risk.[7] In one sample it was found that 75 per cent of men who committed suicide had lost a job or income some years before their death; for women the loss of a personal relationship seemed to be the precipitating factor.[8] This we might expect from the difference in sex roles – the social standing of men is likely to be linked to their job or financial circumstances, whilst that of women is more often derived from the home and friends.

Social isolation is highly disruptive of normal development in children. In adults it can lead to disintegration of personal identity, a loss of contact with realities beyond the self and, when severe, may lead to confusion, memory defects and withdrawal. These depersonalising effects of isolation have been utilised in 'brainwashing' techniques, to make the prisoner more susceptible to a change of ideology.[9]

Our sense of identity and our feelings of 'selfhood' are largely derived from our interactions with other people. We need them to confirm the viability of our existence and we need their support and affection.

At the other end of the continuum, however, the presence of too many others has been regarded as one of the disturbing features of modern life. There is evidence that the arousal levels of animals housed with others are higher than if they are housed alone,[10] and aggressive contact between baboons is about eight times as high in the crowded conditions of captivity as it is in the wild,[11] a finding which has been attributed to the increased frequency of social contacts. Aggressiveness in primates seems to increase with mounting congestion in the living place.[12] It has been suggested that, for man, living in crowded cities creates a situation where he is constantly bombarded by social cues, sights and sounds, impressions and requests for help. There is a confusing excess of potential interaction, so that an 'information overload' is produced, and people are forced to narrow their attentions down to what seems essential.[13] Strangers to the city may be struck by the unfriendliness of shop assistants, the unconcern shown by passers-by to those who, literally, fall by the wayside, the absence of apology when pedestrians collide or bang into each other's parcels. It appears that strangers treat each other more distantly in cities than they do in country areas, and bystanders are less likely in the city to interfere in fights or to offer assistance when needed.[13]

The impersonal behaviour of city dwellers as compared with town dwellers is not necessarily due to lack of time or to the cold nature of the inhabitants. The population of a big city is ethnically and culturally mixed. Appearance, morality and behaviour are of great diversity, which makes it difficult to be sure that intervention is necessary or would be welcome if it occurred. Those who live in a city are also, with some justification, likely to feel more vulnerable to theft or assault and may, therefore, be suspicious of requests for help. A study of responses to requests to use the telephone by supposedly stranded male and female investigators found that many more small town than city dwellers in the USA were willing to admit the investigators into their homes. All the investigators did at least twice as well in the small town as in the city. About 75 per cent of householders contacted in the city refused to open the door and shouted through it or peered through peepholes, whereas about 75 per cent of the small town house-holders opened their doors directly.[14]

Although high density living has been blamed for a variety of ills from mental disorder to crime, the evidence in support of this thesis remains ambiguous and difficult to interpret. The evidence from crowding in animals is interesting but its applicability to man is uncertain. Our capacity for symbolic thought makes the meaning of conditions perhaps more important than the actual conditions themselves. There is a proportionately higher crime rate and mental illness rate in most cities as compared with less densely packed areas,[15] but it is hard to attribute this simply to the number of people. It could be due to a variety of other interacting factors such as deprivation, poverty and the tendency of those who are mentally disturbed to drift down the social scale and end up in the cheapest (and also the most densely packed) areas of a city. Some individuals do appear to find the presence of a large number of others quite congenial. It may be, however, that the possibility of being in constant contact with many people begins to exhaust our resources for coping with them.

Both animals and men have a variety of social techniques which enable them to cope with the presence of others. Because the brain has a finite capacity for dealing with information, it seems possible that the employment of these techniques cannot exceed a certain level. Some social mechanisms have the effect of cutting down on the amount of information we need to extract from any encounter and such devices as dominance and territoriality (in animals) and ritual politeness and role-taking (in human beings) help to smooth the course of social interaction.

SOCIAL TECHNIQUES

By social techniques we mean ways in which people learn to approach others, the ways they interact with them and the means they use for determining the occurrence or non-occurrence of an encounter and the length of time it lasts. The interesting thing about these techniques is that although almost universally employed in our culture, very few of us are conscious of the fact that we are using them. One of the ways in which we can cut down on the information emanating from others is to treat them on the basis of their role.

Roles

The term 'role' is descriptive of behaviour appropriate to a particular position held by someone in a small group or in society as a whole. The occupant of a role – doctor, teacher, parent, comedian, chairman – has available a range of behaviour which is in accord with the expectations of others and with his own expectations. The behaviour associated with a role does not involve deliberate play-acting (although an element of this may be observed in the early stages of taking a new role, say, as a lecturer) but rather is a consequence of adherence to the perceived assumptions of others and oneself about the 'right' way to act in the position concerned. People who violate the norms of a role, say for example, a vicar who tells dirty stories, a bank manager who throws pound notes out of the window, or a scholar who professes ignorance, upset people's expectations and are felt to be disturbing even when no possible harm could result from their actions. Where someone has no clearly defined role this can also be disconcerting. In one study the experimenter established a number of five-man problem-solving groups within which two of the participants were his confederates. In some groups the confederates announced that they were there to listen only, but in other groups they did not explain themselves and remained silent. The latter groups were less effective in their assigned tasks and reported feelings of uneasiness, because of the ambiguous, roleless presence of the silent members.[16] In a group of friends when a normally talkative member of the group is silent, the others often attempt to clarify the situation with questions such as 'Are you all right?' which are a consequence of the silent person's failure to fulfil expectations about his role in that group. Although each role has associated expectations, these have a range of acceptability and are not rigidly circumscribed, so that each individual is allowed a certain latitude in the way in which he fills that role.

A strong personality may take a role in such a way as to

change the expectations that others have of it. Thus the head of a department or organisation may act towards his subordinates in a friendly and encouraging way, where previous bosses have been autocratic and distant. Those in the organisation may then come to alter their expectations of 'the boss' role and expect subsequent superiors to behave in the same way, and feel disappointed when they do not, although they may have accepted the original autocratic role behaviour as the 'correct' way to treat subordinates. Conversely, constant occupation of a role may influence the personality characteristics of the individual Doctors, used to giving the appearance of infallibility at work, may extend this to other areas of their lives and come to behave as if they must be right all the time, lecturers may address dinner parties as if they were audiences and nurses may become brisk and nurturant in their private lives.

Because any individual normally occupies several roles there is always the possibility that the expectations associated with one will come into conflict with those associated with another. A woman who is trying to be wife, mother, social worker and daughter may fail to satisfy simultaneously the demands of her husband, son, client or father. Often this can be avoided by compartmentalising the demands on her time, but there might easily come a Saturday afternoon when her husband wants his shirt ironed, her son wants her to take him to the zoo, a client calls round in tears and her father is waiting for her visit. How well she and those around her cope with this role conflict depends upon their ability to find and tolerate alternative solutions. Most of the time we exist quite happily, automatically juggling with our roles as members of different groups – family, work, sets of friends, committees and so on – as long as we are not required to fulfil more than one role at once. For this, among other reasons, doctors usually refuse to treat members of their own family. Not only would it be difficult to achieve the required degree of objectivity, but incompatible role behaviour might be associated with the positions of father and physician. Role conflict that is latent may become extreme in a crisis situation. After a tornado struck a town in Texas, emergency workers had to choose between duty

o

to the public and concern for their families. Most people did resolve this clash of loyalties in favour of the family and rushed off home to make sure all was well, but disaster was averted because of some important exceptions. Refinery workers stayed on at work until their units were closed down and the Chief of Police stayed at his post for seventy-two hours, because he knew his family was out of town.[17]

Conflict may also occur when different people have different expectations about the same role. University students are expected to behave in different ways by taxpayers, lecturers and other students and so are bound to offend somebody. A person's basic feelings and attitudes may be antipathetic to the role they are fulfilling. A girl may, for example, become a nurse because she enjoys caring for people. She may, however, be so good at her job that she is promoted to a position where she is expected to be an aloof administrator. She can then either creatively re-design the role to suit her personality or stifle her feelings in favour of conformity to the expectations of others, which might make her unhappy enough to resign.

The assumption that people can be depended upon to act in certain ways in certain positions does help social life to run smoothly. It avoids the need to approach each person one meets as an unknown quantity, especially where contact is likely to be short or is confined to specific situations. If we only see the bank clerk over the counter at the bank, we need only assume that he is efficient and trustworthy. To attempt to plumb the innermost recesses of his soul would be expensive of time and likely to cause the formation of a long queue to the irritation of other customers.

This superficiality can, however, make social relationships mechanical and lead to misunderstandings, making deeper relationships difficult to attain. Regarding people as no more than the roles they occupy is to deny their essential individuality

Taking someone at their 'role value' provides us with virtually no information about what they are 'really' like – a fact which most people seem to recognise at some level. One study has shown that when an individual conforms to role expectations he is seen as less like his 'real' self than when he violates role expectations. Tape recordings of a man being interviewed for a job, either as a member of a submarine crew, or as an astronaut, were played over to several subjects who were told that the essential attributes of an astronaut were individuality and self-reliance, whilst those of submarine crew were sociability and ability to work in a team. In half of the supposed interviews the interviewee fulfilled the conditions for the job for which he was applying and in the other half he conformed to the characteristics associated with the other job. Where the characteristics of the interviewee were opposed to the requirements for the job for which he was applying, the interviewee was judged to be more himself.[18] Thus behaviour which fits in with the role expectations tells us little about the individual occupying that role. The prescriptions associated with a role may be used to deny individual responsibility, so that those who abuse the power that their position gives them, or who take orders without question, may claim, as Eichmann did, that they are only 'doing their job' and that they are not 'really' like that at all. This may also be a way of avoiding guilt, if they are at the pre-moral or conventional morality levels. In a recent television programme a mother justified precipitating her 11-year-old son into the world of pop music on the grounds that a mother had to do the best she could for her children.

People who lack confidence and feelings of competence in their own ability may insist on a rigid conformity to role expectations for themselves and other people, but this may place restrictions on deeper personal relationships and stifle individual growth.

Stereotypes

As we have indicated, each individual has some latitude in role performance, and can adapt the requirements of each position to his own propensities to some extent. Stereotypes are rigid and generalised expectations about individuals in, for example, racial, religious or occupational groups which may extend beyond any position an individual occupies and against which description the individual may struggle in vain. Stereotypes are at their most dangerous and widespread in relation to nationalities and religious groups, but even a bank clerk may have difficulty altering the expectation that he will be polite, precise and self-effacing at all times. The stereotyping of the woman's role (by women as well as men) has led to inequalities before the law and a good deal of conflict where a woman feels herself to be capable of behaviour widely held to be inappropriate for a woman, such as being intelligent. Thus some girls tend to cover up their intellectual abilities and expose their physical assets so as to be sure not to be thought unfeminine.

Where stereotypes are widespread in a culture, those at whom they are directed may also come to believe in them, even act them out. A Scotsman may see himself as tight-fisted, and some American blacks really believe that they are inferior to whites, hence the slogan 'Black is Beautiful' designed to give back self-respect.

An important part of understanding the confusing multiplicity of social experience is the capacity to form patterns, to organise information and to classify both people and events. This tendency to lump people into categories on the basis of a small amount of information can lead to dangerous prejudice, especially in times of hostility and conflict. Prejudice feeds on non-neutral stereotypes and is highly resistant to contrary information, so a generous Scotsman is assumed to be an exception to the rule, as is a West Indian who prefers the concerto to the calypso.

The effect of stereotyping is to minimise differences between people within a group – 'They're all alike' – and to magnify the differences between that classification and others – 'They're not like us'. The classification of objects into categories can lead to distortion of perception as shown in an experiment where subjects were divided into three groups and asked to judge the lengths of eight lines all of which differed in length. The first group of subjects were just shown the lines. The second group were shown the lines which were marked either A or B at random, whilst for the third group the four shortest lines were marked A and the four longest B. As predicted the last group judged the shorter lines to be closer in length and to have bigger differences from the longer lines than did the other groups of subjects.[19] If this distortion of perception can occur in relation to objective measures then it can perhaps more readily occur in complex social situations where a minimum of cues can trigger off instant opinions and emotional reactions. Emotional involvement also distorts perception. The size of objects will be judged differently depending on their value to the person making the judgement; highly valued objects will be judged larger than they actually are. Thus an experiment with English people (before decimalisation) found that they consistently exaggerated the difference in size between a two-shilling piece and a half-crown, in comparison to the judgements of the difference in size between two foreign coins.[20] Similar effects are found for judgements of people. American whites who have anti-black prejudices rate differences between skin colours as being greater than do people who are not prejudiced.[21] It appears that this may happen with any quality that is important to an individual. Those who value intelligence may tend to exaggerate differences between those they see as intelligent and those they see as stupid. A similar effect may occur with honesty or common sense or strength of will and so on.

So the less information there is available about someone the more likely he may be judged as having the stereotyped characteristics of a group to which he is seen as belonging; the less emotional involvement there is in the stereotype the more susceptible it is to further information whilst highly emotional stereotypes distort and select information by focusing attention on limited aspects of the situation or by actually seeing it in a way that supports the stereotype. A classic example of this is given in an experiment in which the subjects were shown a drawing and then had to describe it to another subject and he to another and so on until a final report was given. One such drawing showed a carriage in a New York subway train, where two men, one black, one white, were standing together apparently quarrelling. The white man had a razor tucked into his belt. Typically, the final descriptions of the drawing had transferred the razor from the white man's belt to the black man's hand.[22] Interaction of individuals on the basis of roles or stereotypes, although economical in terms of time and trouble, is bound to be on a superficial level.

There are many other techniques which may be used to facilitate, or to discourage social interaction, and to regulate the direction it takes. Many of these involve the use of social reinforcement, the showing of approval or disapproval, interest or a barely concealed boredom. Non-verbal communication plays a large part in the regulation of the behaviour of others. If a person looks us in the eye we assume we have his attention (not always the case, of course). When a person has finished speaking he tends to look up at the other person to indicate he has concluded his contribution for the time being.[23] Looking which is prolonged beyond a certain length of time, however, tends to convey different messages depending upon the context, sexual attraction, hostility or perhaps some disorder in the dress of the observed person.[24]

Physical proximity and bodily orientation can also convey social messages. Turning the body towards someone can indicate a desire to become better acquainted, whilst 'keeping one's distance' physically may indicate a desire not to become involved with the other person.

In the same way as role-taking and role expectations can become rigid and stereotyped, so other social techniques can harden into inflexibility – the persistent refusal to meet another's gaze, a dislike of any kind of physical nearness and so on.

These mechanisms for social interaction are learned in a very subtle way as the child develops by a combination of social experience, imitation, trial and error, and reinforcement ('it's rude to stare').

THE SOCIAL FUNCTION OF GROUPS

Members of groups come together ostensibly to achieve a common goal, whether it is the marketing of a new washing powder, or the collection of molluscs. Groups do, however, come to serve personal needs that go beyond the apparent purpose of the group and there emerge, out of the interaction of the members, shared norms about the correct way to behave.

Groups that are successful in fulfilling individual needs will last long after the reason they came together in the first place has become irrelevant. Hence the continuing existence of 'Old Girls' associations for those who remember school as the happiest time of their life. Moreover, the ostensible purpose for which a group is formed may not reflect the reasons for which members are attracted to the group. Not all members of nudist camps are seekers after the healthy life, and riding to hounds may convey a status and prestige which go beyond the killing of a living creature. Advice to the lonely often includes telling them to join a club for old-time dancing or for tennis. So that although the manifest reason for the group is dancing or sport, its real function may be to provide a hunting ground for friends and/or marriage partners.

In order for a set of people to constitute a group there must be some relationship between the members, each of whom will develop in the course of time a role within that group, even if it is as informal as to be 'the life and soul of the party'. After a number of meetings of the members a kind of group ideology emerges. This ideology grows as a consequence of the interaction of the members and involves the setting up of common standards and values, agreement on the status hierarchy, the delineation of roles and the sharing of assumptions about the world. Once this stage is reached the group has a unity out of which strong loyalties can be created. Formal groups such as are formed in a work situation may have their ideology already laid down by the structure of the organisation, whilst the ideology of informal groups, like friends, evolves out of the interaction and consensus of individual members.

The dual function of groups in providing for both task solution and personal needs is reflected in the emergence of two types of influential people in groups. Bales found that there was one person who led in the area of problem-solving and another who looked after the emotional welfare of the group by providing for the release of tension in making jokes, paying compliments and generally reassuring people.[25] As already indicated in a previous chapter, the style of leadership provided in a group influences the social climate within which the activities of the group take place. An authoritarian leader who sets the goals and takes all the decisions tends to create a work-orientated environment with low personal involvement where individuals are highly dependent upon him for guidance and to some extent lost without him, particularly where work is concerned. A democratic leader may produce a lower performance rate but his group tends to be more cohesive, and because they share, and are familiar with, the goals of the group, they can continue to function when the leader is absent.[26] Some people may prefer authoritarian leadership since it provides for greater immediate security by reducing uncertainty and individual responsibility. Indeed this 'fear of freedom' has been put forward as an explanation for more global trends such as the flight to a dictator in times of great uncertainty and wide individual choice.[27]

The commitment of any individual to the ideology of certain of his groups can be very strong, so that even in the face of information which strongly challenges it he will attempt to assimilate the information into the group's assumptions. This point is nicely illustrated by the events that followed the prediction of the end of the world by a religious sect in America. This group had come together under the influence of a lady who claimed to be in contact with men from another planet who told her that God was going to flood the earth, a catastrophe due to occur at 4 o'clock one morning. The group, however, was to be saved by the arrival of a spaceship on the midnight preceding the flood. Several of the group gave up their jobs, sold their homes and said goodbye to friends in anticipation of the end of the world. On the evening of the spaceship's supposed arrival several members of the sect were gathered in the home of the leader and sat nervously awaiting their rescue. As midnight came and went with no sign of the spacemen, signs of tension and uneasiness were observed. The basic assumptions and beliefs of the group were under heavy fire. Suddenly the lady who was the head of the sect stood up and announced that she had received a telepathic message, to the effect that God had saved the world because the group had had faith. Those who were present when this announcement was made subsequently became even more fervent in their beliefs, but those members of the group who had not been present at the crucial interpretation of events found their attachment to the group ideology to be much weakened.[28] This kind of commitment and the support which group consensus gives to the individual have been used as a means of changing the attitudes and behaviour of individual members.

During World War II an attempt was made to encourage the housewives of America to change their eating habits, so that they saw the eating of offal such as kidneys, liver and brains, as a patriotic duty rather than as a somewhat disgusting preference. Methods used included giving the women a lecture on the merits of such food and the use of group discussion where objections and opinions were aired and the women asked to say whether or not they would be prepared to serve the meat in question to their families. Those who attended discussion groups and made a public commitment were much more likely to change their attitudes and their habits than those housewives who merely attended a lecture.[29]

The important element in estimating how much an individual feels personally involved in a group decision, is whether he took part in the making of it and the extent to which he feels the whole group is agreed on it. Both action and opinion are anchored in social reality; democratic groups whose members take part in the decision-making are thus more likely to be committed to those decisions than groups upon whom decisions are imposed from outside.

This has implications for the wider society. A large faceless bureaucracy may make people feel cut off from effective decision-making so that they have no particular stake in carrying out those decisions. Thus appeals for people to save fuel, say, may be ineffective since they are part of a decision-making process from which those who are asked to co-operate have been excluded. Elections give people the illusion of contributing to social policy, but the illusion is transitory when they see that they have little effect in changing housing conditions, economic inequalities or the price of meat, and so people become uninterested and ill-motivated to assist the unseen and unknown leaders. The recent proliferation of community action groups may reflect the need of individuals to feel involved in and to participate in decisions which are made about their lives.

The decision-making behaviour of an individual in a group will be influenced by whether or not he feels himself to be in competition with the other members. The shared expectations that members have, lead them to adopt different strategies according to the demands of the situation. In a classroom, some children were led to compete by being told that in a group discussion individuals would be awarded marks according to the level of their contribution, whilst other children were told that the performance of their group as a whole would be taken into account. In the latter co-operative condition there was more co-ordination of effort towards the solution of the problem they were discussing, communication was more open and more attention was paid to the contributions of other members. Moreover, those who were co-operating reported that they felt friendlier towards their companions and trusted them more than did those in the competitive condition.[30] Similarly, systems of rewards aimed at improving individual performance (such as piece-work) are detrimental to a task where co-operation is essential.[31] One might thus predict that giving a bonus to a footballer who scores a goal would adversely affect the quality of play and co-ordination of effort, whereas rewarding the whole team for each goal scored should improve it. However, it is possible that co-operation within groups is affected by simultaneous competition between groups. One study measured the differential effects of pure co-operation where the efforts of individuals contributed towards the whole group; group competition, where there was co-operation within the group but also competition with other groups; and individual competition, where it was 'every man for himself'. In this situation it was found that both individual and group competition produced a high quality and quantity of output, whilst pure co-operation led to the lowest, although members in this last condition expressed the most satisfaction.[32]

Some laboratory studies have suggested that when it comes to generating new ideas as opposed to solving problems, groups do rather worse working in unison than do individuals alone.

This appeared to be because of some 'contagion' of ideas, so that the ideas generated by groups were less original. Thinking seemed to become stuck in a groove which restricted the range of ideas.[33] However, in real-life problem-solving groups where each member contributes some particular expertise within a co-operative context, for example in groups of scientific workers, genuine innovations may be produced.[34]

On the whole, the evidence is that people are happier in co-operative groups, but there are exceptions to this, for example, where a high value is placed on individual achievement. A study of morale in army engineers showed that competition led to gains in self-esteem and emotional adjustment where it was successful.[35] Competition may also add interest to a boring task, especially where there is little opportunity for being sociable.

One of the ways in which group decisions differ from the decisions made by individuals is that they tend to be more 'risky', or so a large number of studies have found. Typically, individuals are presented with a series of hypothetical problems such as whether to remain in a steady job with a pension but few prospects, or whether to chance taking a better-paid job with better prospects but with a company that has some chance of failing. Each individual makes a decision alone and is then put into a group to engage in discussion on the topic and reach a group decision. In the majority of cases a 'shift-to-risk' occurs. That is, the group makes a decision that is riskier than the average of individual decisions.[36] This kind of situation has, of course, no real-life consequences, but the same effect does occur when the loss or gain of money is involved. Groups make riskier bets than individuals regardless of whether the loss is a shared one or not.[37]

Several explanations for this phenomenon have been advanced. It could be that groups tend to have a dominant individual who might be both more influential and more inclined to take risks, but in problems where safety is of paramount importance group leaders tend to be more conservative than the rest.[38] In fact the evidence is that the ability of leaders to influence the group is a consequence of the fact that they already represent the direction in which the group is moving.[39] It has also been suggested that when responsibility is spread throughout the group its members feel able to take greater chances.[40] This, however, does not explain why they might wish to do so. Another explanation is that our culture places a value on risk-taking; although there are some problems that draw forth a more conservative decision from the group.[41] What does seem to be of paramount importance is the information that is exchanged during the group discussion. If social norms concerning a particular topic favour either taking a chance or playing safe, these norms become apparent during the course of discussion. Group members can then compare their position on the issue with that of the others and may move accordingly. [41] [42] Where a value is placed on caution, for example in a war game – whether or not to start World War III – groups are no riskier than individuals in the decisions they make.[43]

This tendency of group members to measure their own attitudes and behaviour against those of fellow participants forms part of a 'social comparison' process by means of which other people are used as sources of confirmation of one's world view. The consequences which this can have is shown by the account of the panic in the USA which followed a broadcast of the H. G. Wells story, 'War of the Worlds'. Advance warnings were given that this was fiction, but some people, especially those who tuned in a little late, took the mock broadcasts about invaders from Mars seriously. Some were sensible enough to switch to other radio stations to test the reality of the situation, but others ran into the streets, only to see others running into the streets and a minor panic ensued.[44] It has been suggested that a similar process of 'social comparison' may precede some riots. For example, in New York ghetto areas in midsummer when it is very hot, people tend to congregate in the street. Some nervous shopkeeper may begin to fear trouble and put up his shutters, whereupon the shopkeeper across the road thinks that trouble must be brewing and begins to lock his shop up too. Other people notice, become apprehensive, tension mounts and large groups gather to see what's going on. A cruising police car may stop to investigate the crowd and only a small trigger is needed for violence to start.[45] These kind of incidents arise, then, not out of any 'objective' facts, but out of the use of others as yardsticks for social reality.

Not only might an individual label the 'out there' of the external world by the use of social cues, there is also evidence that an individual may label his internal state according to the social situation he is in. In one experiment, subjects who thought they were helping to test a new vitamin, were actually injected with adrenalin. One group was told that it would make them feel 'jumpy' and 'shaky' with fast-beating hearts. The other group was given no description of the effects to expect. Each of the subjects was put individually with a 'stooge' who, briefed by the experimenters, behaved either euphorically or aggressively. Subjects who had been given no advance explanation for their physiological state were later inclined to describe their feelings as happy or angry, in accordance with the social cues given off by the stooge.[46] This study has implications for the phenomenon of emotional contagion in crowds, where people sometimes become infected with feelings of ecstasy or anger. In view of what we have said about the arousing effect of the presence of others, it would follow that people in a crowd would feel somewhat excited, perhaps without realising why and they would thus be susceptible to social cues.

Social environment and group ideology constitute important influences on the perceptions, thinking and behaviour of an individual. There is a fundamental psychological difference between a man alone and a man in a group. Social contact provides a basis for the confirmation of an individual's existence and for the viability of his view of reality. The reason why this confirmation is so necessary lies in the uncertain and contingent nature of that social reality.

REFERENCES

1 R. Martens, 'Effect of an audience on learning and performance of a complex motor skill', *J. Pers. Soc. Psychol.*, *12* (1969), 252–60.
2 F. H. Allport, 'The influence of the group upon association and thought', *J. Exp. Psychol.*, *3* (1920), 159–82.

222　*Individual Development and Social Experience*

3　J. F. Dashiell, 'An experimental analysis of some group effects', *J. Abn. Soc. Psychol.*, 25 (1930), 190–9.
4　J. Pessin and R. W. Husband, 'Effects of social stimulation on human maze learning', *J. Abn. Soc. Psychol.*, 28 (1933), 148–54.
5　L. Dublin, *Suicide* (New York, The Ronald Press, 1963).
6　J. Cohen, 'Forms of suicide and their significance', *Triangle: the Sandoz. J. of Med. Science*, 6 (1964), 280–6.
7　W. Breed, 'Occupational mobility and suicide among white males', *Amer. Sociol. Rev.*, 28 (1963), 179–88.
8　G. Lester and D. Lester, *Suicide: the gamble with death* (New Jersey, Prentice Hall, 1971).
9　J. A. C. Brown, *Techniques of Persuasion* (Harmondsworth, Penguin Books, 1963).
10　J. W. Mason and J. V. Brady, 'Plasma 17-hydroxycorticosteroid changes related to reserpine effects on emotional behaviour', *Science*, 124 (1956), 983–4.
11　T. Rowell, 'A quantitative comparison of the behaviour of a wild and a caged baboon group', *Anim. Behav.*, 15 (1967), 499–504.
12　D. A. Hamburg, 'Crowding, stranger contact and aggressive behaviour', in *Society, Stress and Disease*, Vol. I : *The psychosocial environment and psychosomatic diseases* (Ed. L. Levi), (London, Oxford University Press, 1971), 209–18.
13　S. Milgram, 'The experience of living in cities', *Science, 167* (1970), 1461–8.
14　D. Altman, M. Levine, M. Nadien and J. Willens, unpublished research (summarised in S. Milgram, op. cit.).
15　G. Carlestam, 'The individual, the city and stress', in *Society, Stress and Disease*, Vol. I : 'The psychosocial environment and psychosomatic diseases' (Ed. L. Levi), (London, Oxford University Press, 1971), 134–47.
16　E. E. Smith, 'The effects of clear and unclear role expectations on group productivity', *J. Abn. Soc. Psychol*, 55 (1957), 213–7.
17　L. M. Killian, 'The significance of multiple group membership in disaster', *Amer. J. Sociol.*, 57 (1952), 309–14.
18　E. E. Jones, K. Davis and K. J. Gergen, 'Role playing variations and their informational value for person perception', *J. Abn. Soc. Psychol.*, 63 (1961), 302–10.
19　H. Tajfel and A. L. Wilkes, 'Classification and quantitative judgement', *Brit. J. Psychol.*, 54 (1963), 101–4.
20　H. Tajfel and S. D. Cawasjee, 'Value and the accentuation of judged differences: a confirmation', *J. Abn. Soc. Psychol.*, 59 (1959), 436–9.
21　P. F. Secord, W. Bevan and B. Katz, 'The negro stereotype and perceptual accentuation', *J. Abn. Soc. Psychol.*, 53 (1956), 78–83.
22　G. W. Allport and L. J. Postman, *The Psychology of Rumor* (New York, Henry Holt & Co., 1947).
23　M. Argyle, *The Psychology of Interpersonal Behaviour* (Harmondsworth, Penguin Books, 1967).
24　E. Goffman, *Encounters* (London, Allen Lane, 1972).
25　R. F. Bales, *Interaction Process Analysis: a method for the study of small groups* (Cambridge, Mass., Addison Wesley, 1950).
26　K. Lewin, R. Lippitt and R. K. White, 'Patterns of aggressive be-

haviour in experimentally created "social climates" ', *J. Soc. Psychol.*, *10* (1939), 271–99.

27 E. Fromm, *The Fear of Freedom* (London, Routledge & Kegan Paul, 1942).

28 L. Festinger, H. W. Riecken Jr and S. Schachter, *When Prophecy Fails* (Minneapolis, University of Minnesota Press, 1956).

29 K. Lewin, 'Group decision and social change', in *Readings in Social Psychology* (Eds E. E. Maccoby, T. M. Newcomb, and E. L. Hartley), (New York, Holt, Rinehart & Winston, 1947), 197–211.

30 M. Deutsch, 'The effects of co-operation and competition upon group processes', in *Group Dynamics: research and theory* (Eds D. Cartwright and A. F. Zander), (London, Tavistock Publications, 1968).

31 L. K. Miller and R. L. Hamblin, 'Interdependence, differential rewarding and productivity', *Amer. Sociol. Rev.*, *28* (1963), 768–78.

32 J. W. Julian and F. A. Perry, 'Co-operation contrasted with intra-group and inter-group competition', *Sociometry*, *3* (1967), 79–90.

33 D. W. Taylor, P. C. Berry and C. H. Block, 'Does group participation when using brainstorming facilitate or inhibit creative thinking?', *Adm. Sci. Quart.*, *3* (1958), 23–47.

34 J. Cohen, 'Contact between minds', in *Readings in Psychology* (Ed. J. Cohen), (London, Allen & Unwin Ltd, 1964), 249–67.

35 J. W. Julian, D. W. Bishop and F. E. Fiedler, 'Quasi-therapeutic effects of intergroup competition', *J. Pers. Soc. Psychol.*, *3* (1966), 321–7.

36 M. A. Wallach, N. Kogan and D. J. Bem, 'Group influences on individual risk-taking', *J. Abn. Soc. Psychol.*, *65* (1962), 75–86.

37 M. A. Wallach, N. Kogan and D. J. Bem, 'Diffusion of responsibility and level of risk-taking in groups', *J. Abn. Soc. Psychol.*, *68* (1964).

38 M. A. Wallach, N. Kogan and R. B. Burt, 'Are risk-takers more persuasive than conservatives in group discussion?', *J. Exp. Soc. Psychol.*, *4* (1968), 76–88.

39 D. E. Krech, R. S. Crutchfield and E. L. Ballachey, *Individual in Society* (New York, McGraw Hill, 1962).

40 M. A. Wallach, N. Kogan and D. J. Bem, 'Diffusion of responsibility and level of risk-taking in groups', *J. Abn. Soc. Psychol.*, *68* (1964), 263–74.

41 R. Brown, *Social Psychology* (New York, The Free Press, 1965).

42 J. Rabow, F. J. Fowler, Jr, D. L. Bradford, M. A. Hofeller and Y. Shibuya, 'The role of social norms and leadership in risk-taking', *Sociometry*, *29* (1966), 16–27.

43 K. L. Higbee, 'Group risk-taking in military decisions', *J. Soc. Psychol.*, *88* (1972), 55–64.

44 H. Cantril, H. Gaudet and H. Hertzog, *The Invasion from Mars: a study in the psychology of panic* (Princeton, Princeton University Press, 1940).

45 E. Sampson, *Social Psychology and Contemporary Problems* (New York, John Wiley & Sons, 1971).

46 S. Schachter and J. S. Singer, 'Cognitive, social and physiological determinants of emotional state', *Psychol. Rev.*, *69* (1962), 379–99.

12

Conformity and Non-Conformity

If a man does not keep pace with his companions perhaps it is because he hears a more distant drummer.
H. D. Thoreau, *Walden*

As we noted in the previous chapter, one of the reasons why other people are important to us is that they provide the reflections we need to maintain our personal identity. A large part of this identity consists of our values, attitudes, beliefs and ideas about the external world and ourselves. However, it is in just these areas that we are in most need of confirmation, since their basis lies not in any absolute reality but rests upon social consensus. Physical aspects of the world such as size, weight, solidity and density are measurable by standard methods, and so subject to verification or falsification. We know that we cannot walk through walls and that if we jump from a high place we will be drawn irresistibly towards the ground. If we wish to know if bricks or wood are better for building a particular kind of structure we can put them both to the test and choose the more suitable material. When it comes to morality, opinion and belief, however, the situation is entirely different. Such judgements as 'good', 'bad', 'correct' or 'incorrect', when applied to human behaviour, have no yardstick universally agreed by all, but are a consequence of the shared assumptions of the members of a group or society and may or may not be assented to by the members of another group or society. These shared assumptions we may call the 'social reality' of the group. Since by its nature social reality is not testable in the way that physical reality is, it can include myths, legends, unrealistic expectations, and will from time to time come into conflict with the social reality of other groups. This situation is perhaps most apparent in times of war when each side is convinced that God is on their side and that the other side is the aggressor. Parents begin the process of social indoctrination by interpreting the world for the child and teaching him the norms and values of a particular society. The basis of comfortable social interaction is the fulfilling by others of our assumption that they will behave according to these norms and will not embarrass us, or question our view of reality, by indulging in 'odd' behaviour. If they conform to our expectations all is well and our view of the world receives confirmation. If they do not, then our interpretation of the way things should be is challenged.

The norms of a group are enforced by its members, usually quite unwittingly, by subtle rewards for 'correct' behaviour, for example showing interest, approval or smiling, and by punishing 'wrong' behaviour by showing irritation, yawning, frowning or open verbal disapproval. These methods of control are, of course, identical to those used by parents on their children. They are thus very powerful means of directing the behaviour of members of a group along the 'right' lines, and individual members come to take on certain characteristics in common, so that differences are less apparent and eccentricities are ironed out.

To say that someone is a conformist is often to imply that he suffers from weakness of the will or has no initiative. Without a certain amount of conformity from us all, however, we could not live in groupings at all. Total conformity, on the other hand, would lead to stagnation, since those in the vanguard of change are inevitably deviants from the established norms of the group or society. Unthinking obedience to every group pressure would endanger individual identity, as the person is forced to don a different cloak in different groups. Accepting group standards without question, however, does provide for security and protection from the ambiguous and complex nature of the world.

Individuality and conformity are not necessarily incompatible. Some groups may have norms about the acceptance of

P

individual differences. Therapeutic and encounter groups may have an ideology which involves tolerance and understanding of individual behaviour even if it is not agreed with. Originality can flourish in a group context as well as being stifled. Some conformity to society's standards is essential for mutual endeavour, but there are times when it may threaten innovations, development and individual freedom.

GROUP PRESSURE

Whenever a person deviates from the accepted behaviour in his group, the other members are likely to exert pressure to bring him back into line whether they and he are aware of it or not. The reason they do this is that non-conformity seems to make people uncomfortable. In a study by Schachter, students in a 'liberal' college took part in group discussions on the treatment of a juvenile delinquent whose case history was presented to them. They were asked to make a judgement on a 7-point scale running from 1 (extreme compassion) to 7 (extreme punishment), about what should happen to the boy. The experimenter inserted three 'stooges' into the discussion groups without the knowledge of the other participants; a 'deviant' who was told to adopt position 7 and stick to it, a 'slider' who was instructed to adopt position 7 initially, but to move gradually in the direction of the majority of group members, and a 'conformist' who went along with the group consensus. (It was assumed that being a liberal college the tendency of the group would be to adopt a median position round about 3 on the scale. This proved to be correct.) Measures of the communication in the group were taken and it was found that many more remarks were made to the 'deviant' than to anyone else, until a point was reached where it was realised that he would not change and he was then ignored. The 'slider' attracted a high number of remarks initially, but communication decreased as he moved to the median position. The 'conformist' received an average number of communications for the group.[1] Boys at an international club who were offered a choice of model aeroplanes, some gliders and some engine-powered, were brought into a discussion about the relative merits of engined and non-engined planes. One boy had previously been instructed to choose a glider, since it was assumed (rightly) that his companions would go for the powered models. During the discussion each boy supported his own choice and later they were asked to choose another boy to work with and a club president. The boy who had chosen the glider was overwhelmingly rejected by the other boys.[2]

Although the mass media paint our society as a 'permissive' one, there appears to be, in fact, wide intolerance of quite harmless non-conformity. Remaining seated during the National Anthem, shaving off one's hair if a woman, and growing it long if a man can provoke extreme reactions from some people, quite out of proportion to any imagined offence. Other sections of society may be equally antagonistic to short hair on men, a mortgage or a nine-to-five job. Where a group is dependent for its continuance upon the consensus of its members about a particular view of the world, then any doubt or questioning either direct or by implication can be a threat to the existence of that group. The antagonism shown during the nineteenth century to Darwin and Freud was so fierce because they challenged the reality which said that man was a rational being, placed on the earth by God and in a different category from other living things. Social norms acquire an apparently independent existence of their own and may take on moral tones – 'every right-thinking Englishman believes that'.

The impetus to the study of conformity was given by a series of experiments conducted by Asch. A group of eight people, seven of whom were confederates of the experimenter, were gathered round a table and required to make judgements about the length of lines, that is, they had to match one of three comparison lines with another line. The eighth man, or victim, was always last to give a decision. All judgements were given aloud. On some trials the confederates had been briefed to give wrong judgements unanimously, so that when it came to the 'victim' he was faced with the prospect of disagreeing in the face of group consensus which challenged the evidence of his own senses. In this predicament about one-third of subjects tested conformed to the majority verdict. Even where subjects remained independent there were signs of tension, hesitation and doubt.[3] Although some independent subjects appeared completely self-confident in giving their judgement, all reported some feeling of being under pressure. Those who withstood this pressure had strategies for coping with it, such as a belief in individuality, psychological withdrawal from the group, conscientiousness about the task, or a belief in their own competence.

Subjects who yielded to the pressure of group solidarity seemed to fall into three categories, those who reported that they actually began to see the majority verdict as correct, that is, they suffered a 'distortion of perception'; those who thought that they must be wrong if they didn't agree with the rest and so underwent a 'distortion of judgement'; and finally those who thought the group was wrong but did not wish to appear different or inferior and so showed a 'distortion of action'. These types of conformity will crop up again in the context of the effects on conformity of the relationship of the individual to the group.

A more sophisticated version of Asch's experiment involving the making of judgements on a variety of topics from arithmetic to art has also shown that about one-third of subjects will conform to a majority decision even when it is obviously wrong, but that this number increases dramatically, to something like 70 per cent, when the material to be judged is highly ambiguous, for example, when subjects are asked to say which of two figures of equal area is the bigger, or when asked to complete a number series which has in fact no solution.[4] It seems that the greater the uncertainty of the subjects and the ambiguity of the situation, the greater will be the conformity.

An earlier experiment supported this finding, since it employed a highly ambiguous situation and showed that a group can establish quite arbitrary norms of perception which persist in individuals even after the group has been disbanded. If a spot of light is seen in an absolutely dark room then it appears to move about, an effect (known as autokinetic) which is not in the external world, and which is likely to be different for each individual in the direction and size of apparent movement. Subjects were asked to view such a light in two conditions : firstly, alone in the room, they were asked to state how much the light was moving, and then they were put into a group to come to a unanimous decision. In the second condition, subjects viewed the light initially with a group which reached consensus on the movement of the light and were then asked to judge it whilst viewing alone. In the first situation individual judgements varied widely and group norms were established round about the mean of the individual estimates. In the second condition individual estimates showed a much narrower range and clustered about the previously established group norm.[5] Thus, in the absence of an objective measure by which to judge, group consensus is likely to have a powerful effect on individual judgement.

Another study has shown how this kind of arbitrarily established norm can be passed on from generation to generation of new members. The same set-up as described in the previous paragraph was used in a four-man group of whom three were initially confederates of the experimenter. The confederates held out for a very high degree of movement (16 ins) and a group norm was established at 14 ins. (In contrast, a control group of naïve subjects agreed on a norm of 4 ins.) After a series of trials the confederates were removed one at a time and replaced by naïve subjects, the group arriving at new estimates with each change. Even after the removal of all the original members of the experimental group, the norm for the movement of the light remained very high and it took eleven generations of subjects before the norm came down to the 4 ins norm of the control group.[6]

The experiments we have described so far have involved a mere verbal conformity. People have been influenced to say certain things about their judgement under the force of group consensus. This is very different from getting someone actually to do something which involves taking some action. Do the same effects occur when group pressure is used to force someone to perform an act that they would otherwise shun? Apparently they do, since it has been shown that subjects in an experiment can be induced to give people what they think are powerful electric shocks when under pressure from the demands of others for conformity.[7]

Most social norms, such as dress fashions and conventions, hair styles or modes of conduct, depend upon the cues which we receive from others. Our only frame of reference is the apparent beliefs and behaviour of others. People who are entering a new situation, such as joining a profession or starting at university, are very dependent upon the behaviour of others as models for their own actions, and as sources of information regarding the accepted things to do. If an individual perceives that his own view of the world is not entirely in accord with that of other people, he may assume, as did some of Asch's subjects, that the majority must be right.

Some individuals are more resistant to group pressure than others. They may derive strength from membership of a group other than the one they are in at the time and whose opinions they value more highly. They may have greater confidence in their own judgement than they have in that of others, especially in areas where they have special competence. The feelings that the person has about his or her own competence and independence are very important. Women, for example, seem to be more conformist than men, but particularly when the topic under discussion is regarded as a male concern such as politics. Past experience of what happens to non-conformists will also be influential – a person is more likely to conform if non-conformity has been punished in his past. In general, most of us feel the need to be found acceptable by others but the strength of this need will depend upon the attractiveness of a particular group and the length of time the association is going to last. Where an individual is forced to be a member of a group he dislikes and disagrees with he is likely to withdraw psychologically from it, and it will have little impact on him during the period of enforced interaction. If he likes the group, but disagrees with it, then the members will have more impact upon him even if he is not committed to further interaction with them.[8] If, however, one person expects to have to work with another person in the future then he is more likely to attempt to change undesirable aspects of the other's behaviour than if they will never meet again.[9]

Conformity has the effect often of reducing individual anxiety. If an individual is anxious about his acceptance by a group he will tend to become more conformist. Physiological indices of arousal show that conformity can reduce tension, but the effect only betrays itself where the individual is in a group which is important to him.[10]

As the results of Asch's experiment indicated, conformity can take more than one form. It has been suggested that in fact there are three types of conformity; compliance, identification and internalisation.[11] Compliance occurs when the individual conforms outwardly to secure something or to avoid being criticised by the group. Rather like Kohlberg's first stage of morality, this is an expedient conformity involving a 'distortion of action' but no change of attitude. Conformity to group norms will, therefore, only occur where the group can supervise the individual's behaviour. An example of this occurred in a clothing factory where a girl employed as a clothes presser initially exceeded group norms of output. Group pressure was brought to bear in the form of harassment and her output dropped. The group was later split up and the girl's output rose to its former level.[12] She had merely complied with the group standard, not accepted it. When identification occurs, the individual accepts the influence of the group because he wishes to remain a member of that group. This may involve a 'distortion of judgement' where the individual relies more on the decision of the group members than on his own perception of the situation. Thus being a 'good citizen' may be seen as an important aspect of being accepted by society, even if it conflicts with private desires. If, however, acceptance by the group ceases to be important, the individual may cease to conform to its values. Internalisation may be considered to have taken place when the values of the group are coincidental with those of the individual. There is no discrepancy between the way the individual and his group see the world. Internalisation may involve the individual in 'distortion of perception' where his views are initially different. Children come to see the world through their parents' eyes as they accept parental values and internalise what was once an external injunction. Attitudes acquired in this way are highly resistant to change since they form part of the personality structure of the individual. For this reason it takes a very drastic experience such as 'brainwashing' or psychoanalysis to affect this type of conformity.

On this formulation then, university students may be said to comply when they take examinations, to identify with each other in matters of dress, behaviour and certain opinions, and to internalise some values of the scholastic life which remain with them long after graduation, such as the value of criticism, the usefulness of research and a logical approach to problems. (It does not always work out like that, of course – some students may pay lip service to the usefulness of research and internalise the value of having a good capacity for beer.) From this is follows that what may appear to be behaviour which is arising out of the 'personality' of the individual may, in fact, be a consequence of external pressures and demands and not necessarily a prevailing characteristic of the person.

The influence of the situation can be seen by reference to another study where subjects were required to give electric shocks of increasing severity (supposedly) to another person. Many more people were able to resist the insistence of the experimenter that they carry out this task when they had a supporter than when they were alone.[13] Similarly in Asch's experiment subjects conformed much less when one other person confirmed their judgement.[14] The feeling that one is not alone increases independence and relieves the deviant individual of the thought that he is either mad or mistaken. This may be the reason why those whom society labels as odd are inclined to seek each other out in support of their particular social reality and form groups such as neurotics anonymous, flat-earthers or witches' covens. Whether one person can induce another to deviate from accepted norms will obviously depend upon their relationship, but even strangers can influence the conformity behaviour of others, especially if they are perceived as prestigious. A study of pedestrians violating traffic signals found that people are more likely to follow a 'high status' well-groomed man than a 'low status' scruffy man across a busy street when the lights are against pedestrians. The same man played both parts and his change from high to low status reduced traffic violations from 14 per cent to 4 per cent.[15]

Although situational effects may be the most important in

inducing conformity or non-conformity, the characteristics of the individual do, naturally, play a part, so the degree to which a person conforms will depend upon some combination of the situation and the individual. It has been suggested that some aspects of human behaviour can be represented by a J-shaped curve which reflects the transitional stages between totally conformist acts and totally non-conformist acts.[16] For

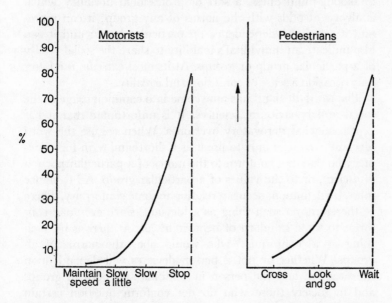

Figure 10   Compliance with traffic signs as a percentage of people observed

example, the vast majority of motorists coming up to a 'Stop' sign will obey it, a certain proportion will slow down a great deal, but keep rolling as they check that the road is clear, a small number will slow down only slightly, and a tiny minority will disregard the sign altogether. The situation is the same to all, but the reaction depends on the individual concerned. For the types of behaviour that have been studied in this way, for example, overstaying time at parking meters, clocking in at work, genuflecting in church, the great majority of people do the 'right' thing, some transgress slightly, a few make a mere gesture to conformity, and a very few behave as though the norm, convention, standard or prohibition did not exist (perhaps at the same time making a gesture of their own).

NON-CONFORMITY

Non-conformity also has three guises. It can come in the form of bloody-mindedness, a sort of professional deviancy which is always at odds with the norms of any group; it can represent a genuine independence on particular issues; and it can also indicate an individual's inability to share the social reality of a particular group or groups. At its most extreme the latter may occasion a sense of confusion and irreality.

The word 'deviant' has now come into common usage in the social and behavioural sciences. It is unfortunate that it has kept somewhat derogatory overtones. When we use the word 'deviant' we mean only to use it as a shorthand term for someone who does not conform to the mores of a particular portion of society, or to the values of a particular group. All deviance must, by definition, occur in relation to some conformity. There is, therefore, no such thing as a 'deviant' since everyone conforms to some standard of behaviour, just as there is no such thing as a 'conformist' who would obey the norms of all groups. Whether or not a person deviates will depend upon the situation and the person in combination. Both in groups and in society those who do not conform question certain accepted interpretations of reality and provide a channel for originality, creativity and change. Deviants disturb the harmonious view of the world of those who accept the norms of the majority without doubting. For this reason, they may be treated with resentment and hostility, ostracised, imprisoned, even shot. Their inability to find a job or perhaps a flat will be upheld as an awful warning to those who are tempted to transgress – 'That's what happens when you . . .'.

Many kinds of behaviour considered deviant in one society at one time have been regarded as completely orthodox by other societies and at other times. Cannabis has been smoked for centuries legally in many parts of the world, whilst still outlawed in this country. Women have worn trousers for millenia in China, but this has only recently become tolerated in the West. Homosexual love was considered a higher form of relationship than marriage in ancient Greece, but remains 'unnatural' in England today. The Vikings wore their hair long, but many people still believe that long hair on men looks effeminate.

Since everyone belongs to many groups, individuals may deviate from norms in one group because they have strongly held views derived from another group. In this way multiple group membership can act so as to transmit new ideas through established institutions. One of the great values of immigration is the opportunity it gives for the cross-fertilisation of customs and ideas, so preventing the stagnation of a society. Individuals may also deviate because they have special knowledge, as did Galileo of the movement of heavenly bodies and Darwin of the Galapagos finches. It has been suggested that some people are allowed greater latitude in disagreeing with their groups than others, through the establishment of what has been called rather elaborately 'idiosyncratic credit'. That is, conformity to the group in the early stages of the relationship confers the privilege of later being allowed to disagree.[17]

Any group which is relatively permanent – a committee, a family or a work group – tends to develop its own ideology, as we have noted. This brings the danger of stereotyped thinking that may become outmoded without continual up-dating. If fresh ways of tackling problems are to be found, there is a constant need for 'new blood', especially in a rapidly changing society. The introduction of new ideas will, however, be very difficult where the group's commitment to a particular social reality is very deep when it may erect defences which deny the validity of alternative interpretations and explanations.

As the experiments on group pressure have shown, people who recognise that the way they feel or think differs from that of the majority tend to blame themselves. So may people whose subjective reality conflicts with the way others say they ought to feel. A woman may have a nice husband, a lovely home and two and three-eighths (as prescribed by the national average) beautiful children. Everyone expects her to be happy, but she is not. In this situation she may well blame herself rather than the institution of marriage or society's norms and feeling guilty and depressed she will perhaps consult the doctor who could unwittingly confirm her view of herself by prescribing anti-depressants.

As indicated earlier, very few people feel able to rely on their own judgement, and so continually cross-reference their experience of reality with that of others. It has been said that many of the effects people get from smoking cannabis, or even injecting heroin, arise not out of the drug alone, but are a consequence of the social cues emanating from the group and the expectations the user has. Thus naïve smokers rarely experience a 'high' on the first or even the second occasion of taking pot. To achieve the desired effects it is necessary to learn from more experienced users how to interpret the physiological changes that occur.[18] [19] [20] [21]

Thus social reality within a group is not only a framework for the group's activities, but also serves to interpret the social experiences of individual members. A non-conformist within a drug-taking group would be someone who refused to accept the group's definition of how he should feel. Acquiring a taste for beer, cigarettes or winkles may follow a similar process. The other group members will try to 'make' the novitiate experience the 'correct' effects by encouraging him to interpret what may be rather unpleasant sensations in a positive way – 'it's great, man'. If these efforts are unsuccessful the group may react with pity, scorn or ridicule.

Those who fail to conform to the norms of the wider society may find themselves labelled as immoral, abnormal, criminal or sick, depending upon the context. Since all these terms depend for their effectiveness on the consensus of the members of society, they have, in fact, no other criteria than that at any one point in time a majority of people agree that they should be used. Labelling a person in this way helps the group or society to dissociate itself from the individual's behaviour and so reduces his status and influence. Harding has called this labelling 'a tool in the service of conservative trends'.[22] The fear of these labels is what encourages people to conceal what they regard as their own deviant behaviour and so live their lives behind a mask of careful conformity. Others may seek out fellow deviants to confirm they are not alone, and so movements like the hippies or the gay liberation front are formed. In this way social change is accomplished. Someone recognises that there is a discrepancy between the way he feels and the way he is 'supposed' to feel. Once he finds out that he is not alone the possibility for social action is present.

Some writers have drawn on studies of conformity and non-conformity in their discussion of mental illness.[23][24] The criteria of whether or not someone is mentally ill tend to depend on how far his behaviour and reported experience falls within what other people regard as normal. Since what is normal in behaviour and experience is dependent upon the social reality of the individual's group, it seems that the criteria of mental illness may not always refer to an illness as such, but merely to the socially unacceptable. In Russia, political deviants are likely to find themselves in a mental hospital. Not very long ago, in this country the defendants in an obscenity trial (the editors of an 'underground' magazine) were remanded for a psychiatric report; the inescapable implication being that those who question prevailing moral and political standards may be accused of insanity.

Labels may serve not only to control but also to relieve individuals of responsibility and retribution. Being able to attach a label such as 'madness' to one's actions can be used to evade responsibility for them, and some individuals may resort to this avenue of escape in times of personal and social confusion. A plea of mental instability could be used to avoid military service, for example. Labels, however, have an unfortunate way of becoming stereotypes. Once categorised as 'mad', a person may find it extremely difficult, even when 'cured', to persuade others that he is not also totally irresponsible, unreliable, violent and undesirable.

Just as some discrepancies between subjective and social reality may be regarded as signs of illness, others may be regarded as signs of 'personality defects'. In studies of crime and delinquency there tends to be a focus on the history and characteristics of individuals who have broken the law, rather than upon the social environment in which they live, and an underplaying of the well-established fact that most people who come before the courts are a selected sample from poorly housed, poorly educated and under-privileged sections of the population. Apart from attempts to improve the security of property, crime prevention usually centres on the 'reform' and 'treatment' of the criminal.

Similarly, in community health projects propaganda is directed at the individual, to encourage him to stop smoking or to go for a health check, whilst the social environment within which these behaviours occur is largely ignored, sometimes for the sake of expediency – like tobacco revenue. Attempts to change the attitudes rather than the social reality within which they exist are, in fact, rarely successful. An example of this is where sailors visiting a particular port were bombarded with information trying to persuade them to visit a V.D. clinic. The campaign met with little success. Eventually it was realised that the principal reason for this lay not in the laziness, fear or apathy of the sailors, but in the fact that the clinic was situated three miles from the docks, and, in the absence of public transport, an expensive taxi ride away. The obvious solution was to move the clinic to the docks or have a mobile unit go on board the ships.[25] The above illustrations demonstrate the widespread tendency of much social engineering, to focus upon the individual rather than institutions as a target for change, in spite of the known inefficiency of the former policy. This may be because those engaged in carrying out social policy are often themselves pillars of society's institutions.

CREATIVITY AND SOCIAL CHANGE

Originality and creativity are often allied, at least in popular speech, with insanity – crazy painters, eccentric professors, mad scientists, unstable musicians, are all part of our social mythology. A recent book by a well-known psychiatrist has taken up this theme with a consideration of the 'psychopathology' of some famous thinkers, writers and artists.[26] This approach is to align 'normality' with banality. There is a statistical sense in which creativity could be considered abnormal, that is, indicating a relatively rare event, but abnormality has connotations beyond the statistically infrequent and sets up the notion that those who have a new idea or question the existing order of things are somehow mentally unbalanced.

There is some evidence that those who remain independent in the face of group pressure do differ in some respects from those who conform. A study of the self-descriptions of 'independents' and 'yielders' in an Asch-type situation revealed that those of the 'independents' tended to include such things as originality, open-mindedness, emotional reactivity and excitability, lack of social ease and the absence of tact. 'Independents' also preferred complex rather than simple patterns and were in favour of uncertainty and contradiction as a challenge to thought. 'Yielders' on the other hand saw themselves as easy-going, helpful, patient, stable, modest and healthy-minded.[27] Some of these adjectives may refer to the degree to which people are sensitive to group pressure, that is, recognise that they may upset the group by not going along with it.

Other studies have also found a relationship between non-conformity and creativity in such areas as scientific research.[28] It is possible that conformists may be doubtful about their own competence and, therefore, fear to step aside from well-trodden paths of thoughts. People who are different merely for the sake of it (the 'professional' non-conformists) are also rarely creative since their behaviour is a calculated opposite to the accepted behaviour. Walking to work on one's hands may be different but is scarcely creative.

The ability to be original in some sense and to challenge old ideas seems to be related to methods of child-rearing which may affect the level of abstract thought that can be achieved. If we recall Piaget's idea of the schema, it may be that schemata are organised at different levels, one of the dimensions being the level of abstractness. Someone who has a high level of abstractness is not tied in his thinking to small concrete details, but is able to see the wider plan and explore it. Someone whose thinking is at a lower level may show stereotyped, rule-dominated behaviour.[29] It is possible to imagine that all levels will exist within one person and that certain environments may engage a particular level of thought at particular times. That is, creativity, like non-conformity is a consequence of some combination of the person and the social situation rather than a talent possessed only by some exceptional people.

The higher levels of abstract thought are said to require a maximum feedback of information about our own behaviour as we explore the world, so that environments which restrict the behaviour of children and adults to a narrow range of activity are likely to constrict conceptual thinking. At least one study has established a relationship between parental training and the conceptual level of children. Boys allowed to explore with a minimum of interference and so gain a maximum feedback of information about both their successes and their failures were found to be at a higher level of conceptual development than boys of the same age who were over-protected and over-dominated.[30] Fairly consistent patterns of child-rearing were found in a sample of architects considered by their colleagues to be the most original in their field.[31] As children they had been given freedom to explore within well-defined but wide limits and had apparently developed a certain independence of the help or approval of others. There was a suggestion that emotional ties to parents were not very strong, which may have liberated them from the fear of loss of affection for exhibiting 'wrong' behaviour.

The school environment may encourage or inhibit exploratory and creative behaviour and thought. Disapproval of question-asking or the following of independent lines of thought, an insistence on obedience and the raising of popularity to a virtue, may all be practices which tend to reduce original thinking. Discovery methods of learning tend to encourage creativity, but are not as appropriate as rote methods for such skills as reading and writing.[32] Creative spelling may have its charms, but can make communication difficult.

An analysis of both creative scientists and original artists suggests that they have many characteristics in common. Freedom to think and act outside the accepted range is the essence of original thought, but this freedom is not one of total normlessness. Rather it is the ability to recognise and be familiar with the rules combined with the capacity to abandon them in favour of new solutions. Indeed, it may be that scientific discovery itself depends upon the tension between tradition

and revolution – between knowing the rules and being prepared to break them.[33] A similar tension may well underlie
the forces that bring about social and political change.

More members of our society today seem to end up in
prisons, community homes, mental hospitals, hostels for
alcoholics or other institutions than ever before. A growing
army of psychiatrists, psychologists, social workers, welfare
officers and policemen attempt to deal with the problems of
the society. This may imply increased concern on the part
of the authorities, but it may also imply a lack of tolerance on
the part of the general public and an attempt to impose homo-
geneity on the population. We may draw an analogy between
the need for individual genetic variability in a population if
it is to survive and the need for variety in behaviour, thought
and belief which will enable us to adapt to a rapidly changing
technology and way of life. Groups of people are, in general,
reluctant to adopt novel solutions unless they are persuaded
that they work in practice. To supply these demonstrations
some members of society need to be free to experiment with
new life styles. The mere recommending of change is (like anti-
smoking propaganda) generally ineffective, although loudly-
voiced and prolonged criticism may eventually win sufficient
converts to effect change.

Socio-political deviants may deliberately or accidentally show
others that there are alternative forms of behaviour. Thus in
Alabama, USA, in 1955, Rosa Parks refused to give up her
seat to a white man on a segregated bus, because her feet
were hurting. For this 'crime' she was arrested, but the event
also triggered off a new phase in the civil rights movement.[34]

Many people believe, with the best intentions, that we
should attempt to rid society of conflict, stress and tension
within and between groups of individuals. However, some
collision between opposing ideas and behaviours is necessary
for individual development and growth, not only in children,
but also in adults and societies. Governments could only
eradicate conflict by the erosion of personal responsibility and
the creation of identical automata. This inhuman prospect is
unlikely since child-rearing methods vary from family to family
and at times within the same family and our inheritance is in-

dividual and our interpretations of reality are idiosyncratic. The environment, moreover, constantly forces upon us reconsideration of what is or is not appropriate behaviour, so that no blue-print for 'ideal' human behaviour can ever be possible.

There are perhaps two things to be considered in the matter of social change. Firstly, if a society can change then this can be either for better or for worse – traditional elements may be more desirable than novel ones or vice versa. Thus individuals in a society should attempt to participate at each moment of choice and seek empirically tested criteria for what is desirable at any one time. Secondly, responsible choice is very difficult since there are always sections of society that want change at any price, whilst other factions will defend to the death the status quo.[35] Planned change based upon knowledge, however, seems preferable to unplanned change based upon opinion.

It is important in considering the future of our society that the existence of agencies for social tidiness should not stifle deviations from quite arbitrary norms of attitude, belief and behaviour by attempts at 'cure' and control. A dynamic and flexible society needs its rebels, and the danger of a compassionate society is that people may be reduced to conformity 'for their own good', with a consequent stifling not only of individual growth, but also of the dynamism of the society itself.

REFERENCES

1 S. Schachter, 'Deviation, rejection and communication', *J. Abn. Soc. Psychol.*, *46* (1951), 190–207.
2 S. Schachter, 'Cross-cultural experimental research: method, problems and factual findings in an international study in group behaviour', *Acta. Psychol.*, *11* (1955), 208–10.
3 S. E. Asch, 'Effects of group pressures upon modification and distortion of judgements', in *Readings in Social Psychology* (Eds E. E. Maccoby, T. M. Newcomb, and E. L. Hartley), (New York, Holt, Rinehart, 1958), 3rd edition, 174–83.
4 R. S. Crutchfield, 'Conformity and character', *Amer. Psychologist*, *10* (1955), 191–8.

5 M. Sherif, 'An experimental approach to the study of attitudes', *Sociometry, 1* (1937), 90–8.

6 R. C. Jacobs and D. T. Campbell, 'The perpetuation of an arbitrary tradition through several generations of a laboratory microculture', *J. Abn. Soc. Psychol., 62,* 649–58.

7 S. Milgram, 'Group pressure and action against a person', *J. Abn. Soc. Psychol., 69* (1964), 137–43.

8 C. A. Kiesler and L. H. Corbin, 'Commitment, attraction and conformity', *J. Pers. Soc. Psychol., 2* (1965), 890–5.

9 C. A. Kiesler, S. B. Kiesler and M. S. Pallak, 'The effect of commitment to future interaction on reactions to norm violations', *J. Pers., 35* (1967), 585–99.

10 K. W. Back, M. D. Bogdonoff, D. M. Shaw and R. A. Klein, 'An interpretation of experimental conformity through physiological measures', *Behavioural Sci., 8* (1963), 34–40.

11 H. Kelman, 'Compliance, identification and internalisation', *J. Conflict Resolution, 2* (1958), 51–60.

12 L. Coch and J. R. P. French, Jr, 'Overcoming resistance to change', *Hum. Relations, 1* (1948), 512–32.

13 S. Milgram, 'Liberating effects of group pressure', *J. Pers. Soc. Psychol., 1* (1965), 127–34.

14 S. E. Asch, 'Effects of group pressures upon modification and distortion of judgements', in *Readings in Social Psychology* (Eds E. E. Maccoby, T. M. Newcomb and E. L. Hartley (New York, Holt Rinehart, 1958), 3rd edition, 174–83.

15 M. Lefkowitz, R. R. Blake and J. S. Mouton, 'Status factors in pedestrian violation of traffic signals', *J. Abn. Soc. Psychol., 51* (1955), 704–5.

16 F. Allport, 'The J-curve hypothesis', *J. Soc. Psychol., 5* (1934), 141–83.

17 E. P. Hollander, 'Competence and conformity in the acceptance of influence', *Psychol. Rev., 65* (1958), 117–27.

18 J. Young, *The Drugtakers* (London, MacGibbon & Kee, 1971).

19 H. Becker, 'On becoming a marijuana user', in *Outsiders* (Ed. H. Becker), (Glencoe, Ill., The Free Press, 1963).

20 K. Lindesmith, 'Problems in the social psychology of addiction', in *Narcotics* (Eds D. Wilner and G. Kassebaum), (1965).

21 H. Isbell and W. White, 'Clinical characteristics of addiction', *Amer. J. Med., 14* (1953), 558.

22 D. W. Harding, *Social Psychology and Individual Values* (London, Hutchinson University Library, 1966), 3rd edition.

23 T. Szasz, *The Manufacture of Madness* (London, Routledge & Kegan Paul, 1971).

24 E. Goffman, *Asylums* (New York, Anchor Books, Doubleday, 1961).

25 A. P. Woudenberg, personal communication.

26 A. Storr, *The Dynamics of Creation* (London, Secker & Warburg, 1972).

27 F. Barron, *Creativity and Psychological Health* (Princeton, New Jersey, Van Nostrand, 1963).

28 R. S. Crutchfield, 'Conformity and creative thinking', in *Contemporary Approaches to Creative Thinking* (Eds H. E. Gruber, G. Terrell and M. Wertheimer), (New York, Atherton, 1962).

29 O. J. Harvey, D. E. Hunt and H. M. Schroder, *Conceptual Systems and Personality Organisation* (New York, John Wiley & Sons, 1961).

30   H. J. Cross, 'The relation of parental training conditions to conceptual level in adolescent boys', *J. Pers., 34* (1966), 348–65.

31 D. W. MacKinnon, 'The personality correlates of creativity: a study of American architects', *Proceedings of the 14th Congress on Applied Psychology, 2* (1962), 11–39.

32 B. R. Worthen, 'Discovery and expository task presentation in elementary mathematics', *J. Educ. Psychol., 59* (1968), 1–13.

33 T. Kuhn, *The Structure of Scientific Revolutions* (Chicago, University of Chicago Press, 1970), 2nd edition.

34 H. Toch, *The Social Psychology of Social Movements* (London, Methuen, 1971).

35 D. W. Harding, *Social Psychology and Individual Values* (London, Hutchinson, 1966), 3rd edition.

13

Coping with Stress

I was much further out than you thought
And not waving but drowning.
Stevie Smith, *Not Waving but Drowning*

The need to keep oneself secure, both physically and psychologically, is fundamental in human motivation. Early in life this security is provided to some degree by parents and the extent to which they are able to make the child feel safe has, as we have seen, important implications for the individual's emotional development. As the child grows into adulthood a variety of strategies are learned for coping with stressful situations. It is probably essential that mild stresses should be experienced in childhood if the individual is to be able to cope with threatening situations later in life.

Most of the human experiences that we have considered so far – childhood, family life, work and social situations – can give rise to sensations that are felt as stressful by the individual. Stress, in engineering terms, is said to be present when a system or structure is under some strain. In psychological terms it may be said to be present when environmental, social or self-generated strains tax an individual's capacity to cope and threaten physical or psychological systems with breakdown.

Animals respond to threat with either flight, fight or freezing. Human beings may also withdraw, attack or become apathetic and depressed, show fatalistic acceptance or chronic anxiety. These various responses may or may not be appropriate depending upon their long-term or short-term efficiency in protecting the person and upon their correspondence to the extent and degee of reality of the threat. The subjective awareness that one is under threat is accompanied by physiological changes such as increased sweating, more rapid breathing, accelerated heart rate and a reduced blood supply to the stomach. These changes which are mediated by the adrenal glands help to divert more oxygen and sugar to the muscles and so prepare the body for physical attack or retreat. These reactions are obviously highly adaptive in the face of the kind of physical emergencies which must have faced our ancestors, but are not so appropriate as responses to a nagging wife or a job beyond one's capabilities – psychological stresses which give rise to the same physiological changes. Actual physical action acts so as to dissipate the hormonal reactions which also occur under stress, but often in our society physical action is barred. Thus the archetypal executive sits behind his desk still smarting from his wife's remarks over breakfast, trying to meet an encroaching deadline, is subjected to some harassment from his boss, and experiences all the effects that would have led Stone Age man to run away or to attack. Our executive, however, has these solutions blocked, since they could lead to an even greater threat of losing his job. The bodily changes, therefore, last much longer and are not compensated for by physical activity. Constant arousal of this kind may eventually give rise to organic changes in the body such as ulcers.

Reactions to stress will vary with differences in upbringing, culture, social class and environment. High blood pressure without organic origin, for example, is a disease associated with stress and is frequent among North American city-dwelling blacks who live in conditions of tension and suppressed aggression, whilst it is rare in Central and Western Africa. One of the greatest killers of middle-aged men in the West is coronary heart disease, which, it has been suggested may arise in part from the conflicts, competition and self-control that our culture presents both at home and at work.[1] Jobs which present constant 'emergencies' may also strain the individual's capacity to adapt. Bus drivers, for example, are especially prone to cardiovascular disease, whilst their colleagues who work as conductors and who, therefore, face fewer emergencies and get more exercise, are less susceptible.[2]

In addition to environmental variables each individual will

have a different definition of what constitutes stress for him, and will also, depending upon constitution and the strategies he has evolved for self-protection, have a different point of collapse. Some people may adapt by the use of external aids which help in the short term, but which may eventually be maladaptive themselves. So some people may ward off anxiety with drugs (whether supplied by a doctor or by a 'pusher'), with alcohol, or with a rigid system of psychological defences, whilst others may acknowledge defeat with a suicide bid.

FEAR AND ANGER

Whether we label sensations as joy, sorrow, anger or fear on the basis of the physiological sensations alone, or on the accompanying words, thoughts, images and social cues, is still uncertain. Man's ability to anticipate future events, however, means that he can feel fear in advance of danger and so the thought can give rise to the same kind of physiological changes as the actuality (a concept not unknown to the authors of pornographic literature). Anticipated fear may be realistic and assist the person to cope with danger by enabling plans to be made in advance. Sometimes the very uncertainty of the future, regardless of actual events, may cause some people to be in a constant state of anxiety and preparedness for dangers that never arrive. Anticipation of dental surgery may lead to as great a secretion of emergency hormones as does the actual physical pain and tissue damage which accompanies the surgery.[3] There are individuals who react to the idea of threat by denying its existence and so may be unprepared for the actuality of danger. Both over-anticipation and failure to anticipate are poor forms of adaptation since they lack correspondence with reality.

Although secretions from the adrenal cortex produce the reactions we have described in either fear or anger, there are differences between these two states. Fear leads to the secretion of adrenalin and gives rise to facial pallor and blood is drawn away from the stomach. In anger nor-adrenalin is secreted and blood is diverted to the face and brain and to the stomach. These differences may be related to the need for active or passive responses as an adaptation to the environment in different species. Animals such as lions which react aggressively to danger have relatively high concentrations of nor-adrenalin in the blood, whilst those such as rabbits and baboons which flee and conceal themselves, have a preponderance of adrenalin.[4] If human beings are highly aroused and able to take action then both adrenalin and nor-adrenalin are produced in large quantities, whereas if they are aroused but must remain passive (as for an interview) then adrenalin only is secreted.[5]

FEAR AND ANXIETY

In some animals fear appears to be an innate response to particular stimuli; it aids survival by leading to flight or fight and, therefore, has selective evolutionary advantage. In human beings a startle response to sudden loud noises and convulsive hand-gripping as a reaction to fear of falling are present from birth. The genetic basis of fear responses in birds has been demonstrated by rearing chaffinches in isolation. When confronted with a model resembling an owl they react with alternate curiosity and approach, and fear and avoidance tendencies, moving back and forth.[6] Toddlers often display a similar alternation of shyness and interest in a strange adult. Human infants develop a fear of strangers at about five months of age, that is, after they are capable of distinguishing the strange from the familiar.[7] Fear of snakes seems to be almost universal amongst primates, such as chimpanzees, and is very common in Man. It is not apparent in children at age 2, but at 3 and 4 years of age there is great caution in the child's reaction to a snake and from then on fear increases in intensity up to adolescence. This could be explained by the fact that children may learn that snakes are likely to be dangerous, but since chimpanzees reared in isolation display a similarly maturing reaction to snakes it appears that this fear may have an innate basis.[8]

Objects that are ambiguous, combining familiar and unfamiliar elements, such as a model of the head of a chimpanzee or a skull, also arouse fear with increasing intensity after the first few months of a chimpanzee's life. Ambiguity and unpredictability may also be at the heart of the common human fears of mice, spiders and darkness. Fear of the dark is a common phenomenon in children from 2 to 5 years old and so is fear of animals around the years of 2 to 4. An investigation of children's fears found that whereas 14 per cent of children in the sample reported that they were afraid of both animals and the dark, only 2 per cent mentioned these things as having been part of the worst thing that had ever happened to them.[9]

Although Freud was inclined to interpret such fears as manifestations of mutiny from the Id (snakes being a particularly suggestive symbol) it seems much more likely that fears of the unfamiliar, the dark, or animals have an evolutionary significance and may, therefore, have an inherited basis. They all represent conditions in which danger is likely to threaten.

Fears can, of course, be learned, as when a particular experience is associated with pain or shock and subsequently comes to be avoided because of the anticipation of unpleasantness (as Albert was conditioned to fear the white rat). Learned fears can be protective where they are realistic, but may become psychologically crippling if they become phobias that prevent people from leaving their homes or entering crowded places. In such conditions the fear may assume a central position in the person's existence so that the whole of his life is built around it. Such an intense fear may be compounded with another, which is the fear that other people will find out and so the sufferer may avoid seeking help or have to invent elaborate excuses for, say, not visiting friends and relatives. The complexity of our social life and our ability for symbolic thought mean that fear can also be aroused by blows to our self-esteem, making a fool of oneself, not being liked and so on. Such fears may be more or less realistic.

It is sometimes thought convenient to distinguish between fear as a reaction to an actually existing external threat, and anxiety as an anticipation of a future event or a feeling containing some element of irrationality. A temporal distinction may also be made between short-term situational anxiety which centres on a particular event, such as speaking in public, and persistent long-term anxieties about social competence or loss of self-control. Anxiety can also be 'free-float-ing', that is, unrelated to any particular event or idea, but existing as a more or less permanent state of the individual. It has been suggested that such chronic anxiety is related to the lack of the development of basic trust in oneself and others in childhood.[10][11] Freud wrote of anxiety as a 'threat to the Ego',[12] believing it to arise from the insistent demands of the Id with which the Ego is unable to cope. It has been shown that approximately 30 per cent of lower-middle and working-class mothers use threats of abandonment, in a few cases even suicide, as a means of controlling their children.[13] In these circumstances it is hardly surprising that some people may suffer from chronic feelings of insecurity. Other people, be-cause of their physical appearance, may be subjected to more potential threats than others: the crippled, the obese, a black man in a white land, for example, may be subjected to a re-latively high number of blows to their self-esteem. A distinc-tion between fear and anxiety may only be meaningful at the extremes so that fear of an external object, such as an enraged lion, may be distinguished from anxiety as a state of constant arousal involving no objective threat. However, most fears such as fear of illness, old age, or loneliness contain both realistic and irrational elements. Moreover, the fact that a particular fear may be peculiar to only one individual, and thus by definition, 'subjective', does not make that fear any the less unpleasant or real to the individual concerned.

As we might predict from arousal theory, low levels of fear or anxiety improve performance on simple tasks. Extreme or prolonged arousal of this kind, however, leads eventually to a total disruption of behaviour and, at the extreme, to panic, loss of the sense of reality, thought-blocking and a disregard for social conventions. An experimental demonstration of 'panic' shows how anxiety disrupts adaptive behaviour. Sub-jects played a game in which they had to press buttons to illuminate a succession of lights on a board and 'escape' through a single exit. When several people played at once only one subject's light could occupy any one position on the board at any one time. Far fewer subjects managed to 'escape' if the players were given electric shocks for not escaping within a time limit. Without electric shocks subjects co-operated and ensured a large number of 'escapes' within the same time. The introduction of shock raised anxiety levels, lowered co-operation and led to maladaptive rushing for the exit, thus blocking it.[14] Anxiety affects the organisation and effectiveness of thought processes, as demonstrated in an experiment in which subjects were asked to report words which were flashed on to a screen. Initially exposure time was too short for recognition, but was gradually increased and subjects were asked to guess at the words on each exposure. Some of those taking part were harassed and criticised and took much longer to guess correctly than did a control group. Moreover, their guesses were much more restricted in range, suggesting a narrow and stereotyped frame of reference.[15]

A common result of anxiety is the development of a rigid 'safe' and patterned way of responding to the complexities and uncertainties of life and cutting down on the intake of new information. This is especially true of occupations where there are frequent crises and high levels of uncertainty, such as hospital work, the police and the army. It is no coincidence that these are situations in which there exist hierarchies of command, formality of interaction and myriad regulations which attempt to counterbalance stress by providing a secure framework. The resultant inflexibility restricts the impact of changes occurring in the wider society and may make it difficult to introduce novel ideas and alternative solutions to problems.

Attempts to change attitudes by using information that is in itself threatening may prove counter-productive by provoking fight, perhaps a verbal attack on the source of the information, or flight in the form of a psychological running away. Thus the news that cigarette-smoking contributes to the causation of cancer may be too frightening to be effective. A study of the effect of lectures on dental hygiene on improving care of the teeth found that a mild threat was more effective than either a low or high threat.[16] People who do not see themselves as vulnerable are more likely to respond with the desired action to strong threats of danger than to mild threats, but those who see themselves as very vulnerable become fatalistic or apathetic if highly threatened and are more likely to respond positively to lower levels of fear arousal.[17]

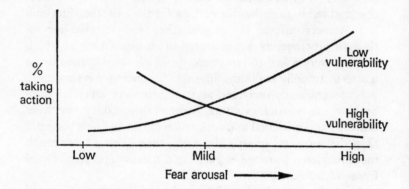

Figure 11   Self-perceived vulnerability and the effects of a fear-arousing communication

COPING WITH THREAT

It has been suggested that there are two stages in any coping process; primary appraisal in which a threat is recognised and secondary appraisal during which some action is decided upon.[18] What one person considers to be a dangerous situation requiring action may not seem so to another. Moreover an action which would not be considered under mild threat may be adopted if the threat is greater. A lecturer would probably not give up his job if lecturing made him mildly anxious, but he would if he began to have attacks of speechless panic.

Identifying the source of a fear is also important if adequate means of coping with it are to be found. If the origin of the threat cannot be identified or if it is too diffuse or powerful to be faced, then a scapegoat may be sought and found. So it is said that the incidence of racial prejudice increases in times of economic instability.[19] It has been reported that, just before the Second World War, stories appeared in English and American newspapers about Nazi atrocities in the concentration camps which led to reprisals being taken against the inmates who were accused of supplying the information to the newspapers. In this situation the people in the camps were unable to direct their hostility at the guards and instead blamed the journalists for publishing the stories.[20]

Anticipation of a feared event can sometimes be beneficial if it helps the individual to come to terms with reality. A study of patients undergoing surgery found that those who showed moderate anxiety before their operation had the fewest post-operative symptoms. Those with very low anxiety beforehand showed great distress afterwards as did those who were highly anxious in anticipation (categorised as chronic worriers).[21] It may be that some advance worrying allows people to consider outcomes and activate their coping strategies, whereas lack of anticipatory worrying leads to greater shock when the event occurs.

Some individuals may be characterised as poor copers by virtue of the fact that they feel as if they have no control over their own lives. They have few means of dealing with problems and are inclined to accept 'fate' as the biggest force in their lives. They thus give up the battle, a strategy which may well cause them less stress than those who struggle on in a difficult situation.[22]

EGO DEFENCE MECHANISMS

When an individual cannot cope realistically with a threat he or she may resort to what are known as 'ego defence mechanisms'.[23] Some of these, such as denial, avoidance and scapegoating, which protect the self from external danger, have already been mentioned. A person may also feel menaced by unacceptable ideas and feelings that arise from the existence of forbidden tendencies within himself. Although sometimes found in severe forms when they may be socially and psychologically disabling, defence mechanisms are resorted to by all of us at times and, by cushioning blows to our self-esteem, serve a useful function. They may become maladaptive when they prevent the individual from coming to terms with reality and perhaps changing some aspects of his behaviour, a course which might improve long-term adjustment.

Individuals may refuse to recognise or admit something by

denying its existence ('I'm not aggressive'), by compartmentalising information or by failing to realise the implications of their actions. Alcoholics who insist they are social drinkers, ladies with a lump in the breast who pretend it's not there, are practising forms of denial. The military chaplain who sees no wrong in blessing the bombers has managed to put his beliefs into separate compartments. A study of denial in polio patients suggested that if not prolonged it may help adaptation. The patients initially called the diagnosis nonsense or cheerfully refused to discuss it. Later they began to ask for information about their illness and became less defensive but more depressed. The authors believed that the initial denial protected them from the full impact of the shock.[24] This kind of denial has been shown to prevent arousal of the adrenal glands. Parents of children dying of leukaemia, who refused to accept the truth showed less evidence of adrenal cortical secretions than did parents who believed the diagnosis.[25]

Raising a problem to a high intellectual plane may also help to reduce feelings of fear and anxiety. Most of us are probably familiar with those people who deal with their emotional feelings by assimilating them to some intellectualised system of beliefs, which lessens their impact. Again this may prevent actual physiological arousal. In one study a film was shown to male students which concerned circumcision rites carried out among Australian aborigines who used a stone implement for the occasion. The audience were divided into four groups: those who saw the film without the soundtrack; those who saw the film and heard a soundtrack which emphasised the anthropological interest of the events shown; those who saw the film and heard a soundtrack which denied that the boys felt any pain or discomfort; and those who saw the film and heard a soundtrack which focused upon the pain and mutilation involved. Before, during and after the film all the students had their blood pressure, heart and respiration rates and skin resistance measured. The results showed that those students who had been in the group which heard pain emphasised manifested the greatest physiological arousal, closely followed by those who had heard no soundtrack. Those students who had heard the soundtrack denying pain or intellectualising the ceremony showed little deviation from the base line measures.[26]

Such protective devices may well be essential in some jobs, such as medicine, where a clinical, intellectual approach or the use of 'sick' jokes and humour help the individual to cope with the pain and suffering around him. In other situations, such as pretending that someone dead is really alive, or refusing to admit that spitting blood could indicate illness, denial may well be maladaptive in the long run.

Another defence commonly used to justify one's behaviour or beliefs is rationalisation. Emotional or unacceptable arguments may be dressed up in pseudo-logical or fashionable clothing. Rationalisation allows one to claim worthy and acceptable motives for what may really be regarded as somewhat disreputable behaviour, like the psychologist who claimed he went to strip clubs to study the audience. It may be that this attempt to find praiseworthy explanations for one's actions begins in childhood when children are expected to give socially acceptable accounts of themselves.[27] Fear of the disapproval of oneself is as powerful in guiding explanations as that of other people. So we may come to believe in our own rationalisations.

People may regress to earlier successful ways of behaving if they cannot cope with present situations. Hospital patients commonly become childishly dependent and protect themselves against anxiety by relying on their substitute parents (doctors and nurses) to make everything well again. Regression is also used by children who are jealous of a newly arrived brother or sister – they attract attention by returning to an earlier 'babyish' mode of adjustment. Wives and husbands may react to marital crises by going home to mother. Where a person is very disturbed by the recognition of some trait in themselves that they have learned to regard as unacceptable (whether other people find it so or not) they may, in order to keep this at bay, over-value the opposite characteristic. Thus, it has been suggested that advocates of extreme sexual purity have difficulty in coming to terms with their own sexuality. Fear of aggression in oneself may be displayed in an exaggerated sweetness and politeness. This is not to say that all moral atti-

tudes arise out of their opposites, but rather that the excessive
zeal with which certain individuals pursue the sins of others
suggests an emotional rather than a rational basis.

One way of coping with aggression aroused, say, by parents
or bosses, may be to displace it on to inanimate objects
(hurling an ashtray across the room) or on to scapegoats or
subordinates. Husbands unable to answer back at work may
come home and shout at the children. Hospital patients who
cannot complain to doctors or nurses because of their dependent position, may quarrel with visitors or berate ward
orderlies. It also seems possible for a person to project his or
her own feelings outwards and this is found in an extreme
form in those who see themselves as surrounded by hostile
conspirators. The behaviour of this type of suspicious individual
may so antagonise other people as to bring about a self-fulfilling prophecy. Pleasant emotions may also be projected so that
the world is viewed through rose-tinted spectacles, and someone
in love may be unable to see why everyone else is not
enamoured of the adored object.

Anna Freud has postulated two forms of identification which
may act as a defence against anxiety.[28] Identification with a
'lost object' can occur when the person loses someone important to him. Thus a child whose father dies may adopt some
of his father's mannerisms as though to compensate for his
absence. Identification with 'the aggressor' may occur when
the target of dislike is too dangerous to attack and where withdrawal is impossible. Bettleheim has described concentration
camp inmates who almost outdid the guards in brutality towards their fellow prisoners.[29] They thus protected themselves
from the profound terror of utter powerlessness by identifying
with the supreme power of the guards. Black policemen in
New York may react to their conflicts by being harsher towards blacks than their white colleagues. The alternative –
identification with the victim – is not really open to them once
they have donned police uniform. Some writers have postulated that large groups may use self-deception to distort or deny
disturbing information, as the Germans denied or rationalised
Nazi brutalities, and Americans denied the truth of the My
Lai massacre in Vietnam.[30] The fact that young black Ameri-

cans tend to express a higher level of self-esteem on personality tests than whites of the same age has been interpreted as compensation and protective rationalisation against widespread discrimination and actual or feared failure.[31]

AGGRESSION

One alternative response to defence is attack. We will define aggression as any action or thought whose aim is physical or psychological injury.[32] Aggression is usually considered to be undesirable, but in animal societies it plays an important part in survival by establishing territories and dominance hierarchies. In Man, it is claimed by some psychologists to be the source of ambition, competition and achievement.[33] In animals most contests over territory or dominance consist of psychological warfare – the males roar, show their teeth, wave antlers, plumes, crests, neck ruffs or exhibit the erect penis, according to species. Animals with sharp teeth usually push rather than wound each other. These means of avoiding hurt may have cultural concomitants in Man such as the convention that you do not kick a man when he's down, and the 'rules' of warfare.

Aggression is another piece of behaviour which has been involved in the 'Nature/Nurture' controversy. Early textbooks of psychology list 'pugnacity' as an instinct, and Freud, depressed by world events, decided that Man had a destructive drive, 'Thanatos', which complemented his sexual drive, 'Eros'.[34] Some ethologists claim that men, like geese, have an aggressive drive.[35]

In animals, aggression within the species is adapted in form, timing and extent to the situation and is precipitated by environmental cues, such as the red breast in robins, and by internal changes which are appropriate to the season of the year. If two members of the same species are fighting and one is defeated, he acknowledges his defeat with a sign which has the effect of switching off the opponent's attack, for example, rolling over to expose the under-belly. Those who support the view of innate aggressive tendencies in Man point out that modern weapons (since the invention of the long bow)

R

have put opponents out of sight of such signals of admission of defeat, and that is why modern warfare is so dangerous. Some birds, if they do not receive signals which would put a stop to their behaviour, become murderous – a robin will attack a model of a robin until the model is torn to shreds, because it can emit no signal to stop the onslaught.[36] Konrad Lorenz has maintained that Man is the only species capable of murdering its own kind because we have no built-in inhibitory devices to limit our aggression. It seems unlikely, however, that energy is specifically diverted into a particular channel called aggression.[37] Moreover, if we really had no inhibitions about killing, it seems reasonable to assume that murder would be much more frequent and attempts to find alternatives to war much less pursued.[38]

It has been suggested that aggression in Man arises when energy which is being directed toward some end becomes blocked by some frustrating circumstance.[39] If this block is overcome or circumnavigated by force, this success may encourage further aggressive behaviour when frustration next arises. Success in fighting is known to be a powerful reinforcer of aggression. In one study the preliminary bouts of a timid mouse, in a contest with more dominant ones, were 'fixed', and the timid mouse became more aggressive the more fights he won.[40] (A technique not unknown to the promoters of professional boxing.) Culture is also a powerful influence on the form and timing of aggression in Man. Non-technological human groups have methods such as ritual confrontations, public insults and peaceful tournaments which channel hostility without doing much harm. More sophisticated nations may send diplomatic notes or withdraw ambassadors. It seems that most individuals do learn to inhibit their tendencies to hostility unless circumstances in some way condone or encourage their display.[41] The rare occasions on which animals do kill their own kind are usually in environments manufactured by men. For example, although healthy primates in the wild rarely fight, in zoos, possibly because they are overcrowded, they do display a similar type of 'pointless' aggression to that seen in Man. Many animals will attack if cornered or frightened. It may thus be that certain social conditions exhaust Man's capacity to cope with hostility and make him a potential murderer.

Different patterns of upbringing also produce different patterns of behaviour. The childhood of the Iatmul head hunters of New Guinea was characterised by humiliation and pain. Bullying and ritualised aggression were the essence of their culture, and as adults the more human scalps they acquired the higher became their prestige and pride. In contrast, the Hutterites, a religious sect in America, advocate total pacifism, aggression is discouraged and gentleness rewarded. According to a Freudian or Lorenzian formulation, their 'innate' aggression should emerge in some other, covert, way. But this does not appear to be the case.[42] As we have already noted in a previous chapter, imitation can play a part in encouraging aggression. Rather than aggression being an inevitable concomitant of frustration, it seems as if it is only one of a number of ways in which a person may react to disappointment or goal-blocking. In an experiment with 10- and 11-year-old boys, the boys were made angry by having their on-going activities interfered with. They were then divided into three groups. Group 1 were shown a film involving some violence, Group 2 were shown a non-aggressive film and Group 3 saw no film at all. The children were then observed in a free play situation. Some of the boys from Group 1 showed high levels of aggressive behaviour compared with those in the other two groups, but those previously rated as 'highly imaginative' showed little aggression in contrast to a 'low imagination' group. The author suggested one way of reacting to frustration may be by means of fantasy.[43] In another study black civil rights workers were exposed to white racist speeches and so aroused to anger. They were then divided into two groups to listen to a comedian. In Group 1 the comedian told jokes against whites, whilst in Group 2 the jokes were on 'neutral' topics. The first group subsequently expressed less anti-white hostility than did the other group.[44] Thus humour may provide an alternative form of tension release. The idea of 'catharsis', the release of pent-up tension in a discharge of emotion, is a very old one, existing in 'folk wisdom' in the idea that it is better to have a good cry than to bottle things up. This has led Lorenz among others to suggest that it would be a good idea to have local centres where people could give vent to their hostility in a harmless way.[45] The results of studies on imitation and reinforcement suggest, however, the converse : that allowing people to express their hostility will, in fact, encourage it.

Whether a situation will call out an aggressive response depends upon the meaning of the situation to the individual, the strength of the emotion aroused, past learning experiences, level of moral development and whether the social situation appears to condone or condemn violence. Thus aggression is by no means a spontaneous response to frustration or to tension arousal, but is dependent upon some primary appraisal of the extent of threat in the situation, and the best means of coping with it.

Nevertheless Man can clearly become aggressive in response to frustration, and our highly complex society makes it impossible for anyone to be completely without some frustrations. Ambition, hard work and competitiveness are encouraged in all, but the plum rewards go only to a few. Man's capacity for symbolic thought means he can see enemies where none exist, and our capacity for group loyalty has led Koestler to postulate that man is at his most dangerous when most conscious of his group membership and thus hostile to 'outsiders'.[46]

It may be that a more realistic way of looking at aggression is to regard it as having twin roots : a biologically based drive, shared with animals, which is a response to threat and which we have to learn to control, and an instrumental means of achieving goals which is learned within a culture which encourages competition and uses violence as a form of control.

PSYCHOSOMATIC REACTIONS

Conflict or aggression which is aroused but not expressed in overt action, may be expressed inwardly and lead to physical damage. Many of the present-day killers – coronary heart disease, ulcers, certain forms of cancer – appear to have as part of their aetiology some form of psychological stress.[47] Prolonged stress may give rise to long-term adjustments known as a 'general adaptation syndrome'[48] which halts those activities of the body that are concerned with growth, reproduction and resistance to infection. These long-term effects of stress make people increasingly vulnerable to breakdown and may in part account for some of the more extreme effects of deprivation mentioned in the early chapters of this book. If, for example, animals are housed together in increasing numbers, with diet, temperature, sanitation and space remaining constant, then as the room available for each animal becomes less, maternal and infant mortality rates rise and there is increased susceptibility to disease, including diabetes and some forms of cancer. The amount of the 'emergency' hormones in the blood increases in each animal as the numbers in the group grow larger.[49] [50]

Generalisations from animal studies to human reactions must always be viewed with some sceptism, but evidence is not lacking to indicate that psychological factors, which are a consequence of a competitive, conflict-full and complex way of life, are implicated in a number of illnesses.[51] The social value placed upon control of the emotions in the West, for example, has physiological consequences which have been instanced as a contributory factor in coronary heart disease.[52] Certain events in the life of a person may put them especially at risk. Rejection in love, a setback at work and loss of social prestige, precede, more frequently than one would expect by chance, the onset of the symptoms of cardiovascular illness.[53] Prolonged emotional strain associated with job responsibility seems to be particularly important in predisposing a person to breakdown.[54] Ulcers are more common in the widowed and divorced than in married people, and ulcerative colitis is almost exclusively a disease of the western world, although diet as well as stress may well play a part in this. Men seem to be more susceptible than women to stress – duodenal ulcers are ten times more common in men, although the incidence in women increases after the menopause, suggesting that the female sex hormones may have a protective role in this respect. The men of middle management, caught frustratingly between the upper and nether millstones of industry, are especially prone to ulcers. Paradoxically, in appalling situations, without hope, choice or responsibility, some illnesses appear to become less common. In Nazi concentration camps there is evidence that prisoners suffering from ulcers prior to incarceration found their symptoms went away and asthma patients in the same situation reported that their attacks diminished.[55]

Often those people who feel themselves to be under strain may attempt to cope by means which only serve to exacerbate the disorder, for example, excessive alcohol intake and smoking. This is not to say that societies should attempt to eliminate all stress from life. Moderate or even high short-term arousal is felt as pleasant and stimulating. Many sports are popular because of the excitement associated with the taking of risks. The pursuit of new disturbing ideas has always been attractive to scientists and writers. Man seeks tension as well as, at times, seeking to avoid it. It has been suggested that physiological arousal itself may aid the coping process rather than hinder it.[56] One study found the most efficient problem-solvers to be those who showed the greatest heart-rate changes. People who were of above average I.Q. and intellectually confident manifested more cardiovascular activity during problem-solving than those of lower I.Q. who were less confident.[57] It has been postulated that the absence of arousal in response to imposed stress should be regarded as a sign of psychological impairment.[58]

We have already noted that the nervous system functions best at some optimal level of stimulation which will vary from individual to individual. Apart from this the meaning of any situation is not the same for everybody in that situation. Thus what constitutes stress for one individual may be experienced by another as mildly stimulating. Apart from individual differences in physiological arousal, early experience and the existence of efficient coping strategies will determine whether or not some particular set of circumstances becomes exciting or disturbing. Change of any kind involves the person in efforts to adapt and may therefore impose some strain on coping devices.[59] However, as we have seen, it is only through attempts to adjust to novelty that individuals achieve emotional and cognitive growth. Each person will be able to handle novel events at a different level and at a different pace. Thus when people are bored they may well go out and seek for excitement and potentially 'stressful' situations, but having no control over the rate or type of change which occurs imposes much greater forces on cognitive, emotional and physiological systems.

REFERENCES

1 J. J. Groen, 'Social change and psychosomatic disease', in *Society, Stress and Disease*, Vol. I: The psycho-social environment and psychosomatic diseases (Ed. L. Levi), (London, Oxford University Press, 1971), 91–109.
2 R. M. Oliver, 'Physique and serum lipids of young London busmen in relation to ischaemic heart disease', *Brit. J. Ind. Med.*, *24* (1967), 181–7.
3 I. L. Shannon and G. M. Isbell, 'Stress in dental patients: effects of local anaesthetic procedures', *Tech. Rep. No. SAM-TDR* 63–29 USAF School of Aerospace Medicine Texas 1963.
4 D. Funkenstein, 'The physiology of fear and anger', *Sci. Amer.*, *192* (1955), 74–80.
5 A. F. Ax, 'The physiological differentiation between fear and anger in humans', *Psychosom. Med.*, *5* (1953), 433–42.
6 R. A. Hinde, 'Factors governing the changes in strength of a partially inborn response as shown by the mobbing behaviour of the chaffinch (*fringilla coelebs*), I: The nature of the response and an examination of its course', *Proc. Roy. Soc.*, Series B, *142* (1954), 306–30.
7 D. O. Hebb, 'On the nature of fear', *Psychol. Rev.*, *53* (1946), 259–76.
8 D. O. Hebb, 'Emotion in man and animal', *Psychol. Rev.*, *53* (1946), 88–106.
9 A. Jersild, 'Children's wishes, dreams, fears, daydreams pleasant and unpleasant memories', *Psychol. Bull.*, *30* (1933), 552–3.
10 E. Erikson, *Childhood and Society* (New York, W. W. Norton, 1950).
11 K. Horney, *The Neurotic Personality of our Time* (London, Routledge & Kegan Paul, 1937).
12 S. Freud, *New Introductory Lectures on Psychoanalysis* (London, Hogarth Press, 1933).
13 J. J. Bowlby, 'Separation, Anxiety and Anger', *Attachment and Loss*, Vol. II (London, Hogarth Press, 1973).
14 H. H. Kelley, J. C. Condry, A. E. Dahlke and A. H. Hill, 'Collective behaviour in a simulated panic situation', *J. Exp. Soc. Psychol.*, *1* (1965), 20–54.
15 L. Postman and J. S. Bruner, 'Perception under stress', *Psychol. Rev.*, *55* (1948), 314–24.
16 I. L. Janis and S. Feshback, 'Effects of fear-arousing communications', *J. Abn. Soc. Psychol.*, *48* (1953), 78–92.

17 H. Leventhal, 'Fear communications in the acceptance of health practices', *Bull. N.Y. Acad. Med.*, *41*, Series 2 (1965), 1144–68.

18 R. Lazarus, *Psychological Stress and the Coping Process* (New York, McGraw-Hill, 1966).

19 G. W. Allport, *The Nature of Prejudice* (Reading, M.A., Addison Wesley, 1954).

20 B. Bettleheim, *The Informed Heart* (Glencoe, Ill., The Free Press, 1960).

21 I. L. Janis, *Psychological Stress* (New York, John Wiley, 1958).

22 D. Mechanic, 'Some problems in developing a social psychology of adaptation to stress', in *Social and Psychological Factors in Stress* (Ed. J. E. McGrath), (New York, Holt, Rinehart, 1970), 104–23.

23 A. Freud, *The Ego and the Mechanisms of Defence*, revised edition (London, Hogarth Press, 1968).

24 H. M. Visotsky, D. A. Hamburg, M. E. Goss and B. Z. Lebovits, 'Coping behaviour under extreme stress', *Arch. Gen. Psychiat.*, *5* (1961), 423–48.

25 C. T. Wolff, S. B. Friedman, M. A. Hofer and J. W. Mason, 'Relationship between psychological defences and mean urinary 17-hydroxycorticosteroid excretion rates. I : A predictive study of parents of fatally ill children', *Psychosom. Med.*, *26* (1964), 576–91.

26 J. C. Speisman, R. S. Lazarus, A. M. Mordkoff and L. A. Davidson, 'The experimental reduction of stress based on ego defense theory', *J. Abn. Soc. Psychol.*, *68* (1964), 367–80.

27 R. J. McCall, 'The defence mechanisms re-examined : a logical and phenomenological analysis', *Catholic Psychological Record*, *1* (1963), 1.

28 A. Freud, *The Ego and the Mechanisms of Defence*, revised edition (London, Hogarth Press, 1968).

29 B. Bettleheim, *The Informed Heart* (Glencoe, Ill., The Free Press, 1960).

30 E. M. Opton, Jr, 'Mental gymnastics on My Lai', *The New Republic* (21 February 1970).

31 J. D. Grambs, 'The self concept: basis for re-education of Negro youths', in *Negro Self-concept: implications for school and citizenship* (Ed. W. C. Kvaraceus), (New York, McGraw-Hill, 1965).

32 U. Bronfenbrenner and H. N. Ricciutti, 'The appraisal of personality characteristics in children', in *Handbook of Research Methods in Child Development* (Ed. P. E. Mussen), (New York, John Wiley, 1960).

33 A. Storr, *Human Aggression* (London, Allen Lane, 1968).

34 S. Freud, *Civilisation and its Discontents* (London, Hogarth Press, 1929).

35 K. Lorenz, *On Aggression* (London, Methuen, 1966).

36 D. Lack, *The Life of the Robin* (Cambridge University Press, 1943).

37 R. Hinde, 'Some recent trends in Ethology', in *Psychology: a study of a science*, Vol. II (Ed. S. Koch), (New York, McGraw-Hill, 1959), 561–610.

38 J. Cohen, *Homo Psychologicus* (London, George Allen & Unwin, 1970), Ch. 8.

39 J. Dollard, L. W. Doob, N. B. Miller, O. H. Mowrer, R. R. Sears, C. I. Hovland and R. T. Sollenberger, *Frustration and Aggression* (New Haven, Yale University Press, 1939).

40 J. P. Scott, *Aggression* (Illinois, The Chicago Press, 1958).

41 L. Berkowitz, *Aggression, A Social-psychological Analysis* (New York, McGraw-Hill, 1962).

42 E. Sampson, *Social Psychology and Contemporary Society* (New York, John Wiley, 1971).

43 E. Biblow, 'The role of fantasy in the reduction of aggression', *Diss. Abstr. Int., 31* (1970), 6B 3699.

44 D. I. Singer, 'Aggression arousal, hostile humor, catharsis', *J. Pers. Soc. Psychol., 8* (1969), 1–14.

45 K. Lorenz, *On Aggression* (London, Methuen, 1966).

46 A. Koestler, *The Ghost in the Machine* (London, Hutchinson, 1967).

47 J. J. Groen, 'Social change and psychosomatic disease', in *Society, Stress and Disease*, Vol. I : 'The psychosocial environment and psychosomatic diseases' (London, Oxford University Press, 1971).

48 H. Selye, *The Story of the Adaptation Syndrome* (New York, Acta Inc., 1952).

49 J. Axelrod, R. A. Meuller, J. P. Henry and P. M. Stephens, 'Effect of psychosocial stimulation on the enzymes involved in the biosynthesis and metabolism of noradrenalin and adrenalin'. Paper presented to the American Psychosomatic Society (Washington DC, March, 1970).

50 E. L. Bliss and J. Ailion, 'Response of neurogenic amines to aggregation and strangers', *J. Pharmacol. Exp. Therap., 169* (1968), 258–63.

51 C. D. Jenkins, 'Psychologic and social precursors of coronary disease', *New Eng. J. Med., 284* (1971), Part I, 244–55; Part II, 307–17.

52 S. Minc, 'Psychological factors in coronary heart disease', *Geriatrics, 20* (1965), 747–55.

53 H. Kits van Heijningen and N. Treurniet, 'Psychodynamic factors in acute myocardial infarction', *Int. J. Psychoanalysis, 47* (1966), 370–4.

54 H. I. Russek, 'Stress, tobacco and coronary disease in North American professional groups', *J.A.M.A., 192* (1965), 189–94.

55 J. J. Groen, 'Social change and psychosomatic disease', in *Society, Stress and Disease*, Vol. I : 'The psychosocial environment and psychosomatic diseases' (London, Oxford University Press, 1971).

56 J. I. Lacey, 'Somatic response patterning and stress: some revisions of activation theory', in *Psychological Stress* (Eds M. H. Appley and R. Trumbell), (New York, Appleton-Century-Crofts, 1967).

57 S. J. Blatt, 'Patterns of cardiac arousal during complex mental activity', *J. Abn. Soc. Psychol., 63* (1961), 272–82.

58 J. Kagan and H. A. Moss, *Birth to Maturity: a study in psychological development* (New York, John Wiley, 1962).

59 R. H. Rahe, J. D. McKean, Jr and J. A. Ransom, 'A longitudinal study of life change and illness patterns', *J. Psychosom. Res., 10* (1967), 355–66.

14

Growing Old

As you walk towards the darkness you must laugh.
Katherine Hepburn, interview in *The Times*

There is an underlying assumption involved in our treatment of the old – that they are all alike, that they, therefore, have a lot in common and need no company but each other. This assumption bears little relationship to reality. The biological changes which accompany the ageing process have different consequences for different people and act upon individual differences of heredity and experience. The very wide variety of reactions to ageing means that any generalisations should be carefully scrutinised. All societies, however, have certain attitudes towards the old which exert social pressure on the individual to conform to expectations. These socially acquired attitudes guide not only the expectations of others but the self-image of the ageing person, so that people in the same age range may share superficial attributes which relate to the kind of behaviour regarded as fitting for that age range in that society. Thus as we get older we may cease to wear bright clothes, go to parties or fall in love, not because we are incapable of these things, but because they may not be regarded as 'suitable'.

Putting actual numbers to the concepts of 'middle age' and 'old age' is very difficult. A man of 30 may be an 'old' footballer, whilst a man of 60 may be 'young' for a judge. Life expectancy in a society and the age at which people have children will also affect the age at which they are regarded as 'old'. People may look older or younger than their years, and internal feelings may bear little relationship to outward behaviour or appearance.

It is extremely difficult to distinguish between any changes in psychological characteristics which are a consequence of ageing *per se* and those that result from physical disease and social expectations. If old people are revered as sources of traditional knowledge and wisdom, old age may be seen as the satisfactory culmination of a life. In our society old people are likely to feel under-valued and a nuisance. The knowledge explosion means that even the middle-aged may know less about technology than schoolchildren. Geographical and social mobility and the growth of social services mean that many of the traditional functions of the old have become impossible to fulfil or have been taken over by official agencies.

During the ageing process, physiological, social and psychological changes interact and it is possible that at least some of the adverse consequences of ageing may not be inevitable accompaniments of the process, but result from the way the individual reacts to the recognition of physical changes and the structure of the society in which those changes take place.

Much work in this area has been directed to what makes a 'successful' old age. By 'successful' most writers seem to mean growing old gracefully without too many regrets and without bitterness (and presumably without being a nuisance). It is obvious that this will depend heavily upon past and present life style and personal relationships. It has been suggested that those who age successfully can live at their own pace, are not pressurised at work, but maintain some minimum of activity; that they have a background of close and harmonious relationships with relatives; and, if living alone, that they can cope well and do not become isolated from the wider society.[1] On the whole, having a full and varied life seems to be the best preparation for ageing. The person will have learned a variety of problem-solving strategies which will aid adaptation, although those who have been very active may fear the restrictions on activity which come with age. Easing through life with a minimum of social involvement and a network of diffuse and neutral relationships can also be an effective preparation for coping with changed social roles and loss of personal relationships.

Bromley has made a useful division of adulthood into six

phases which take into account physiological, social and psychological influences on behaviour. The first phase from 20 to 25 years of age is concerned mainly with marriage and career prospects. The second phase from 25 to 40 sees the consolidation of social relationships and the occupational role. This is the time of greatest productivity in work and highest social activity with a lot of emotional investment in life. The end of this period will probably bring some deterioration in vision and in some aspects of intellectual ability. The years from 40 to 60 are accompanied by changes in family life, and hormonal changes bring about the menopause in women. There may be a decline in health which limits the scope of activities and there is a tendency to increased self-awareness and reflection on life. In the fourth phase, from 60 to 65 physical changes accelerate and although competence is retained in tasks which depend upon experience, a decline is shown in tasks dependent upon speed or new learning. Social activity begins to subside. The period from 65 to 70 usually brings with it the necessity to adjust to the end of working life and a more dependent status of lesser value to the society. Personal relationships are very important in providing companionship and stimulation. In the final phase, which Bromley designates as being from 70 years onwards, there are considerable individual differences, but there is inevitably some decline in ability to deal with everyday affairs and a general continuing slowing down. Most people die, however, before showing extreme signs of senility.[2]

PHYSIOLOGICAL CHANGES

As we become adult the significance of biological factors lessens in relation to childhood, but after middle age physical changes again exert important influences on behaviour. Reactions to these will depend upon the past experience of the individual and the coping strategies he or she has learned. From an evolutionary point of view the survival of the individuals of a species is only necessary until reproduction and the rearing of offspring has taken place. Biological development in childhood is an orderly, genetically regulated sequence which comes to an end with adulthood. The processes of ageing may represent not a continuing development but rather a gradual disintegration of the 'programme'. Although on a philosophical and social level we may regard old age as the culmination of a lifetime's development, in biological terms it may well represent the consequences of developmental processes having come to an end.[3]

Physical dexterity tends to decline continuously from the teens onward, and in industrial tasks, workers, as they get older, compensate for their waning powers by working nearer to the limits of their capacity. The work norms that are established in mixed age groups usually adjust the pace of the younger men to that of the older. Older men may also keep up productivity by missing out on what they regard as inessential parts of a task, such as safety checks. If they do have accidents these are more likely to be due to simplification of a task or slowness of response rather than carelessness.[4]

Visual acuity also diminishes after the age of about 25 and for most people this is a continuing decline. The pupil of the eye becomes smaller and so the effect of poor lighting on vision increases with age. The old need more light than younger people and also take longer to adapt to the dark.[5] This has implications for night driving – an older person will take relatively longer to re-adapt to darkness after having been dazzled by the headlights of an oncoming car.

Hearing loss increases quite rapidly after the age of 45, on average, especially in men, with the higher frequencies being the first affected.[6] Stress associated with learning a new task produces longer lasting autonomic reactions in older people.[7]

For some women, the menopause, which occurs on average at about the age of 45 can bring susceptibility to internal disorders and emotional upsets. Most women appear to adjust well, but hormonal imbalance at this time may produce more body hair, lowered voice pitch, greater skin pigmentation and flabby breasts. Other distressing symptoms can be the well-known 'hot flushes', sweating, headaches, irritation, insomnia, giddiness, restlessness and frigidity.[8] The meaning which the woman attaches to the menopause, fears of loss of femininity or sexual attractiveness, undoubtedly influences the appearance and severity of such symptoms, perhaps more than the physiological changes themselves. The age of the menopause coincides for many women with the time at which their children become adult and when their husbands may be pre-occupied with work, so that, biological changes apart, the period is one requiring considerable adjustment to a change in social role, and bringing the danger of social and emotional isolation. Men also go through a period of change in the endocrine system at approximately the same age, but the effects are much less obvious and less well understood than those taking place in women.[9]

COGNITIVE CHANGES

There has been a multitude of studies comparing age groups on a variety of intelligence tests. The type of results obtained depend to some extent upon the methodology of the studies. For example, one can carry out a longitudinal study repeatedly testing the same group of individuals at different ages, that is, measuring age *changes*, or one can take groups of individuals of different ages and compare them, that is, measuring age *differences*. Neither of these methods is completely satisfactory since they confound differences in educational experience and social expectations with cognitive changes, and the longitudinal method has the added disadvantage of subject loss. The majority of studies, however, show a general decline in I.Q. score with age, some of which may be related to physical changes, but much may be accounted for by environmental factors. A dull repetitive job may deaden a lively mind whereas people in occupations which involve high-level mental activity show very little decline and sometimes an improvement in score.[10] Deprivation of sensory and social stimulation which may attend the restricted lives of the aged will tend to produce apathy and confusion and memory defects which will affect test scores.

On average, those tests involving perception and dexterity show a decline from the teens onwards, whilst those tapping comprehension and verbal ability may not decline until the age of 50. Tests of vocabulary or of general information show little change and may improve with age. Those tasks requiring a novel solution or persistent effort are most affected by advancing age.[11] In old age there is a tendency to return to a simpler, more concrete style of thinking which has tempted some writers to talk in terms of a reversal of the Piagetian stages.[12] This view implies some kind of systematic disassembling of the cognitive structures whereas the reality is probably more like a slow and random crumbling. The cognitive changes that occur late in life do not manifest a systematic movement through a series of stages as seems to be the case in childhood. Moreover, the decay of the physical brain seems to follow a random rather than an ordered sequence. Post-mortem examinations show that the brains of older people weigh less, have larger internal spaces and furrows between the convolutions, more areas missing and have fewer neurons than do those of young people.[13]

There are wide individual differences in the stability of mental functioning. Some individuals appear to deteriorate not at all whilst others may show a rapid decline with age which may be indicative of impending death.[14]

Tests of intelligence, as we have already suggested, are not entirely reliable instruments and there are a number of factors involved in the testing of old people particularly which must serve to qualify any conclusions that are drawn. Speed is at a premium in many I.Q. tests and this will handicap old people. Poor vision may delay understanding of a test item and poor hearing may make instructions difficult to follow and so cause anxiety or lowered motivation. The aged may have little motivation in any case to try hard since they may see such tests as childish or pointless, or they may have worries about showing up in a bad light which can make them reluctant to respond. Physical conditions which may be undetected such as mild arteriosclerosis, heart disease or arthritis can affect concentration, motivation and writing speed. Most of the evidence for a decline in I.Q. score comes from cross-sectional studies of age differences in score which are complicated by differences in social and educational advantages in younger age groups. At the present time there are no I.Q. tests that have been standardised on adequate samples of old people, and often they assume knowledge of school subjects which a 60-year-old has left far behind.

There is some evidence that those of higher initial intelligence are more likely to retain their intellectual powers into old age, which may be due to continued use and to greater flexibility of mental processes. (It could be biased by the fact that it is just this type of person who does the testing.) Significant differences in learning ability have been found between people who left school early and those who continued study thereafter, even with initial I.Q. score held constant.[15] There is also neurophysiological evidence which indicates that there is less brain cell deterioration among those people who have maintained a high level of either physical or mental activity.[16]

Two areas of functioning in particular do show clear evidence of succumbing to age. One of these is reaction time, which increases, a fact which is related more to decisional processes than to physical slowness,[17] and the other is short-term memory – an older person takes longer to learn a list of words and has greater difficulty in retaining instructions.[18]

Laboratory tasks, however, cannot reproduce the complexity of daily life. The real-life environment transmits a constant flow of information which must be dealt with. The amount of information which can be handled at any one time seems to decline with age; in terms of communication engineering, 'channel capacity' grows smaller. This means that relevant pieces of information are likely to be missed. People over the age of 60, for instance, have a disproportionately high number of car accidents (although fewer than people in their 20s).[19] Although it has not been shown that this is a consequence of reduced channel capacity, car-driving does require rapid and constantly maintained processing of information which becomes increasingly difficult with age, although the knowledge that this is so may lead to a greater caution and more realistic appraisal of abilities than is the case with younger people. If a task supplies too much information, or demands a very complex response, this 'behavioural load' may give rise to tension, irritation and a tendency to shed some of the load by ignoring or distorting some of the incoming stimuli.

Old people may have a tendency to compensate for intellectual weaknesses such as poor memory by vigorous denial ('Of course I remember you') or by filling in the gaps fictitiously. Because it becomes increasingly hard to invent new solutions to problems they are more prone to rely on the tried and trusted strategies they already know. This may, on occasion, produce stereotyped or inappropriate behaviour.

ADJUSTMENT TO AGEING

It has been said that the last stages of life offer the alternatives of 'integrity' or 'despair'[20] – if the individual does not achieve self-acceptance now, the chance will be lost for ever. How acceptable we are to ourselves is very dependent upon our perception of the reactions of other people and this is as important in old age as it is in childhood. Solitariness can be psychologically disrupting for the old as for the young. An individual's self-image includes his or her recognition of which roles and what opportunities are still available. In old age these are limited not solely by biological changes, but also by social definitions of what kinds of behaviour are appropriate and which enforce definition and recognition of the self as old.

In our society there are the initiatory stages of middle age and retirement which gradually redefine the self-image. All the individual's past experience will also affect reactions to ageing, from affectionate and stimulating contacts in infancy, through degrees of success and failure at school, work and in the family. The person who has, through social interaction, learned to think of himself or herself as intrinsically valuable will obviously be armoured against some of the more negative aspects of old age as compared with someone who has struggled all his life against feelings of insecurity and inadequacy which are likely to be exacerbated at this time.

Middle Age

In our society, this may be said to correspond to Bromley's third and fourth stages, say from 40 to 65 (bearing in mind that any definition of middle age tends to be some years in advance of the age of the writer giving the definition). The

s

awareness of oneself as falling into this category seems to be linked with the recognition of physical changes, such as greying hair, hair loss, facial wrinkles and expanding flesh, and social cues, such as attempts to find a new job when the age limits for applicants rule one out, or merely realising for the first time that one has grown-up children.

Studies in Kansas found that some middle-aged people suffered from a crisis involving depression in the early 50s, but that recovery from this usually occurred within a few years.[21] This depression may result from a tendency at this time to compare one's achievements with those of others of a similar age and find oneself lacking. In a materialistic society it is not surprising that such comparisons tend to focus upon size of car and house. Promotion prospects at work may also become an obsessive concern, especially for men in middle life who begin to hear behind them the loud and eager voices of younger men.

The awareness that one's options are gradually diminishing may cause people to reassess their position and suddenly change the course of their life. A successful company director may become a social worker, or a high-ranking police officer may embark on a new career as a teacher. Others may feel that it is too late to start again and adjust their ambitions to narrower channels. Some people in middle age have to face sudden changes such as premature retirement or the consequences of a heart attack and are faced with the task of redesigning their life style.

Since Man is essentially a striving and exploratory creature, the attainment of the limited material goals set up by society may leave people feeling aimless at the mid-point of their lives. Women have finished bringing up their children and a man may have accumulated all those possessions which advertisers tell us we need. Sex differences in attitudes to middle age have been found. A study of one hundred middle-class men and women found that despite the effects of the menopause women were less concerned than men about their body or their health. Indeed, on the whole, women welcomed middle age as a time of new freedoms when latent abilities could be developed, whilst men tended to feel under pressure at work and worried about boredom and responsibilities. As they get older, however, both sexes are inclined to see themselves as increasingly frail and become over-concerned and hypochondriacal about body functions.[22]

Through adolescence and early adulthood there is an implicit expectance that life can only get better and better, so many things to look forward to, so many things to achieve, but, on the whole, in middle age people cease to feel this way. There are three common reactions to the notion that there is less time left than has gone before. One is resignation, a reluctance to take risks or seek excitement so that there is no fear of exceeding one's capabilities; another is defensiveness, a retreat into rigid, narrow-minded self-righteousness which protects the person from the recognition that other life patterns could have been more desirable; the third reaction is to see middle age as a time of new opportunities. This may sometimes take the form of a 'final fling' into social and sexual activity, or be represented by occupational and intellectual changes.

Changes that occur in the individual's body image may precipitate him or her into a search for reassurance that physical attractiveness still remains. In men this tends to be connected with fears about their potency, but for women the knowledge that there is no fear of pregnancy may give a new impetus to their sex life. Those who associate sex solely with reproduction or with youth may abandon completely this side of life.

It has been suggested that the critical aspect of failure to come to terms with ageing is not necessarily a sense of decline or insecurity but rather self-assessment as to whether or not fulfilment in life has been, or is likely to be, achieved.[23]

Retirement

Retirement from a full-time occupation usually occurs at a time arbitrarily imposed by employers. It takes little account of an individual's capacities, and is a social, not a biological, landmark. Retirement benefits used to be intended only for those who could no longer work, but now define the time when people should no longer work. Since our culture sets a high value on a productive life, the effect of being retired, however much it may have been looked forward to as a distant prospect, may in practice come as a shock and a blow to self-esteem, especially for those who still feel fit and competent. Younger people tend to anticipate that retirement will be like one long holiday, but former leisure activities now become the only activities and are, moreover, likely to be more difficult to pursue on a pension than on a full salary. A whole new pattern of life has to be established.

The label of retirement does provide a role, a pattern of behaviour, but in doing so, may hasten the ageing process by forcing individuals to mix with and identify with other old people.[24] Retirement may pose no problems for some types of people. For example, those whose work lies in creative fields, such as artists or scientists, may never retire. Indeed many, such as Verdi, Titian, Goethe, Haydn and Freud did some of their best work towards the end of their long lives. Academics and businessmen who are highly involved in work which continues to supply status and interest after official retirement are also in a happy position. Paradoxically, those who have had a purely instrumental approach to work, seeing it as a necessary evil, seem to be less upset by retirement, probably because their sense of identity tends to be bound up with other activities. It is white-collar and skilled workers who experience most problems on retirement, since their jobs tend to be associated with particular skills, tools and social techniques which are not available after retirement, as the academic's books still are or the stock market reports for the ex-tycoon. If work has been the central defining activity of life, then the loss of it can be very disturbing. Life may become empty and meaningless and the individual may experience great difficulty in developing new interests and relationships. There may also arise conflicts with the wife, whose image of housewife is still intact and who may see her husband as interfering and a nuisance if he attempts to take over some of her tasks.

For those who had had a wide range of interests outside their job, retirement will also present little difficulty as it merely means altering the emphasis of the activities. It appears to be the meaning that is attached to activity in retirement that is important in retaining self-respect, not its nature. If what a person does is seen by him as valueless and time-filling, then it gives him no dignity. Unfortunately, the kind of amusements that are organised for old people, with the best of intentions, such as bingo and tea parties, are trivial and easily construed as an arrangement to fill in time until death. Many pensioners have a lot to offer the community in caring, advice and accumulated knowledge, but we tend to assume that all the caring must flow one way, that we must 'look after' the elderly, an attitude which can only lead to the assumption that they are incapable of looking after themselves, whether this is the case or not and thus to the ultimate disregard of the very positive contribution they might make.

Old Age

Changes in emotional and social expression at this final stage of adulthood are again ambiguous. They are partially a consequence of biological disruption, but also stem from reduced social expectations. It has been suggested that one mode of adjustment to old age is 'disengagement'.[25] By this is meant that it is not so much other people who withdraw from the elderly, but that ageing individuals co-operate in a mutual process of social disengagement in order to limit demands on their diminished energy and strength, so that social activities become ever more restricted and the time spent with other people is reduced. This withdrawal is said to begin in the 50s and is well established by the age of seventy. The results of disengagement may be increasingly self-centred and idiosyncratic behaviour. However, although some people may prefer this mode of adjustment, it is quite evident that others may find old age more bearable in the midst of many social contacts. Disengagement represents only one of several possible way of adjusting to ageing. It is important, therefore, that society should provide opportunities both for those who wish to disengage and for those who wish to remain socially and occupationally active.[26] Disengagement may be a typically middle-class response, whilst remaining socially active may be more likely among lower economic groups.[27] [28]

There does seem to be some flattening of emotions in old age with fewer extremes of joy and sadness, but whilst some become self-pitying and irritable, others become calm and tolerant.

Young people tend to think that the principal fears of the old must relate to death, but in fact they are usually more concerned about conditions of living and have quite realistic fears about illness or financial insecurity. Indeed, loneliness, ill-health or insecurity may mean that death is seen as a desirable escape from a life which has become intolerable (the high suicide rate amongst old people mentioned in the last chapter is clearly of relevance here).

One technique widely used by the old to escape from current reality is reminiscence, the repetitive recalling of past events, often combined with difficulties in remembering recent experiences. Although this may be infuriating for the listener, it may well have a positive function in that it helps to maintain and strengthen the person's self-esteem by affirming his or her past value. Reminiscence, it has been suggested, may protect people from depression and be associated with survival. One study found that 'reminiscers' were more likely to be still alive a year after first testing than were 'non-reminiscers'.[29] Those old people who rarely reminisce seem to retain only unhappy memories[30] (which may or may not mean that they have led unhappy lives, but that their life is recollected as having been unsatisfactory). Reminiscence may reflect an awareness of approaching death and an attempt to review and reorganise past living.

Sexual behaviour in the elderly is likely to excite ridicule or disgust even in these supposedly tolerant times. Old people who say they are still sexually active or interested are seen as amazing, dirty, or indulging in wish-fulfilment. Jokes abound about the inabilities of old men faced with nubile young women (although interestingly enough there are virtually no jokes about old women and young men). A longitudinal study of thirty-one couples aged between 60 and 94 found that at the beginning of the study 70 per cent of the males were sexually active and 80 per cent reported a continuing interest in sex. Ten years later (after which time some of the subjects were obviously unable to participate) only 25 per cent were still sexually active but 70 per cent were still interested.[31] This discrepancy between activity and interest increases with age and is probably related to lack of opportunity in terms of sufficient privacy and suitable and willing partners. It may well be a factor in the high rate of exhibitionism amongst elderly men. Sexual overtures or love affairs between old people often give rise to bawdy comments. Also the common tendency to house old people in segregated sections of institutions or, where they live with relatives, to allow insufficient privacy, may encourage the old to feel that their sexual feelings are distasteful or abnormal and they are thus denied a cheap, but priceless, pleasure.

Nearly half the inmates of our mental hospitals are over 60 years of age. This is not necessarily due to greater proneness to mental illness, but may, in part, be a consequence of sensory and social deprivation. Loss of hearing, poor eyesight, taste and smell and lack of stimulation from others can reduce the level of brain arousal to well below the optimum for efficient functioning and produce confusion, lack of concentration, forgetfulness and even hallucinations.

The less social interaction we have at any age the easier it is to become increasingly egocentric and fail to adapt to the point of view of others. Even in advanced and humane institutions there appears to be a tendency for some staff to establish a 'social distance' between themselves and the mentally impaired elderly, by means of emotional detachment, physical segregation and unconscious dehumanising, so that the inmates are seen as passive objects to be manipulated rather than as living human beings. Unwittingly this attitude may exacerbate the social and sensory isolation of the patients and make them worse.[32]

The placing of old people in institutions may, in itself, come as a severe blow to the self-image, as the person has now been defined as the sort who belongs with old people. But some individuals are reported as preferring the daily routine that institutions provide and the opportunity to mix with others of the same age.[33] The same study found that all the people interviewed wanted some privacy and some control over what happened to them and that they preferred to turn for help to 'significant others' rather than to professionals provided for that purpose.

The entry of an old person into an institution constitutes a stress situation, as the individual is required to adapt to a radically different way of life. It has been found that old people in institutions in Holland were less satisfied with their lives than those who lived at home or with relatives[34] and there is some evidence that entrance to geriatric homes decreases life expectancy.[35]

Moving inmates from one institution to another may also have serious consequences such as depression, illness and even death.[36]

We have already discussed the extent to which social cues may serve to label our own behaviour and sensations. Because of the negative stereotype of the elderly that most people in our society share, any sign of mental or physical disability may tend to be ascribed to age, both by the individual concerned and by those around him. Momentary lapses of memory or fleeting pains will perhaps not be accepted as universal human inevitabilities but rather will be put down to advancing years ('I must be getting old'). Our society has virtually no positive expectations of the elderly, and they may be implicitly encouraged to become dependent and helpless. Regression may be reinforced in geriatric patients by rewarding dependency, by teasing, denial of privacy and curtailment of personal freedom. Old people who try to be independent may be discouraged from being self-sufficient ('It's dangerous for you to go out alone', 'A person your age should be sitting back and letting young people do the work'). Such treatment can only encourage the infantile tendencies that we all possess. Some of the characteristics associated with old age, such as dependency, querulousness and lack of curiosity, might arise in any age group which was consistently undervalued, discouraged from thinking for itself, overprotected and denied opportunities for constructive behaviour. That some of these social factors can be offset has been shown by attempts to provide a different kind of environment. In one such study, old, infirm and apathetic patients in a geriatric hospital were encouraged to take part in a programme which provided a stimulating and demanding social situation, where the expectations of the staff were high and independent behaviour was rewarded. In relation to a control group those individuals who had participated in the programme showed significant gains in activity, responsibility and general health and satisfaction.[37]

Although it is apparent that there are wide individual differences in adaptation to the ageing process there have been attempts to set these within broad frameworks. A study of eighty-seven old men differentiated five modes of adjustment.[38] First, constructive – where the person showed a continuing enjoyment of life in all its aspects, had warm human relationships, retained flexibility of mind and self-esteem which was related to a realistic knowledge of his own capabilities. The men in this group reported a satisfactory life with few problems; second, dependent – individuals in this category tended to be passive and reliant on others, but were well adjusted and realistic about themselves except for a tendency to be rather over-optimistic. They reported life styles of self-indulgence combined with a lack of ambition. Third, defensive – people in this group were said to show a tight emotional control, conventional behaviour and stereotyped thinking about old age and death. They were envious of the young and warded off anxiety by a compulsive kind of activity. Fourth, hostile – these men were aggressive, prejudiced, complaining and suspicious and were said to lack insight and be pessimistic. They saw old age as synonymous with poverty, starvation and inevitable deterioration and reported a background of unstable work record, downward social mobility and lack of affection in childhood. Fifth, self-hating – for this group death was seen as a merciful release from an incompetent and unhappy life full of failure. The men were reported as depressed and lonely and as having experienced financial and social failure. The categorisations of this study suggest a focus on individual coping devices as responsible for the self-image of the men. However, one should bear in mind that an individual may have little control over some events such as the loss of loved ones, social disadvantage and financial level. Moreover, western society tends to place more value upon the well-off and those who have a steady job, so that those who show neither attribute may well become depressed and lonely. Such findings may, however, provide evidence for the idea that there is a basic core of personality which is maintained throughout life (even though current emotions are likely to colour the memories that an old person has of his past life, that is, if he is feeling cheerful at the time of the interview he may report his life as having been a happy one, whereas, if depressed, he may report feelings of futility and failure). The crises and triumphs of experience do not seem totally to destroy some essential inner core and, except in cases of mental disorder, the person seems to become, in a strange sense, more like himself as the superficial layers of social roles fall away.

Those who adjust most satisfactorily to old age seem to be those who adjusted best at earlier stages of life although the manner of adjustment will vary greatly. For some it may be pottering around the garden whilst for others a constant round of family visits may be more important. Although in general, successful adaptation to ageing is aided by physical health, an optimal amount of stimulation, a clear set of social roles, self-esteem and, of course, financial security, it is inter-personal relationships which seem to have most relevance for a contented old age.

Officialdom tends to treat old people as if they fall into a special category, but throughout life, from infancy to old age, it can be seen that those experiences which make us feel loved, valued, competent and growing in knowledge and understanding, serve to promote enthusiasm for life, but those experiences which block exploration, which make us feel anxious and un-loved, promote a narrow and rigid attitude to life and diminish our humanity. Thus it is not so much that the elderly have different needs, but rather that physiological changes and social expectations make it more difficult for them to maintain that fine balance between human needs and the ability to satisfy them.

REFERENCES

1 R. H. Williams and C. G. Wirth, *Lives Through the Years* (New York, Atherton Press, 1965).

2 D. B. Bromley, *Human Ageing* (Harmondsworth, Penguin Books, 1973), 2nd edition.

3 D. B. Bromley, 'The effects of ageing on intelligence', *Impact of Science on Society*, *21* (1971), No. 4.

4 A. T. Welford, *Ageing and Human Skill* (London, Oxford University Press, 1958).

5 S. K. Guth, A. A. Eastmen and J. F. McNelis, 'Lighting requirements for older workers', *Illuminating Engineering*, *51* (1956), 656–60.

6 R. S. Woodworth and H. Schlosberg, *Experimental Psychology* (London, Methuen, 1954), revised edition, Ch. 12.

7 M. H. Powell, C. Eisdorfer and M. D. Bogdonoff, 'Physiologic response patterns observed in a learning task', *Arch. Gen. Psychiat.*, *10* (1964), 192–5.

8 E. Hurlock, *Developmental Psychology* (New York, McGraw Hill, 1959), 2nd edition.

9 L. J. Bischof, *Adult Psychology* (London, Harper & Row, 1969).

10 J. Latimer, 'The status of intelligence in the ageing', *J. Genet. Psychol.*, *102* (1963), 75–88.

11 I. Bilash and J. P. Zubeck, 'The effects of age on factorially "pure" mental abilities', *J. Gerontol.*, *15* (1960), 175–82.

12 W. R. Looft, 'Egocentrism and social interaction across the life span', *Psychol. Bull.* (1972), 73–92.

13 D. B. Bromley, 'The effects of ageing on intelligence', *Impact of Science on Society*, *21* (1971), No. 4.

14 R. W. Kleemeier, 'Intellectual changes in the senium, or death and the I.Q.'. Presidential address. Division on maturity and old age, American Psychology Association, New York (1961).

15 J. D. Nisbet, 'Intelligence and age: retesting with 24 years interval', *Brit. J. Educ. Psychol.*, *27* (1957), 190–8.

16 O. Vogt, 'Study of the ageing of nerve cells', *J. Gerontol.*, *6* (1951), 164–5.

17 W. T. Singleton, 'The change of movement timing with age', *Brit. J. Psychol.*, *45* (1954), 166–72.

18 D. Wechsler, 'Intelligence, memory and the ageing process', in *Psychopathology of Ageing* (Eds P. H. Hock and J. Zubin), (New York, Grune & Stratton, 1961), 152–9.

19 R. A. McFarland, G. S. Tune and A. T. Welford, 'On the driving of automobiles by older people', *J. Gerontol.*, *19* (1964), 190–7.

20 E. Erickson, *Childhood and Society* (Harmondsworth, Penguin Books, 1965).

21 B. O. Neugarten, *Personality in Middle and Late Life* (New York, Atherton Press, 1964).

22 B. L. Neugarten, 'The awareness of middle age', in *Middle Age* (Ed. R. Owen), (London, BBC Publications, 1967), 54–65.

23 C. Buhler, 'Meaningful living in the mature years', in *Ageing and*

Leisure (Ed. R. W. Kleemeier), (New York, Oxford University Press, 1961).

24 Z. S. Blau, 'Structural constraints on friendship in old age', *Amer. Soc. Rev.*, 26 (1961), 429–39.

25 E. Cumming and W. E. Henry, *Growing Old: the process of disengagement* (New York, Basic Books, 1961).

26 T. Tissue, 'Disengagement potential: replications and use as an explanatory variable', *J. Gerontol.*, 26 (1971), 76–80.

27 N. Kogan and M. A. Wallach, 'Age changes in values and attitudes', *J. Geronotol*, 16 (1961), 272–80.

28 D. L. Phillips, 'Social class, social participation and happiness: a consideration of "interaction" – opportunities and "investment" ', *Sociol. Quart.*, 10 (1969), 3–21.

29 A. McMahon and P. Rhudick, 'Reminiscing', *Arch. Gen. Psychiat.*, 10 (1964), 292–8.

30 C. N. Lewis, 'Reminiscing and self concept in old age', *J. Gerontol.*, 26 (1971), 240–3.

31 E. Pfeiffer, A. Verwoerdt and H. S. Wang, 'The natural history of sexual behaviour in a biologically advantaged group of aged', *J. Gerontol.*, 24 (1969), 193–8.

32 A. J. de Long quoted in D. B. Bromley, 'Person perception and the study of human ageing'. Paper read to the Brit. Society Soc. and Behav. Gerontol. (University of Keele, 24th March, 1973).

33 E. Kahana, 'Perspectives on service needs and service preferences of older people', *Amer. J. Orthopsychiat.*, 43 (1973), 278–9.

34 A. Macoen, 'Levensvoldrening van individueel en collectief gehnisreste Bejaarden', *Nederlands Tijdschrift voor Gerontologie, 1* (1970), 35–41.

35 M. A. Lieberman, 'Relationship of mortality rates to entrance to a home for the aged', *Geriatrics, 16* (1961), 515–9.

36 D. Miller and M. A. Lieberman, 'The relationship of affect state and adaptive capacity to reactions to stress', *J. Gerontol, 19* (1964), 492–7.

37 R. N. Filer and D. D. O'Connell, 'Motivation of ageing persons in an institutional setting', *J. Gerontol.*, 19 (1964), 492–7.

38 S. Reichard, F. Livson and P. G. Peterson, *Ageing and Personality: a study of 87 older men* (New York, John Wiley, 1962).

Index